LANDSCAPE AND IDEOLOGY IN AMERICAN RENAISSANCE LITERATURE

In this provocative and original study, Robert E. Abrams argues that in mid-nineteenth-century American writing, new concepts of space and landscape emerge. Abrams explores the underlying frailty of a sense of place in American literature of this period. Sense of place, Abrams proposes, is culturally constructed. It is perceived through the lens of maps, ideas of nature, styles of painting, and other cultural frameworks that can contradict one another or change dramatically over time. Abrams contends that midcentury American writers ranging from Henry D. Thoreau to Margaret Fuller are especially sensitive to instability of sense of place across the span of American history, and that they are ultimately haunted by an underlying placelessness. Many books have explored the variety of aesthetic conventions and ideas that have influenced the American imagination of landscape, but this study introduces the idea of the placeless into the discussion, and suggests that it has far-reaching consequences.

ROBERT E. ABRAMS is Associate Professor of English at the University of Washington. He has published widely on American literature and culture in journals such as *ELH*, *American Literature*, *Philological Quarterly*, and *Nineteenth-Century Literature*.

LANDSCAPE AND IDEOLOGY IN AMERICAN RENAISSANCE LITERATURE

Topographies of Skepticism

ROBERT E. ABRAMS

University of Washington

CAMBRIDGE
UNIVERSITY PRESS

PUBLISHED BY THE PRESS SYNDICATE OF THE UNIVERSITY OF CAMBRIDGE
The Pitt Building, Trumpington Street, Cambridge, United Kingdom

CAMBRIDGE UNIVERSITY PRESS
The Edinburgh Building, Cambridge, CB2 2RU, UK
40 West 20th Street, New York, NY 10011–4211, USA
477 Williamstown Road, Port Melbourne, VIC 3207, Australia
Ruiz de Alarcón 13, 28014 Madrid, Spain
Dock House, The Waterfront, Cape Town 8001, South Africa

http://www.cambridge.org

First published 2004

Printed in the United Kingdom at the University Press, Cambridge

Typeface Adobe Garamond 11/12.5 pt.   *System* LATEX 2$_\varepsilon$ [TB]

A catalogue record for this book is available from the British Library

Library of Congress cataloguing in Publication data
Abrams, Robert E.
Landscape and ideology in American renaissance literature : topographies of skepticism /
Robert E. Abrams.
p.   cm. – (Cambridge studies in American literature and culture; 140)
Includes bibliographical references and index.
ISBN 0 521 83064 8
1. American literature – 19th century – History and criticism.   2. Skepticism in literature.
3. Alienation (Social psychology) in literature.   4. Place (Philosophy) in literature.
5. Landscape in literature.   6. Geography in literature.   I. Title.   II. Series.
PS217.S5A26   2003
810.9'353 – dc21   2003053188

ISBN 0 521 83064 8 hardback

For my mother, Pearl B. Abrams,
and in memory of my father,
George J. Abrams, 1905–1979

Contents

vii

Illustrations

Acknowledgments

My original interest in American literature and culture was inspired by two especially gifted high school teachers, Mr. R. A. Ducharme and Mr. Joseph Katz, whose "American Thought" seminar many years ago in Roslyn High School in Roslyn, New York, proved the equal in intensity and rigor to any course that I took thereafter.

Terence Martin helped to convert the advanced study of American literature into a genuine adventure, and Martha Banta and Charles Altieri, each in their different ways, were inspiring and helpful colleagues who read preliminary portions of this study, and whose conversation and friendship at an early stage of my career were treasured. Marshall Brown and Charles Johnson were also helpful in reading and commenting on early chapters of this book, and Daniel Burgoyne served as my alert and generous research assistant in the preparation of chapter 1. Alan H. Rose has been both a good friend and an intellectual co-conspirator as well as a source of endless insight into the bewilderments of contemporary software. At Cambridge University Press, Ray Ryan answered my numerous questions with unflagging graciousness and precision, and the anonymous readers of my manuscript alerted me to sources, problems, solutions, and lines of inquiry that I would otherwise have overlooked. Above all I am profoundly indebted to Ross Posnock, whose incisive criticism, encouragement, and wise counsel were nothing less than essential to the completion of this study.

My little Persian cat, Minsk, provided companionship and diversion throughout long hours of writing, although I was never quite sure whether I was playing with him, or he was toying with me.

Margaret Coughlan's warmth, charm, patience, and support have been priceless.

An earlier version of chapter 1 originally appeared as "Critiquing Colonial American Geography: Hawthorne's Landscape of Bewilderment," in *Texas Studies in Literature and Language* 36:4, pp. 357–79. Copyright © 1994 by the University of Texas Press. All rights reserved.

An earlier version of chapter 2 originally appeared as "Image, Object, and Perception in Thoreau's Landscapes: The Development of Anti-Geography," in *Nineteenth-Century Literature* 46:2, pp. 245–62. Copyright © 1991 by The Regents of the University of California. Reprinted by permission of the University of California Press.

A small section of chapter 3 initially appeared as part of "'Bartleby' and the Fragile Pageantry of the Ego," in *ELH* 45:3 (1978), pp. 488–500.

I am grateful to all journals for permission to reprint.

Finally, I am grateful to the English Department at the University of Washington for generous Hilen Fund support of my research expenses.

Introduction: the ubiquity of negative geography

> These continents . . . are soon run over, but an always unexplored
> and infinite region makes off on every side . . . further than to sunset,
> and we can make no highway or beaten track into it, but the grass
> immediately springs up in the path.
>
> Thoreau, *A Week on the Concord and Merrimack Rivers*[1]

From F. O. Matthiessen's landmark study to present scholarship and criticism, mid-nineteenth-century American literature is sometimes said to
represent nothing short of a *renaissance* in written expression and national
self-understanding. Although this approach is by now an old one, and although it has given rise over the decades to countless studies, debates, shifts
in canon formation, and revisions in the meaning of the term, the idea of
an "American Renaissance" survives to mark a period of intense national
self-scrutiny and reassessment of prevailing assumptions.[2] A major dimension of such reassessment, however, involves a radical transformation in
the envisagement of American landscape and space that has never been
satisfactorily explored.

On the one hand, according to maps and paintings of the American continent deeply rooted in European history and geography, an unequivocally
differed elsewhere of wild, historically uncompromised space ostensibly
looms up along a frontier-edge. From there the eye seems ushered into
a desolate counter-world outside civilization and administrative control
that keeps alive the promise (or the fear) that the world as settled, organized, and absorbed into history reaches inevitable territorial limits. By
the middle of the nineteenth century, however, such dualistic geography
becomes increasingly untenable and unconvincing. Far-off depths that are
said to lead into free, culturally uncompromised space, but that in fact have
long been inhabited by native tribal populations, now seem on the verge,
from the other end, of becoming nationalized and settled. Moreover, in
a post-Kantian era grown alert to the inevitably mediated character of all

reality – including whatever is projected to the other side of horizons and frontiers – numerous writers begin to recognize that from the very out-set of American continental discovery, far-away prospects leading beyond "settlement" have actually been envisaged through maps and other medi-ating frameworks fraught with underlying ideological presuppositions. A cherished objective correlative for an historically uncompromised reserve of freedom begins to lose its credibility and power.

It is precisely within this context that midcentury American writers such as Henry David Thoreau develop a dramatically altered understanding of the relationship between compromised, culturally organized space and a counter-dimension of latitude and vista. In the massive retheorization of space that occurs in texts such as *A Week on the Concord and Merrimack Rivers*, even as "continents" seem "soon run over," "always unexplored" space continues to make "off on every side," no matter where one stands. In contrast to the clean, unequivocal projection of *terra incognita* to else-where, a ubiquitous dimension of obscurity remains diffused throughout all positively conceived presence and landscape feature somewhat the way a Rorschach inkblot gives rise to and yet inevitably overflows whatever lit-erally seems to be occurring there. We might term this obscure dimension an abidingly *negative* geography or space which constitutes the dark, alien aspect of all positively conceived landscapes and spectacles, subtly altering everything encountered and known.

No doubt wilderness – not diffusively negative space making "off" from the eye "on every side" – seems the quintessential locus of the American sense of otherness, mystery, and perceptual depth. From William Bradford's dreary envisagement of the pre-New England forest to Thomas Cole's pow-erfully painted landscapes of desolation and withered foliage in the Catskill Mountains, a quarantined reserve of wild, forlorn space, apparently spread-ing beyond the restrictive frameworks of culture and history, represents a major dimension of American sense of landscape. But if such space seems to usher the eye into an emphatically differed elsewhere, we have certainly learned in retrospect just how culturally aggressive such envisagement of wild, desolate space has been from the very beginning. In his 1630 account of early New England settlement, for example, Bradford depicts a "hideous and desolate wilderness" lying outside "all the civil parts of the world."[3] Historians, however, have become sensitive to what such phraseology ef-faces and obscures. In contrast to Bradford's desolate pre-New England of "wild and savage hue,"[4] sixteenth- and seventeenth-century accounts by Verrazzano, Champlain, and others of the coastal flatland from the

Saco River to Narragansett Bay reveal a well-populated region, already cleared in many places for agriculture, and evidence suggests that Algonkian peoples inhabited this region for more than two thousand years.[5] Or consider the case of Thomas Cole, whose paintings of Catskill dreariness caught from steep, dizzying precipices and perilous angles of vision actually combine many different sketches composed in the mountains, brought back to his New York City studio, and there cunningly enhanced, abridged, or synthesized to produce the most spectacular visual effects.[6] From Bradford to Cole and beyond, representations of American wilderness have proved in many respects to be artfully mediated and staged.

Contemporary scholarship emphasizes the culturally aggressive theatricality of such wilderness representation while stressing the repressed counter-history of indigenous populations in places much too facilely considered to be placeless, uncultivated and wild. David Laurence, for example, observes that in choosing "the word 'wilderness'" to describe the continent first sighted off the coast, "Bradford names space according to what is, after all, a European category . . . He reconstructs Algonkian country exactly as Europe's margin, in an aggressive act of definition . . . that effaces what was there."[7] In effacing Algonkian clearings and villages, Bradford rhetorically clears the ground for unimpeded colonial settlement, and in still other ways as well, the reciprocal relationship between representations of the wilderness and the socio-economic imperatives first of colonialism and then of an expansionary national enterprise have been noted. Scholars and historians have emphasized, for example, the way "the continent's wilderness" becomes "the central icon" in the nineteenth-century effort to ground American nationalism in a visual symbology expressive of sublime national prospects.[8] And numerous other ideological agendas, cultural preoccupations, anxieties, and obsessions have been detected at work in visualizations and descriptions of wilderness, from its eroticization and feminization (often accompanied by violent fantasies of rape and guilty desecration) to the projection into wilderness of biblical imagery and metaphor.[9]

No doubt as Lawrence Buell cautions in his comprehensive study of "nature writing" and "the formation of American culture," scholarship that simply emphasizes the "power of imagination, textuality, and culture" to shape and fantasize wilderness according "to its will" must be qualified. Although "the constraints of" art and language "make zero-interference impossible" in the would-be envisionment of wilderness, the range of interpretative and aesthetic possibility extends, Buell observes, from aggressively "prefabricated imagery" and confident orientation in the service of ideology and culture to more complex, subtle art forms which manage to invoke "reciprocal" give-and-take between received cognitive schemata and what they cannot entirely fix in their sights.[10] Moreover, the recently published new edition of John W. McCoubrey's seminal study, *American Tradition in Painting*, reemphasizes how often in wilderness landscapes painted by nineteenth-century artists such as Thomas Cole and George Caleb Bingham, aesthetic strategies that "traditionally bottle up, control, and make habitable pictorial space" are relinquished. Certainly in many of Cole's landscapes, vast skies and towering, mountainous masses tend to dwarf whatever familiar domestic objects order, arrange, and impart a human sense of scale to the foreground. And in Bingham's misty river-boat scenes, forlorn human figures, as McCoubrey observes, are deliberately placed in vulnerable positions and passive, languorous attitudes that scarcely bespeak their "mastery over the spaces they occupy."[11]

Still, even Buell confesses that "zero-interference" with an unwarped primordial elsewhere is ultimately "impossible" to achieve on canvas or in "nature writing." And Bingham, like Cole, is not invariably credited with situating his forlorn wilderness scenes radically outside human interests and historical perspectives.[12] At best aesthetic technique can invoke a space of minimal spectatorial mastery within which the eye fails to find definitive orientation and bearing. Morever, the invocation of such minimally mastered space by no means entails an inevitable solicitation of the gaze into wilderness. McCoubrey himself calls attention to the survival, long after the provocative wilderness paintings of the nineteenth century, of a nomadic and largely undomesticated sense of space in a painting such as Jackson Pollock's *Autumn Rhythm* (1950), where ever-improvisational "trajectories" of "swirling lines of splattered paint" across the canvas resist the eye's struggle to objectify them into familiar, categorically stable visual schemata, or even to discern a "repeated . . . pattern" among "minimal masses" of visual order that quickly dissipate.[13]

When, precisely, do American painters and writers turn away from wilderness desolation per se in their invocation of freer, less domesticated, more nomadic modes of space? A fundamental proposition of my study is that at the very moment when the vast wilderness painted by Cole, Bingham, and others – however provocatively it may emerge on canvas – nevertheless seems doomed by history to invasion and extinction, an alternative, subtler, more freely floating antithesis to mapped, domesticated space, not evident in prior painting and cartography, begins to emerge in antebellum American art and thought. Such an alternative dimension begins to challenge official geographical premises, to wreak havoc with the logic of the scale map, and to mark a ubiquitous and pervasive rather than a westwardly receding limit to the settlement of interpretative and linguistic power in an era officially committed to the doctrine of "Manifest Destiny" and to the nationalization of alien land.

A radical paradigm shift in sense of geography and space begins to occur: a recognition of pervasive limitation to the power of socio-cultural "settlement" – not properly reducible into a westwardly receding edge – that a writer like Thoreau emphasizes even as he earns his living by surveying the boundaries of farmlands and wooded lots in and around Concord, Massachusetts. No doubt to Thoreau the surveyor, "wood-lots" and precise property divisions, taking shape in his "eye" as well as "on paper," appear to organize the countryside all around him.[14] But during the winter of 1857–58, even as he complains about the effects of surveying topography on his perception of landscape, his deepening acquaintance with a number of different tribal languages so alters his impression of the surrounding New England countryside that "another and wholly new" consciousness of landscape and space starts to emerge to him.[15] To learn native tribal languages is to grow sensitive to an unsuspected landscape of hidden detail and sensory nuance alien to that registered in Currier and Ives lithography or in *The Farmer's Almanac*. It is to discover, for example, "twenty" hitherto unsuspected "words for the tree and its different parts" that "are not in our botanies."[16] In the shift from one language and frame of reference into another, natural feature itself begins to alter. A tree witnessed through the lens of native tribal phraseology possesses unsuspected "parts," uses, and meanings falling unconsciously outside the field of vision of an English-speaking observer, who is predisposed to conceive of maples and great firs differently, and who is likely to encounter the entire New England wilderness through the lens of a vocabulary rooted in a mixture of European folklore, biblical myth, Western capitalist economics, and positivistic science.

So what, then, is radically *there* within that wilderness – or even in nearby places and farmlands of longstanding settlement? On the one hand, "landscape," observes W. J. T. Mitchell, tends to become a congealed repository of cultural interpretation and power deceptively visited back in upon the observer as frozen, fixed, and "independent of human intentions." Landscape in this sense not only deceptively naturalizes culturally mediated "fact" as if it were "simply given and inevitable," but "also makes" this seemingly independent life-world "operational by interpellating its beholder in some more or less determinate relation to its givenness as sight and site."[17] The ostensibly objective "givenness" of surrounding texture and visual feature, however, is precisely what begins to waver when one culturally mediated experience of landscape is measured and tested against another, as if variations of what seems there could alter and shift like variations within a Rorschach inkblot.

The geographical premises that are starting to become challenged, critiqued, and reassessed by a writer like Thoreau have a long history. On the one hand, in emphasizing the inevitably parochialized, interpretative, if alterable character of landscape, Thoreau anticipates our own increasing sensitivity to the culturally parochialized if changeable character of whatever seems to take place as "sight and site." Maps in particular, we are now told, project "cultural practices, preferences, and priorities" into landscape; they inevitably entail, it is argued, a specific "construction of reality," their seemingly neutral "images laden with intentions and consequences," their power to convince a matter of visual "rhetoric" that "permeates all layers of the map."[18] Yet in emphasizing the inevitably interpretative character of mapped, visualized landscape, a nineteenth-century author like Thoreau not only anticipates contemporary sensitivity to the ideological power of apparently neutral geography, but also invites a look back into history, where the alliance of an aggressively projective cartography with the European invasion of alien worlds lies at the heart of the legacy that he is striving to interrogate and to critique. Early maps defining "New World" space for European eyes, for example, prove part and parcel of what Edmundo O'Gorman, among the earliest of scholars to emphasize this process, terms "the invention of America" in print and shaping idea rather than its simple "physical discovery."[19] Such envisagement of New World space proves in many respects to be shaped and molded through a set of representational and discursive practices rooted in European interests, economic priorities, and cultural assumptions, from the tendency of venerable authoritative volumes such as Pierre d'Ailly's *Imago Mundi* and Pliny's *Natural History* to govern Columbus's accounts of New World discovery, and to do so even when empirical evidence seems to resist textual authority,[20] to the development, from the seventeenth century onward, of an abstract and standardized cartography reducing rich and variegated possibilities of landscape to a "single mathematical and mercantile scheme": a "uniform scientific writing" capable of quantifying "the increasing territorial wealth . . . of the mother country" and of converting vast stretches of colonized space into fungible, exchangeable commodity.[21]

What must not be discounted in such "invention" of American space, however, or at least from the perspective of early English settlers along the Atlantic coast, is the way mapped, administratively consolidated territory seems to withdraw from the eye into a dismal and mysterious counter-space ostensibly spreading beyond the confines of organized human history.[22] Herein lies Governor William Bradford's "hideous and desolate wilderness" of "weatherbeaten face" and "savage hue" whose "wild" character ostensibly exists in contradiction to "all the civil parts of the world."[23] This tendency to polarize wilderness into the dark Other of civilized order lies rooted in the religious and cultural history of northern and western Europe, where well into the seventeenth century, as historian John R. Stilgoe observes, "wilderness" is felt to shadow humanly organized space as its alien antithesis. Such antithetical space emerges, for example, as the luridly heathen antiworld of witchcraft and bizarre event in Shakespeare's *Macbeth*. In common folklore as well, a dismal antiworld spreads inchoately away from roadway, cultivated field, and all sense of pattern and structure into misty moorlands and lonely marshes where wanderers can become bewildered and lost.[24]

From the perspective of early English colonists along the Atlantic coast, "wilderness" in this sense seems to spread fearfully and antithetically westward, there to mark an edge of certainty where nameless rivers and unmapped prospects recede into conjecture, and administrative and ecclesiastical authority disappears. Yet especially from the late eighteenth century onward, as attitudes toward wilderness shift in keeping with the rise of Romanticism in Europe, wild, uncultivated space begins to exert a certain fascinating appeal in painting and verse. Such space becomes an inviting aperture beyond repressive systems of meaning and artificial laws as well as a window into divine processes operating outside "associations of human agency."[25] No doubt as Angela Miller emphasizes, a residual revulsion toward wilderness and desert landscape persists in American art and writing.[26] In *Sketches of Scenery and Manners in the United States* (1829), for example, Theodore Dwight insists that dreary prospects of "vast magnitudes," "overhanging" precipices, and "useless extensions of height" all draw the eye into a bewildering, irrational nature of wayward form and inhuman desolation that can be mitigated only by "our recurring to the calmer . . . more encouraging objects" of everyday domestic order.[27] The reassuring imposition, as Miller observes, of a recognizably "cultural and social text on nature" – to the degree that natural scenery becomes "stage-like," well composed, and fraught with signs of human artifice such as those that dominate the visual center of a painting such as Asher B. Durand's *Sunday Morning* (1860) – corresponds, it is widely felt, to the "civilizing mission" of the nation. It is precisely well-composed painting or lithography of this sort, available in handsome prints or on impressive museum canvases, that tends to be

encouraged by the increasingly influential New York societies for the promotion of art and culture such as the National Academy of Design, the
American Art-Union, and the Union League Club.[28]

In dramatic contrast, however, there is the case, as we have seen, of
Thomas Cole, many of whose wilderness landscapes seem intended to
evoke, as Bryan Jay Wolf proposes, a world of "alien strangeness" that
transcends normative "systems of meaning."[29] If Cole's landscapes of
"strangeness" precede the steadily growing influence, at midcentury, of
a more "stage-like" portraiture of American nature, a widespread taste for
wild, desolate scenery develops toward the end of the period as well. David
C. Miller, for example, emphasizes that beginning in the 1850s, drearily
wild scenery – especially of "swamps, marshes, and uninhabited beaches" –
assumes unprecedented power in American art and writing. Such scenery,
Miller proposes, starts to become darkly corresponsive in its marginal,
off-to-the-sides obscurity to hidden layers and unaddressed possibilities
of consciousness and personality. Indeed, in ushering the eye away from
"an increasingly urbanized and technological environment," lurid scenes
of swamps and marshlands in particular seem intended to expose the repressed underside of rational Western culture: that is to say, the profusion
of rank, indescribable foliage, the fetid smells and sulphurous gases of the
swamp-world, all seem to lead into a wayward and uncontrollable materi-
ality not amenable to rigid conceptual stabilization, fixed pattern, precise
measurement, and dependable visual category.[30]

Such aesthetic cultivation of wild scenery, however, leaves in its wake a
point of departure in domesticated, everyday space from which its more subversive tendencies remain quarantined. It is ultimately within a *sequestered*
elsewhere of dreariness and seclusion that art forms with power to disrupt –
and perhaps to enlarge – commonplace patterns of understanding confine
their disruptive tactics. However isolated from everyday reality these tactics
may be, they often become, as we have seen, latently stage-managed, with
Albert Bierstadt as well as Cole charged with cleverly fabricating a theater
of spectacular visual effects.[31] Moreover, the very impression of desolation
so powerfully conjured up in a painting such as Frederic Edwin Church's
Twilight in the Wilderness (1860) tends to erase, as we have seen, all trace
of a richly indigenous tribal history, so that what seems empty, dreary, and
simply vacant in such a painting masks an underlying historical amnesia.
And, finally, even as the trace of native tribal memory is erased from apparent expanses of wild scenery and inhuman solitude, such expanses seem
doomed to historical invasion from the other end. As early as 1836, in his
"Essay on American Scenery," Cole ruefully observes that the "sublimity

Figure 1   Thomas Cole, *Snow Squall, Winter Landscape in the Catskills, c. 1825.*

of . . . wilderness" is destined to "pass away," notwithstanding the memorialization of wild nature in paintings whose function is to "preserve" a
window beyond compromised human spaces into "purer" prospects.[32]

In contrast to such would-be preservation of an opening into the wild,
midcentury America writers begin to develop an alternative, less escapist
aesthetic whose liberating power lies immediately *within* rather than *beyond*
culture and history. On the one hand, in novels, tales, and sketches becoming burdened by the recognition, as Emerson puts it in "Experience," that
"we have learned" that we "see . . . mediately," never "directly,"[33] the shadow
of interpretative bias starts to fall self-consciously everywhere, spreading
throughout far-off wilderness prospects and domesticated scenery alike.
Indeed, in texts ranging from Thoreau's *A Week on the Concord and Merrimack Rivers* to Margaret Fuller's *Summer on the Lakes, in 1843*, the horizon
of historicized, culturally molded space becomes as difficult to establish as
the indeterminable edge of Giovanni Piranesi's dream-prisons, in the blurry
recesses of which it is hard to tell exactly where, or even if, structured, imprisoning space ends, and an outside dimension begins. In keeping with

just such a sense of space, Hawthorne cautions that "we, who are born into the world's artificial system, can never adequately know how little in our present state and circumstances is natural, and how much is merely the interpolation of the perverted mind and heart of man."[34] Within space in which the line between the domesticated and the wild grows troubled and confused, one travels far from home, and perhaps visits a renowned site of wilderness splendor like Niagara Falls, only to discover, as Margaret Fuller puts it in *Summer on the Lakes*, that "I merely felt, 'ah, yes, here is the fall, just as I have seen it in the picture.'"[35]

Yet even as it is acknowledged that out-and-out escape from a mediated, inevitably historicized world into a counter-world of pure unwarped wilderness "can never adequately" be achieved, phraseology such as Hawthorne's "merely the interpolation of the perverted mind and heart of man," or Fuller's "merely . . . as I have seen it in the picture," asserts a certain residually skeptical pressure of its own. The impossibility of breakthrough into a visible, positively conceived dimension of pure primordial otherness notwithstanding, everything visually encountered, coherently described in language, or conceived through the lens of cartography remains latently vulnerable and frail. For example, Thoreau observes that although on maps and in surveyors' plans, the woods seem "lotted off distinctly" and "boundaries" are "accurately described," wooded lots and precise boundaries "fade from" the lush countryside during an afternoon gaze across rolling meadows into far-off shadows. As attention shifts and consciousness of the countryside alters, what ultimately is *there* in any absolute, permanent sense? What is *there*, for that matter, at the site of Hawthorne's superstitiously lurid scarlet "A," which dwindles over the centuries into a mere "rag of . . . cloth" on the floor of a Customs House attic?[36] The tendency of writers like Thoreau and Hawthorne is to redirect a conceived point of crisis – where known, settled space collides with a residually "unsettled" dimension – from the receding threshold of western wilderness into the vulnerable depth of all culturally accredited presence, where textures and features of everyday life remain as latently frail as the lost legibility of once decipherable hieroglyphics.

The first part of my study of such a redirected crisis point includes chapters on Hawthorne's colonial American fiction, Thoreau's journal entries and formal prose, and fiction written by Melville in the decade after *Moby-Dick*. All such writing, I hope to demonstrate, ultimately rejects the proposition that an alien, specifically edged counter-world of primordial wilderness or, in Melville's case, of oceanic desolation marks the visible limit of sociocultural power. In Hawthorne's sketches and romances of colonial New

England life, for example, everything that the eye takes in and accredits as real, from a comunally feared symbol "A" to "specular evidence" for witchcraft, takes coherent shape only *against* what on closer scrutiny exceeds clarity of perspective and turns ambiguous and obscure. Similarly in Thoreau's writing, a pervasive sense of depth and perceptual vista ubiquitously gives rise to – and yet falls away from – meaningful spectacle and pattern wherever the eye turns. Similarly in fiction by Melville written after *Moby-Dick*, humanly structured, interpretative space turns precarious and frail, and assumes hesitant shape within a Rorschach-inkblot obscurity, in a multitude of environments and situations.

My initial chapters on Hawthorne, Thoreau, and Melville are meant to build upon one another, with Hawthorne's revisitation of the colonial New England past and its geographic premises leading into more contemporary meditations on landscape and sense of space in works such as Thoreau's *A Week on the Concord and Merrimack Rivers* and Melville's "The Piazza." All of the writing that I explore in these chapters, however, is marked by two fundamental developments: (1) an emerging sensitivity to the difficulty of disentangling pure "nature," as Hawthorne puts it, from the "interpolation of the perverted mind and heart of man"; (2) a complementary sensitivity, on the other hand, to the way mutation in human perspective opens up a spaciousness of its own this side of any breakthrough into an unwarped, radically extra-cultural dimension. Spaciousness of this sort, however, introduces an irremediably *negative* dimension into all positively conceived presence in the sense that shifting cognitive profiles can grow as incommensurable with one another as shifting visualizations of the same optical illusion, leaving an "x" factor in their midst that transcends all positive, well-focused visibility.

In my fourth chapter, I explore the socio-political implications of this negative, aspecular dimension as it emerges in ambiguous writing during a period in American history in which maps, paintings, travelogues, and lithographs all conspire to tell a cultural narrative of national "settlement" expanding incessantly westward, there to dispel desolation and the unknown. In opening up, in contrast, a permanently negative dimension of the real, more enduring than any receding wilderness, American literary ambiguity challenges a series of mediating mechanisms that otherwise characterize representational forms officially defining American space in the era of Manifest Destiny. In contrast, for example, to popular bird's-eye or mountaintop views of spreading American prospects, which project enormous spectatorial power in lithographs such as James T. Palmatary's *View of Chicago* (1857), American literary ambiguity undermines faith in the single comprehensive perspective, and in the process liberates a sense of indefinite existential promise – free-floating, inscrutable, and dark – from the imprisoning fixity of any central, apparently all-clarifying gaze. Moreover, in contrast to the characteristic envisagement of American "progress" as a succession of ever more advanced historical scenes extending into the depths of pictorial space, as in Asher B. Durand's *Progress (The Advance of Civilization)* (1853), American literary ambiguity displays discontinuous, incongruously juxtaposed versions of a single object or form that follow no innate narrative order. In the case, for example, of Hawthorne's notoriously mutable scarlet "A," which emerges at various moments in his novel as a conspicuous and fascinating sign of shame, a benevolently transformed emblem of Hester's abilities, or an innocuous rag of faded cloth, the drift of cultural history potentially emerges as incalculable vicissitude *in* perspective rather than as a steadily perceived progression of scenes that can be tracked by a stable gaze down the corridor of time. Finally, in contrast to crispness of image, absolute faithfulness to formal category, and precision of geometric pattern noticeable in popular lithographic prints of the period, the counter-style of the ambiguous entails a softened provisionality of pattern and figure taking hesitant shape against a backdrop that exerts irremediable pressure against any coherent, interpretative foreground.

My fifth and sixth chapters trace through the consequences that ensue when such an ineradicably ambiguous sense of space is allowed to enter into the exploration of three specific issues plaguing antebellum America: Indian removal, slavery, and industrial-revolution poverty. Absence of a central, cohesive perspective, a hallmark of the ambiguous style, proves fundamental to my discussion throughout both of these later chapters. But in my fifth chapter, I specifically explore the way what I have designated as the second aspect of the ambiguous style – incongruous shifts in vision following no single developmental progress, and so privileging no particular version of what remains mutable and volatile – potentially challenges the whole premise of Indian removal. According to the official American narrative of settlement and westward expansion, "Indian Removal" obeys and is justified by a linear, temporalized logic: an ostensibly inferior world-order giving way unequivocally to more advanced cultural space.[37] Dramatically in contrast, it is precisely the reciprocal exposure of alternatively perceived, mutually alien human universes toward one another – to the point where each starts to emerge as contingent and edged – that develops in texts sensitive to the trauma of the Euro-American incursion into native tribal worlds such as Margaret Fuller's *Summer on the Lakes* and "Chief Seattle's Speech" (or at least its earliest printed translation).

As for the third important aspect of ambiguous aesthetic style – softness of figure, form, and identity against a backdrop of uncertainty – chapter 6 of my study demonstrates the relevance of this figure-against-background provisionality to spaces of destitution inhabited by the enslaved and the abjectly poor. In reflection of the erosion of economic and cultural power within these spaces, that is to say, an otherwise comfortably inhabited, culturally foregrounded world of form and feature, elsewhere apparently saturated throughout a communally orchestrated experience of the sensuous, deteriorates and become enfeebled. Language itself threatens to lose power to orient and describe within situations of outrage and shock. The texts that I explore in this chapter include Frederick Douglass's two antebellum slave narratives, in which commonplace patterns of descriptive language fall under enormous pressure, and Rebecca Harding Davis's "Life in the Iron Mills," her pioneering literary envisagement of the industrial-revolution poor.

The question arises: why does Davis, at the outset of her text, announce that "from the very extremity" of the dismal, crumbling *mise-en-scène* of her story, "the most solemn prophecy which the world has known of the Hope to come" ultimately issues?[38] Indeed, throughout the antebellum decades, when statuary, well-composed lithographic scenes of pastoral farmlands and rolling meadows, maps, paintings, and monuments appear to be focalizing and stabilizing what one contemporary witness calls "the idea of country in a visible shape,"[39] why does American writing nevertheless raise the specter of a frail and fluctuating reality that cannot, at bottom, be integrated and steadied wherever the eye turns, whether toward settlement or wilderness?

No doubt at a more general, more abstract level of analysis, scholarship has repeatedly emphasized the underlying frailty of value and meaning across the instabilities of American society and history. Wayne Franklin, for example, suggests that as early as Bradford's *Of Plymouth Plantation*, in which the would-be line of "argumentation" is forced repeatedly to deal with "competing views" – with ostensibly marginalized (but vigilantly attended to) cultural and ideological alternatives represented by "secular settlers like Morton and Weston," by "presumed schismatics like Roger Williams," by "the early Quakers and by the native tribes" – "the center of American" reality proves, at bottom, to be "a point" of "opposition" and "untidiness" rather than of "convergence."[40] Still more recently, Timothy Powell has emphasized that the national "will to monoculturalism" notwithstanding, the "multicultural complexity" of the nation actually results in an "infinitely complicated aporia that cannot be resolved in the name of ideological consistency or logical clarity." In such studies, however, the gathering of "different" American "voices," as Powell puts it, into a "fluid, infinitely complicated, never-ending dialogue" tends to remain a matter of conflicting ideological agendas, of arguments and counter-arguments, or of the way, in a novel such as John Rollin Ridge's *The Life and Adventures of Joaquin Murieta*, "multiple imagined communities," as Powell observes – Tejon Indians, white nativist racist mobs, or the shaky alliance of Indians and Mexican-Americans provisionally forged by Murieta himself – interact, trouble one another, collide.[41] I would go still further and emphasize that as early as mid-nineteenth-century American writing, a dynamic of incongruous perspectives and frames of reference in collision, and, along with that, a strong sense of the underlying frailty of visible cultural form, percolates into what Raymond Williams, in exploring Antonio Gramsci's theory of hegemony, terms the subtlest depths and recesses of the "lived social process." Here "forms of practical consciousness" that seem equivalent to the "pressures and limits of simple experience and common sense" are said, according to hegemonic theory, to hold sway over the senses, and to govern the most fundamental "shaping perceptions" of objects, situations, and human beings themselves.[42] It is precisely this shaped sense of moment at its most fundamentally lived through, experienced, and perceived that begins to prove mercurial and frail in the writing that I am about to explore.

In such writing, the deep matrix of communal assumption and belief – the atmosphere of credence, perceptual proclivity, taste, judgment, and shaping presupposition in which the superstitious luridness of a scarlet "A" either seems frightening and real, or withers innocuously away – mutates, turns noticeably incommensurable with itself, and fails to become thoroughly saturated throughout its material base. A mobile and fluxional history opens up in the depth of the false steadiness of culturally constructed objects and named events. To peer into such flux is to confront the fundamentally aleatory, uncentered drift of the caring, concern, judgment, and perception through which these most fundamental phenomena take evanescent form.

Herein lies existentially open-ended space more permanent than the vanishing wilderness. But on such terms, what remains of the concept of human community? How, that is to say, does a community become *intelligible to itself* – and *tangible to itself* – within such frailty and flux except on terms imparting more trans-historical coherence to it than it actually possesses, and endowing it with more apparent steadiness throughout its material base than it actually sustains? Or is it more proper to say that community, at bottom, has no steady, coherent focal center, and that its constitutive potential, not given a priori, is not convincingly summed up by the engravings, monuments, public rituals, and memorable speeches that seem to mirror a community intelligibly back to itself?

Throughout antebellum American writing, the question of an absent communal focal center within a forever shifting and incalculable reality rises to the surface. The wild, incipiently revolutionary mob that spills into the streets in "My Kinsman, Major Molineux," for example – no longer exactly British, if not precisely anything else, with some figures wearing "the Indian dress," and "many fantastic shapes without a model"[43] – might be said to be coming into the terrible realization of the awesomely fluid process whereby the whole context of communal assumption and shaping belief in which a "Major" assumes credentialed, thickly historicized existence can suddenly evaporate, leaving a forlorn, existentially denuded, Lear-like figure in its wake.

The conclusion of this study explores the political implications of imagining human beings deprived of firm, reassuring placement within historical contexts and milieus, if still immanently *inside* – without customary evasion and defense – the terrible contingency and fluidity of their history. In such writing, the perennially open-ended question of to be or not to be, which otherwise recedes into the deceptive steadiness of objects and material spectacles, mapped geographies and thickly historicized selves, is thrown into relief. Such a question opens up immanently *within* history rather than outside it in the dreariness of a wilderness toward which Hester Prynne at one point directs Arthur Dimmesdale's gaze, insisting that "there thou art free!"[44] In dramatic contrast, freedom emerges as a much more historically immanent potential across a range of antebellum American texts. In emphasizing, as W. J. T. Mitchell puts it, that the very "medium" in which "we 'live and move and have our being'" is itself "transitional" and "in motion,"[45] such texts throw this transformative potential into the clear light of day, albeit with a clarity that at bottom resists focalization, and that entails mutation rather than clarifying steadiness in any mediated point of view.

To attempt to direct attention toward what mutates, eludes focus, and grows incommensurable with itself is no doubt to open a black hole in one's vocabulary. In an effort to remain more thickly embedded in historical particularities, contemporary studies often pursue an alternative tactic. In making the assumption – as an enabling *point d'appui* rather than as a would-be focus of study – that landscapes and milieus are inevitably encoded, metamorphic, and contingently constructed, contemporary studies go on to situate themselves in the thick of particular transformations of context. In a recent study exploring "gender and geography in contemporary women's writing," for example, Krista Comer emphasizes the way postmodernism opens up a new form of landscape writing – "transnational, postmodern, feminist" – in which women regional writers "deploy representations of western lands" to "challenge and change" the way we think about "social and political topics" such as "racial history" or "relationships between human and non-human nature."[46] No doubt my own study is intended to derive much of its interest from the circulation of what we would now call a "postmodern" sense of landscape through a variety of "social and political topics." But readers will discover that in my studies of midcentury American texts, a sense of the contingency of landscape and historical milieu looms up as a major issue in and of itself.

Why is this so? Certainly the social space of fluidity, hybridity, and contingency that the modern nation is said to unify and to render coherent sometimes does, in and of itself, remain a major preoccupation within contemporary scholarship. Homi K. Bhabha in particular stresses that within this "crowded" social space of "juxtaposition" and "contradiction," freighted with "incommensurable meanings and judgements," a "discourse" that "moves between cultural formations . . . without a 'centered' . . . logic" must become self-consciously highlighted and affirmed. Ultimately, such a discourse moving "between cultural formations" without a "'centered' logic" does not so much confidently "change the way we think" as it performs a different kind of cultural work. That is to say, such a discourse fosters respect for what Bhabha terms "ambivalent and chiasmatic intersections" of context and meaning, if only to acknowledge the underlying "perplexity of living" within an indefinitely "disjunctive, liminal" space that "resists" confident "teleology" along a single line. "Change" occurs within space of this sort such that "adding-*to* does not add up." Change often serves to supplement, complicate, and multiply the sense of the possible and to diversify the envisagement of conceivable directions.[47]

Midcentury American texts emphasizing the reciprocally incommensurable character of contingent, culturally mediated realities are properly read, this is to imply, both against a decisively linear, progressivist idea of change, and against the pressure to repress the difficulties of "living" in a "disjunctive" social space through standardized envisagement of milieu. No doubt such conformist pressure grows remarkably strong during the antebellum decades, even as it arguably becomes still more powerful after the Civil War. Mechanisms of cultural homogeneity during the antebellum period include the power press and lithographic engraving, which make possible the unprecedented mass production of prints and picture-book collections claiming to typify and to epitomize American experience and life. Along with such would-be codification of Americana in picture books and in popular lithography, the railroad, telegraph, steamship, and turnpike all help to foster a networked, well-administered sense of space. Moreover, in the antebellum US, a prevailing ideology given to splicing, as Lauren Berlant emphasizes, the national and the sacred, "the political and the utopian," seeks to privilege the national frame of reference over local investments and attachments.[48] Dramatically in contrast, in a kind of negative centripetalism that mimics if only to alter this powerful ideological referral of historical and parochial differences toward what Berlant terms a utopian "realm of ideality and wholeness"[49] – or, at the minimum, toward the would-be iconographic portraiture of normative national experience epitomized by Currier and Ives lithography – the writing that I explore, from "My Kinsman, Major Molineux" to "Chief Seattle's Speech," opens up the prospect of differences colliding to the point of dissonance. Phraseology such as the all-gathering "universal hum" of the crowd in "My Kinsman, Major Molineux," its collective sound "nearly allied to silence," or warnings that at the midmost arctic "Pole" of converging meridional readings, "the needle indifferently respects all points of the horizon alike," or admonitions that life-worlds "come and go like the waves" within the ever-fluid ocean, deny the possibility of a single authoritative focal center sustaining itself in the midst of converging or mutating social realities.[50] Nevertheless, in contrast to a defensive, fragmentary regionalism – still another important factor in its own right during this period – the notorious ambiguity of writings by Hawthorne, Melville, and others entails the deliberate intersection of voices, perspectives, and frames of reference to the point of mutually exposed contingency.

To explore the socio-political implications of such a deliberately centripetal but non-synthesizing style is precisely to *historicize* such texts. On the one hand, the "object" of New Historicism, starkly defined by Giles Gunn, "is to resituate the text in the socio-political and economic sites of its production and thus to unmask the ideological factors that have concealed its true purpose."[51] But to "resituate" texts such as "My Kinsman, Major Molineux" in midcentury American politics and culture is to grow sensitive to the way they react, through their own unmasking procedures, to the powerful American tendency to usher all differences toward a grand magisterial dimension of "wholeness." Midcentury American texts mimic this centralizing tendency by drawing various milieus, contexts, and frames of reference toward one another, if only in such a manner that at the point

PART I

Hawthorne, Thoreau, and Melville and the diffusion of estrangement

CHAPTER I

Critiquing colonial American geography:
Hawthorne's landscape of bewilderment

He endeavored to define the forms of distant objects, starting away
with almost ghostly indistinctness, just as his eye appeared to grasp
them . . .

. . . The torches were close at hand; but the unsteady brightness of
the latter formed a veil which he could not penetrate. The rattling of
wheels over the stones sometimes found its way to his ear, and confused
traces of a human form appeared at intervals, and then melted into
the vivid light.

Hawthorne, "My Kinsman, Major Molineux"[1]

The notoriously elusive and ambiguous atmosphere of Hawthorne's colonial New England fiction, in which "objects" seem to start "away with
almost ghostly indistinctness" and setting so often becomes murky and
"confused," remains a misunderstood – if widely discussed – dimension
of Hawthorne's craft. We have been told over the years that such an aesthetic of shifting perspective and multiple meaning has important cultural
as well as political implications. But the tendency has been to explore these
implications only at the cost of ignoring the more disturbing if intriguing aspects of Hawthorne's own art. In a number of influential readings,
for example, Hawthorne's historical fiction becomes the site not where disparate perspectives remain incommensurable with one another, but, rather,
where a hermeneutic style entailing the interaction, mutual adjustment,
and reciprocal qualification of differences, all in the name of faith in some
"ultimate hermeneutical complementarity," or at least resulting in "varying
agreements" of "the people," ultimately displays the very logic of political stability itself in America.[2] That a volatile and perceptually unsettled
text like "My Kinsman, Major Molineux," where competing frames of reference dissonantly clash and "objects" fade into "ghostly indistinctness,"
might cause one's sense of the historical moment to turn incongruous and
fluid – and might, in fact, be registering the underlying absence of a single, unifying focal center in the agitated colonial culture out of which

the national republic has issued – is the counter-possibility that I would like to raise. Indeed, I would argue that much of Hawthorne's colonial New England *mise-en-scène* emerges precisely in this turbulent, unsettled manner to challenge more integrative models of national formation and development and to throw into relief the irremediable provisionality of any particular settlement of culturally mediated truth.[3]

Certainly in Hawthorne's literary revisitation of the colonial New England experience, an ambiguous atmosphere of doubt, uncertainty, and mutating perspective develops not within a socio-political vacuum, but, rather, within the context of an historical counter-struggle to define, map, and politically consolidate a colonial "settlement" throughout a landscape initially innocent of "the New England which they were here planting in the wilderness" (*Scarlet Letter* 249). The would-be consolidation of potentially shaky faith in a "commonwealth . . . so newly constructed," for example, is the paramount objective of the vigilantly orchestrated state ceremonials that conclude *The Scarlet Letter* (230–31). But in revisiting these earliest origins of New England settlement during increasingly troubled decades leading up to the Civil War, when the geo-political integrity of the post-colonial nation is itself becoming vulnerable and threatens to scatter like "the fragments," as Hawthorne puts it, "of a shattered dream,"[4] a text like *The Scarlet Letter* becomes haunted by what centuries of map-making and official historical account have never really suppressed: not simply the underlying collision, in the depths of American history, of mutually incongruous vocabularies and interpretative frameworks, but, furthermore, the underlying frailty of all culturally accredited appearance as it seems to assume persuasive spectatorial shape within its ostensible empirical base.

In tales and romances of colonial New England life, Hawthorne evokes a far more frail and evanescent sense of the cultural appearance-world – one much more overtly dependent upon constitutive forms of eyesight and interpretative assent that potentially subside into oblivion or incongruously collide – than the steadier, more inert reality that seems registered and firmly preserved in antique maps and in old engraved prints. No doubt in contrast to the mutable and perplexing atmosphere of Hawthorne's historical fiction, colonial American maps, the would-be indices of spreading administrative dominion over an initially alien topography, seem to bespeak a firmer, more settled world. Through their guiding meridians and grids, increasingly exact property divisions, political boundaries, toponyms, and carefully laid-out diagrams of towns, such maps scarcely register the "ghostly indistinctness" and "confused traces" of "objects" as they sometimes strike the eye in "unsteady," ambiguous ways. Indeed, from "at least the seventeenth century onward," observes J. B. Harley, Western carto-graphical science "increasingly promoted what we would describe today" as a "positivistic" model of "knowledge" according to which objects and forms in space appeared to enjoy a neutral, scientifically accessible exis-tence expressible through precise measurement and exact printed imagery. Harley emphasizes that such "positivistic" confidence in the printed two-dimensional image and in "mathematical" precision led from early onward to the promotion of certain culturally authorized ways of envisaging a colo-nial landscape and to the dismissal of other perspectives into it – especially those significant to "other, non-Western . . . cultures": "The primary effect of the scientific rules was to create a 'standard' . . . that enabled cartog-raphers to build a wall around the citadel of the 'true' map. Its central bastions were measurement and standardization, and beyond there was a 'not cartography' land where lurked an army of inaccurate, heretical, sub-jective, valuative and ideologically distorted images."[5] Ambiguity of the kind that we encounter in Hawthorne's colonial New England landscapes, in contrast, tends to undermine this positivistic, ostensibly "normal" space of "measurement and standardization" as shifting perspectives overtly con-tend for control of a "visionary and impalpable Now."[6] In contrast to the fixed, inert imagery of official maps and charts, we enter into Hawthorne's notoriously problematic topography where figures and objects, forms and situations emerge in contradictory and incongruous ways.

What develops is scarcely a space of spreading scientific illumination and political "settlement," advancing militantly against the wilderness, from whose precincts a shifting and disorderly array of "inaccurate, heretical, subjective, valuative and ideologically distorted images" has been unequiv-ocally excluded. Quite the contrary, absence of "standard" visualization and description opens Hawthorne's retrospective envisagement of the colonial New England experience to much experimentation and free play as situa-tions and figures in space – the dreamy topography of "Young Goodman Brown," the odd spectacles and crazy events through which Robin Molineux wanders – resist becoming stereotypically rendered and defini-tively pinned down. All this is no doubt illuminating and intriguing: American historical reality is thrown open to a proliferation of other-wise sub-official and marginalized accounts, and its emergence accord-ing to shifting modes of human constructive agency is exposed. But it is worth noting that such exposure spawns considerable anxiety in Hawthorne's writing. An "impalpable" rather than an orienting sense of immediacy, caught in the crosswinds of shifting perspectives, often sur-faces negatively as "sad destruction, disturbance, incongruity that meets the eye; . . . everything that seemed so true . . . in its proper atmosphere, and nicely adjusted relations . . . a hideous absurdity" from another point of view.[7]

Recognition of the underlying frailty of "everything" that seems "true" only in "its proper" interpretative "atmosphere" – of the way the "clerical band," for example, loses its "reverence" and becomes a thing voided of mystique in "Indian" eyes (*Scarlet Letter* 199) – spreads throughout the most familiar cultural appearances and textures instead of emerging exclusively along a precarious edge of "settlement" fronting the wilderness. A colonial incursion into the wilderness may appear to aim its space of "settlement" against a counter-space of unsettled, cleanly differentiated Otherness. But it is the diffusion rather than the geographical isolation of what remains still unsettled that we encounter in Hawthorne's literary reorientation of colonial New England space. Significantly, even as Dimmesdale returns home from the forest,

> he took an impression of change from the series of familiar objects that presented themselves . . . The minister's deepest sense seemed to inform him of their mutability. A similar impression struck him most remarkably as he passed under the walls of his own church. The edifice had so very strange . . . an aspect, that Mr. Dimmesdale's mind vibrated between two ideas; either that he had seen it only in a dream hitherto, or that he was merely dreaming about it now. (*Scarlet Letter* 216–17)

Wilderness may appear to withdraw from an oriented, consolidated space deeper and deeper into elusive, unsettled recesses. But a free-floating sense of the unsettled turns ubiquitous and inescapable in Hawthorne's colonial New England landscape. Everywhere throughout such a landscape, discrepancy creeps in between mediating abstractions and what they never quite encompass, contain, and explain in this incongruous and "impalpable Now."

In contrast to the topographically sequestered Otherness of the colonial map, such a ubiquitously unsettled and "impalpable Now" cannot be quarantined to an exoticized elsewhere. Rather, Hawthorne exposes deep within the daily textures and features even of a "righteous Colony of the Massachusetts" (*Scarlet Letter* 54), where New Jerusalem is ostensibly becoming incarnate in a developing array of civic institutions, ceremonies, customs, and symbols, an irremediable gap between the communally foregrounded gestalt – the letter "A" emergent out of scarlet cloth, the ostensibly patterned, well-choreographed public ceremony taking shape in the eye – and an inevitably more unsettled and obscure backdrop out of which all culturally relevant appearance issues. In Hawthorne's revisionary history of New England "settlement," even the incursion of a "righteous Colony" into the wilderness becomes haunted by this ubiquitous gap between crisp figure and unsettled ground, between ostensibly coherent shape and its latently more ambiguous empirical basis, which serves as a kind of omnipresent frontier – albeit a subtle, easily neglected one – along which all apparent cultural order turns problematic and frail.

In Hawthorne's reorientation of the colonial New England landscape, then, the wilderness proffers a false aperture into separately unsettled space. More properly speaking, everything that the eye strives to take in, shape, contextualize, and endow with meaning overflows and potentially betrays the formative power of a concept or name, a pattern or specular image.

    Let me emphasize the pervasiveness of an inevitably more obscure, unsettled reality than whatever seems to become directly visible and concretely known. To project this residually unsettled challenge to culturally enfranchised coherence specifically into the "wilderness" is not only to attempt to quarantine a ubiquitous sense of obscurity, but furthermore to endow what properly challenges eyesight and overflows any specific description with an ostensibly visible, named specificity of its own – the "wilderness" – which such obscurity does not ultimately entail. Indeed, "wilderness" as specifically gazed at and experienced by Hawthorne's colonial characters tends to become the projective repository of particular ideas, schemata, and assumptions that have been culturally acquired. No doubt wonder, curiosity, and fascination at times gravitate toward the forest as what appears to lie unconditionally beyond a more restrictive, more culturally organized space. Hester Prynne, for example, asks Arthur Dimmesdale:

Is the world then so narrow? . . . Doth the universe lie within the compass of yonder town, which only a little time ago was but a leaf-strewn desert, as lonely as this around us? Whither leads yonder forest-track? Backward to the settlement, thou sayest! Yes; but onward, too! Deeper it goes, and deeper, into the wilderness, less plainly to be seen at every step; until, some few miles hence, the yellow leaves will show no vestige of the white man's tread. There thou art free! (*Scarlet Letter* 197)[8]

On close examination, however, space "less plainly to be seen at every step" continues to bear diminishing traces of recognizable, patterned feature as far as visibility extends. Ultimately, such a prospect suggests the difficulty of differentiating a radically unpatterned and unadulterated space from what eyesight persists in patterning, assessing, categorizing – often according to categories and schemata deeply ingrained within it – all the way out to any conceivable horizon. Indeed, the very maze-like suggestiveness of the forest, Hawthorne observes in "Roger Malvin's Burial," invites much projective speculation as feeble "light" coming down "among the trees" remains "sufficiently dim to create many illusions" in "expecting fancy."⁹ The lurid phantasmagoria of a still heavily superstitious New England population, latently fraught with all sorts of unexamined presuppositions and attitudes, readily pours itself into such dimly lit, suggestive space. Breakthrough into an unwarped primordial dimension beyond artifice, interpretation, bias and cultural influence scarcely occurs under such circumstances.

Certainly no breakthrough into an unwarped primordial dimension develops in the landscape of "Young Goodman Brown." Quite the contrary, such a text goes far toward revivifying, argues Michael Colacurcio, what it actually would "have been like" to encounter and to perceive the world through seventeenth-century Puritan categories and schemata. Hawthorne's narrative resists, Colacurcio proposes, any ahistorical search for "ultimacy of . . . interest and explanation." It invites, instead, a backward projection of the reader into antiquated concepts, vocabularies, and beliefs – if also into crises in institutional procedure and descriptive phraseology precipitated by them – that once culturally mattered at a time when "specter evidence" and the possibility of witchcraft were solemnly deliberated in courts of law. By extension, sense of space itself undergoes historicization in fiction seeking to reconstruct a "dramatically believable version of 'how it might have felt' to live in . . . Puritanism's . . . troubled years" in the late seventeenth century.¹⁰

The ostensibly alien, frightening wilderness into which Brown enters at nightfall, such an argument suggests, is itself culturally shaped, however shaped by deeply rooted superstitions and widespread communal fears regarding what purportedly lurks beyond the confines of civilized, rational, everyday experience. Still, as Hawthorne himself emphasizes in a statement that would appear to provide the appropriate gloss for Brown's seemingly extra-cultural experience within the forest: "We, who are born into the world's artificial system, can never adequately know how little in our present state and circumstances is natural, and how much is merely the interpolation of the perverted mind and heart of man."¹¹

No breakthrough into unequivocally differed, ahistorical space can be expected to develop in art governed by such a proposition. Quite in contrast to absolute wilderness desolation as ostensibly registered in a nineteenth-century American painting such as Thomas Cole's *Snow Squall, Winter Landscape in the Catskills* (c. 1825–26), fiction like "Young Goodman Brown" unmistakably projects a culturally shaped (and shaping) consciousness all the way into the wilderness.[12] Goodman Brown, his mind steeped in European folklore and duly catechized by Deacon Gookin, gazes into a forest the archaic imageries and textures of which have obvious roots in medieval folklore and Old Testament legend. Brown's wilderness is culturally molded – scarcely timeless, universal, and unwarped – spreading before his eyes at twilight as a "heathen wilderness" molded by racism and superstition into sensational, lurid theater where "there may be a devilish Indian behind every tree."[13] Biblical associations and superstitious folk motifs suffuse everything, from the serpentine stick on the ground that almost seems to come alive (as in the story, Hawthorne duly notes, of the "Egyptian magi" in Exodus 7:9–12) (79), to the suspicion that "a basin . . . hollowed" in rock may be actually be filled with "blood" – not "water" – fit for a Satanic forest ritual much like dark ceremonies depicted in medieval woodcuts ("Young Goodman Brown" 88).

No doubt much of what Brown seems to see emerges as uncertainly arisen from out of vague shape and flickering form like figuration provisionally witnessed in a Rorschach inkblot. "Sudden gleams of light" flash over an "obscure field" (85), and for a moment Brown appears to distinguish the faces of his neighbors engaged in a "witch-meeting" (89). "Indistinct" forest sounds, however "confused and doubtful," seem to become "the accents of" familiar "town's-people," although "the next moment, so indistinct were the sounds," that Brown "doubted whether he had heard aught but the murmur of the old forest" (82). As dubious events come in and out of focus in Brown's dreamy perceptions, the constitutive play of inference and conjecture throughout suggestive wilderness obscurity becomes sufficiently blatant, or so it would appear, to be readily pierced through by an enlightened, post-superstitious reader. And yet such a breakthrough is curiously impeded by Hawthorne's narrative. Quite in contrast to a painting such as Cole's *Snow Squall, Winter Landscape in the Catskills*, no emphatically differed counter-space, its alien vista spreading wildly and unequivocally outside the perimeters of time-bound, culturally compromised vision, assumes visible, concrete shape in Hawthorne's tale. Rather, mixed and mingled textual signals make it difficult to determine precisely where the interpretative breaks off and where an ostensibly differed realm of wilderness begins. What may be "indistinct" forest "sounds," for example, are nevertheless placed by this prevaricating text within quotation marks to become words and conversations that Brown actually seems to hear. A chance-like swell of rock – or is it the shape of an actual "altar"? – flickers in and out of view in the uncertain light at the far end of a field (84).

Equivocally *between* language and noise, artifactual and natural shape, semiosis and nonsense, what actually takes place in this tale uncertainly wavers: it falls neither inside nor quite outside the "interpolation of the perverted mind and heart of man." Rather, as in the case of moldering architectural feature that has become marginally decipherable amidst the edges and crevices of the Tarpeian Rock in *The Marble Faun*, mixed narrative signals evade disclosing "what portion of it was man's work, and what was Nature's," but leave "it all in . . . ambiguity and half-knowledge."[14]

Hawthorne, then, blurs the jealously sustained opposition between "man's work" and "nature's," the civil and the wild, so fundamental to cartography and sense of space in seventeenth-century New England. In subversion of this antithesis, we are invited to waver in a kind of epistemological twilight between visually foregrounded shapes and images that have lost cultural persuasiveness over time (but nevertheless are accorded a certain retrograde respect by Hawthorne's reconstructive narrative) and what fails to take independent, timeless shape outside them.

No breakthrough into differed, extra-cultural space develops. *The Scarlet Letter* similarly registers a realm of "nature" heavily suffused with interpretation and cultural projection, from the tendency of Puritan theologians to "interpret all meteoric appearances, and other natural phenomena," as prophetic "revelations" directed to the New England community (154) to the demonization of the forest in myth, gossip, and fantasy into a place of witchcraft and devilish magic. Such a wilderness assumes shape through imaginations steeped from early childhood onward in the heavily allegorized nature of Puritan verse, lesson-books, and emblematic engraving (wherein a creek readily becomes a "Slough of Despond," and explicit verbal captions are sometimes blatantly affixed to bushes, dells, rocky ravines, and brooks). In *The Scarlet Letter*, the transfer of such heavily allegorized topography from printed engraving to immediate forest scenery emerges almost as an unconscious cultural reflex. Thus, "to Hester's mind," the "forest . . . imaged not amiss the moral wilderness in which she had so long been wandering." Similarly, when little Pearl takes "A Forest Walk" with her mother, the sunshine fades, and "'Mother,' said little Pearl, 'the sunshine does not love you. It runs away and hides itself'" (183). Shortly thereafter, the little girl situates herself on one side of a brook in the forest, Hester and Arthur stand on the other, and "'I have a strange fancy,' observed the sensitive minister, 'that this brook is the boundary between two worlds'" (208).

As these seventeenth-century characters transact their affairs just outside the "settlement," the "mystery of the primeval forest" (183) itself becomes mapped, bounded, and allegorized through their most seemingly spontaneous acts of eyesight and conversation. And even at its most ostensibly alien, such a wilderness sometimes proves to be the unconscious repository of hidden meanings and associations. When, in "Roger Malvin's Burial," the aging Reuben Bourne leads his family deep into what seems sheer "howling wilderness" (339), he unwittingly travels – so he at last discovers to his horror – over unconsciously remembered, subliminally mapped topography that he has traveled before, and that beckons him, however unconsciously, back to where he left Roger Malvin to die.

Space in Hawthorne's fiction thus extends indefinitely westward into forest gloom – but toward no definitive egress from memory, association, learned category, and cultural schemata. No matter how deeply Goodman Brown travels into the forest, "he was himself," Hawthorne emphasizes, "the chief horror of the scene" ("Young Goodman Brown" 83). Still, this side of a breakthrough into an unwarped primordial wilderness, flourishing outside mediated structure, that never actually occurs in Hawthorne's bookish, richly allusive, heavily meditative fiction, we can to a degree "loosen these iron fetters, which we call truth and reality, and make ourselves" at least "partially sensible what prisoners we are" ("New Adam and Eve" 247).

That is to say, without breakthrough into an ahistorical wilderness of unwarped primordial feature becoming visible outside mediation, we can nevertheless discover the way all mediated visibility remains latently feeble, fragile, and alterable. Consider Hawthorne's disclosure of the unsuspectedly frail visibility even of a letter "A" assuming shape in the Salem Custom House within "cloth" so "frayed and defaced" that the letter is not initially perceived there. Hawthorne emphasizes that what he picks up, handles, and fingers "assumed the shape of a letter" only "on careful examination." What he examines initially emerges not as an "A" but only as "a certain affair of fine red cloth, much worn and faded." Once "fine" but now a "rag," "faded," a fragment of junk, and yet piquing the curiosity with its "wonderful skill of needlework," what eventually comes into focus as the semiological shape "A" initially invites the eye into a more open-ended, intriguing interplay of textures and possibilities. Only by degrees retrospectively reduced into a single, coherent form with an inferable function to play at a former moment in New England history (through a process recapitulating the whole struggle to recontextualize the initial ambiguity of nameless, excavated things waged by nineteenth-century archeology), shape "A" is initially embedded in a more volatile backdrop of incongruous aspects, values, and figures. Ultimately possessing much of the turbulence of an enigmatic object in a Jasper Johns painting, the strange, wayward thing encountered in the "mysterious package" seems in part an "ornamental article of dress," if also a letter in the alphabet, and yet also, following the fate of all material things that only appear to be obedient registries of social value and meaning, something of a wayward enigma: a strange X-factor amidst garbage and debris "which . . . I saw little hope of solving" (*Scarlet Letter* 31).

So what, ultimately, *is there*? How does a nineteenth-century customs official whose duty is the appraisal of foreign artifacts coming into his purview such that they can be commodified, pigeonholed, and taxed within the economic and cultural system that he represents – whose job is the re-contextualization of the object somewhat like the translation of a hieroglyphic mark from a former to a current interpretative system – name, use, and conceive of what he here encounters? What surges so waywardly out of the depths of the artifact in such a liminal, free-floating condition between official contexts? Why propose elsewhere to focalize "a story" around a volatile, wildcard thing such that "from different points of view, it should appear to change," or why stress that "were we to sit here all day, a week, a month, and doubtless a lifetime, objects would . . . still be presenting themselves" in "new" and disruptive ways?[15] The latently soft, alterable character of objects prevails not simply in the wilderness of "Young Goodman Brown," but everywhere throughout cultural space – if often more subtly, and only in ways that become evident by measuring the mutations of an object's meaning, appearance, and value over time. Still, objective spectacle never fully encompasses and controls – even as it remains the powerful shaping lens through which historicized, culturally immersed creatures come to behold and to fix in seemingly dependable ways – the otherwise obscure immediacy through which they are passing, the forces that act upon them, the material substances that they seem to witness, handle, and trade. On the one hand respecting the powerful persuasiveness and enormous practical consequences of the "big, heavy, solid unrealities" that we describe in our conversations, yearn for, buy, or sell, Hawthorne nevertheless treats such phenomena as potentially fading, problematic forms within "this visionary and impalpable Now, which, if you once look closely at it, is nothing" (*House of Seven Gables* 229, 149).

A certain underlying vagueness ("if you once look closely at it") pervades everything imaged forth, charged with value, and given an office to play in cultural space. No doubt cultural appearances are often designed to preempt insofar as possible the otherwise wayward play of eyesight across textures and surfaces meant to become the stable repositories of communal value and meaning. In the opening marketplace scene of *The Scarlet Letter*, for example, we witness an official struggle (by no means entirely successful) to leave little interpretative breathing room amidst meticulously controlled cultural appearances, from Hester's "A" itself, which becomes the object of a long and tendentious sermon designed to fix its meaning unmistakably in everybody's eyes, to the strict spatial choreography that segregates the patriarchy high on the balcony from the common people looking up from below. In this tight schematization of communal appearance and display, the Reverend John Wilson, we are told, "looked" as though one of the "portraits which we see prefixed to old volumes of sermons" had actually managed to "step forth" from print into living social space (*Scarlet Letter* 65).

The gap between the official printed image and the denser complexity of the living social moment is thus narrowed as tightly as possible in the quaint, public pageantry of the "righteous Colony of the Massachusetts" (54). Only in stark contrast does the eye seem to gaze into the dangerous if fascinating suggestiveness of a "primeval forest," "less plainly to be seen at every step," where edges soften and appearances turn obscure. But even the forest in such seventeenth-century *mise-en-scène* becomes a controlled, communally quarantined realm of "mystery." For it emerges as an edged, bordered anti-world observable by turning in a certain westward direction only, and so to that degree it becomes a site of sequestered "mystery" that has become topographically situated and contained.

The counter-tendency of Hawthorne's fiction, I have been proposing, is to suggest a more intertwined, more equivocal, less definitively bordered sense of space in which the residually alien character of reality – its slippage out of tight verbal and imagistic control into the incalculable – cannot be quarantined to the far side of a mapped cultural edge. Rather, what eludes descriptive and perceptual mastery intertwines itself with all that the eye gathers in, seems familiar with, and seeks to pattern and define. Up to a point, no doubt, the ceremonial pageantry of a "righteous Colony" can be contrived to resemble as tightly as possible the rigid, schematized world of the hornbook image and the frontispiece engraving. But beyond that point – "if you once look closely" – numerous discordant, quirky details will begin to show up, to clutter and to contaminate what is being culturally foregrounded, to mark its visual limits, and to provoke the further play of curiosity into unsuspected recesses, nooks, and crannies.

This side of the theoretical boundary segregating civil from wild space, how successfully can detail that overflows official patterns of explanation and disrupts ostensible epistemological consensus actually be driven from sight? "As perceivers," writes anthropologist Mary Douglas in exploring the inevitable residuum of messy, troublesome detail that haunts and pervades ostensibly coherent spectacle, we no doubt seek to

select from all the stimuli falling on our senses only those which interest us, and our interests are governed by a pattern-making tendency, sometimes call *schema* . . . In a chaos of shifting impressions, each of us constructs a stable world in which objects have recognisable shapes, are located in depth, and have permanence. In perceiving we are building, taking some cues and rejecting others. The most acceptable cues are those which fit most easily in with the pattern that is being built up. Ambiguous ones tend to be treated as if they harmonised with the rest of the pattern. Discordant ones tend to be rejected.[16]

Eyesight even at its most seemingly fundamental and spontaneous, Douglas theorizes, tends to make whatever it perceives conform as much as possible to theoretical constructs and formations. Aesthetic registries of this drive to abstract theoretical constructs out of the potentially more complex density of raw sensuous immediacy include a wide variety of visual forms, from engraved portraiture "prefixed to old volumes of sermons" to Currier and Ives prints. Such schematized prints and engravings proffer a cleansed, iconographically controlled space from which "discordant" and "ambiguous" detail has been banished. To a degree such imagery seems to persuade. In episodes such as the opening marketplace scene of *The Scarlet Letter*, however, Hawthorne's more probing and venturesome narrative reaches through foregrounded, well choreographed communal display toward what remains fleeting, subliminal, neglected – if covertly festering – within it. Quite in contrast to a Currier and Ives engraving, an easily overlooked gesture or a momentary agitation of the eye is permitted to intrude into and to mar the theoretical, set-piece character of such spectacle, from Dimmesdale's hand held oddly over his heart even as he sits with other dignitaries on the balcony to the sudden, "writhing horror" in Chillingworth's features upon spying Hester Prynne ("After a brief space," writes Hawthorne, such "writhing horror" of facial feature hastily disappears) (*Scarlet Letter* 61).

Such details may seem peripheral, marginal, and fleeting – come and gone in the space of a micro-second. But as they twinkle into view and rapidly fade, they proffer quick, darting glimpses into a more complicated moment than is finding its way into foregrounded, officially authorized pageantry (and into orthodox patterns of public attentiveness such pageantry invites).

Within the detailed depths of this moment, a nervous hand over a heart or a hastily suppressed agitation of the eye marks the horizon of what has been officially foregrounded into shared, communal theater. Similarly, "a burning blush, and yet a haughty smile" (52) struggle for dominion in Hester's nuanced, conflicted face, which ultimately remains too intricate to be flattened into a "worthy type of her of Babylon" (110).

To "look closely" into such a moment is to see visible objects and human figures escaping pat categories and settled forms. In Hawthorne's complexly rendered *mise-en-scène*, the nearby world (intensely scrutinized) starts to become the site of textbook feature only imperfectly realized, of schemata at best provisionally abstracted out of "discordant," subliminal "cues" that must be repressed if tidier, officially authorized images of reality are to prevail. Ultimately, the ragged outermost fringe of administered, organized spectacle, where official cultural formations start to become unstable and unsettled, emerges not specifically along the wilderness frontier, but ubiquitously throughout even the most meticulously choreographed public theater.

Deep within the space of a letter "A" or of ritualized appearance, reality remains more discordant and ambiguous. But the limited sway of the interpretative image over whatever it appears to stabilize in its sights is never more strikingly emergent than when shifting profiles, configurations, and patterns begin noticeably to proliferate at precisely the same place. Such volatility of specular potential is explored in Hawthorne's *American Notebooks* by extreme but instructive examples, anticipating modern optical illusions, such as "letters" forming "words" at a distance but then appearing to metamorphose into human "figures": "Letters in the shape of figures of men &c. At a distance the words composed by the letters were alone distinguishable. Close at hand, the figures alone were seen, and not distinguished as letters" (183). A hermeneutic power vacuum develops at the nodal center of optical illusions of this sort as no way emerges to determine what is the important, central, and relevant reading, and what is the wayward, aberrant one.

One might argue that selective power over the properly foregrounded gestalt, however destabilized in optical illusions, is precisely what prevails throughout daily social experience. The sense of the immediate, "concrete" moment, writes Susan Stewart in her provocative book on *Nonsense*, is normally solidified and stabilized by a felt "horizon of the situation" determining "what will be allowed to 'exist' or 'appear'" within it "and what will remain invisible, white, a blankness." The task at hand will guide mutually involved participants toward the selection of relevant gestalten, the adoption of a shared descriptive vocabulary, and the foregrounding of significant detail, and "none of this," adds Stewart, "is accomplished privately. We must see our situation as 'intersubjective,' holding to an idea that others share in a 'vivid present' and that this present is a matter-of-course, accessible to everyone else in the same way in which it is accessible to us. We . . . 'stand in each other's shoes.' "[17] Yet in certain episodes in Hawthorne's fiction in which colonial New England society emerges, on closest scrutiny, less as a "settlement" than as a volatile convergence of competing interests and frames of reference, this sense of "intersubjective," shared space lapses into something very much like Stewart's definition of "nonsense": space in which the sense of what is concrete and immediate "spirals away from any privileged signification" and no longer seems "coherent and integral" (*Nonsense* 209).

A threat of "nonsense" certainly hovers over the concluding marketplace scene of *The Scarlet Letter*, in which a visiting "party of Indians," Spanish mariners, and "people . . . from the country" mingle with the Puritan townsfolk amidst what is becoming somewhat other than homogeneously shared public space. Rather, "various thoughts, moods, and interests" proliferating "across the wide and bustling square" ultimately scatter the overall logic of the spectacle. What unfolds is officially a state-choreographed occasion designed to celebrate the "election" of a new governor. Certainly Dimmesdale's sermon inside the chapel, mingling theology with politics, and foretelling the special destiny of "the New England" state "which they were here planting in the wilderness," appears to those who have organized this gathering to provide its appropriate gloss. Yet even as Dimmesdale holds his audience spellbound inside the chapel, an overflowing crowd continues to circulate throughout a larger marketplace scene of diverse, simultaneously unfolding activities. Here "little Pearl," having quit her mother's side, makes some who are present "cheerful by her erratic and glistening ray." In a still further dispersal of interest and perspective, "many people present, from the country roundabout," direct their gaze toward Hester wearing her letter, provoking, in turn, the curiosity of the visiting "party of Indians," for whom the "brilliantly embroidered badge" seems to promote Hester into "a personage of high dignity among her people." Spanish mariners, moreover, transgress "without fear or scruple" a less than uniformly enforced code by consuming "draughts of wine" (*Scarlet Letter* 226–49).

The overall cultural moment as Hawthorne envisages it turns somewhat schizophrenic in behavior, perspective, and mood, although it is true that power to name this occasion "Election Day," to marginalize the activities of "Indians" and Spanish mariners within it as sub-official and secondary, and to control at least its official meaning and gloss, remains clearly vested in those gathered inside the little Protestant chapel.

In "My Kinsman, Major Molineux," however, even power over the official meaning and interpretation of events proves more problematic and uncertain. A "vivid present . . . accessible to everyone . . . in the same way" is scarcely what develops. Rather, reaching back "not far from a hundred years ago" (209) into the cultural and political turbulence of the 1730s, Hawthorne undermines the tendency of providential American history to project singleness of national consciousness and unity of communal purpose back into more inchoate, unsettled times.[18] What is reopened, instead, is the "commotion" and "confusion," the dispersal of public allegiances, and the mixture of fear, hope, populist sentiment, and yet residual monarchial loyalties characterizing a prior cultural moment that on closest view proves too incongruously scattered across competing value systems and life forms to be tidily summed up in a unified perspective and a single descriptive vocabulary. It is true that during the central, climactic scene of the text, a more or less organized group of subversives seems temporarily in charge. But many others who are present, "inactive, except as . . . spectators," merely look on. Meanwhile, women run "along the sidewalks," reacting to the unfolding "confusion" with "mirth" – or, conversely, with "terror" – while from still other quarters of the city, "voices hailed each other from house to house, all demanding the explanation, which not a soul could give" (227–28). A public and widespread "horizon of the situation" – some shared "intersubjective" reading of events valid for this community *in toto* – simply does not emerge.

Robin ultimately enters into an unfolding historical situation without a clearly self-reflective, dependably "intersubjective" gloss. At such a moment of interpretative turbulence, "the forms of . . . objects" might very well seem to start "away with almost ghostly indistinctness" (221). For in such an atmosphere, much that might otherwise seem self-evidently concrete, settled, and fixed, from the "little province-bill of five shillings" (that has suddenly depreciated so steeply in value) (209), to the "swinging" picture of a "British hero" before an inn (212), to the violent spectacle of the Major's disgrace itself, will at best sustain unstable meaning and value. How, then, to objectify into some truly public, "intersubjective" scene – some unambiguous concrete registry of communal perceptual consensus – the wild and feverish spectacle that whirls and swirls beyond easy perceptual capture at the turbulent pith of this text? At the center of its "confusion," "discord," and "unsteady brightness," where "moonbeams" are "disturbed" by "redder light" and nothing is easily settled upon, the Major looms into unsteady focus at the confused intersection of competing lighting effects (and frames of reference) like "some dead potentate . . . majestic still," the "ashen" gravity of the old man's face caught in the midst of hilarity and frenzy, signs of his dignity surviving amidst signs of his disgrace, as if the objective were to expose a tumultuous spectacle at the uncertain nexus of colliding tones, gestalten, and judgments rather than to reduce and flatten its impact (226–30). From one perspective, a humiliated old man de-mystified of office and rank, his "face . . . pale as death," his "eyes . . . red and wild," and his lips "quivering," is allowed momentarily to emerge in vividly delineated vulnerability. But the narrative lens through which such detail is momentarily highlighted remains elusive and unstable. The foregrounded detail of agony and anguish fades back into "confused traces" (228), and we lurch quickly away into a wholly different aesthetic universe, with a separate set of mediating conventions, as "the congregated mirth roared up into the sky! The Man in the Moon heard the far bellow; 'Oho,' quoth he, 'the old Earth is frolicsome to-night!'" (230). From this intrusion of a jocose Man in the Moon into the narrative back toward solemn, Augustan cadences initiating what seems straightforward colonial history – "After the kings of Great Britain had assumed the right of appointing the colonial governors, the measures of the latter seldom met with . . . ready and general approbation" (208) – the text fluctuates in orientation and tone. Copious allusions, clues, and analogies no doubt proliferate. The name "Robin" and the midsummer madness of the tale summon up the festival antics of *A Midsummer Night's Dream*; the initial scene is reminiscent of Charon's ferry crossing the Styx into the underworld; the climactic scene looks forward to the Boston Tea Party. But how to gather this allusive hodgepodge together? Just as the "universal hum" of the otherwise distinct, coherent voices of the crowd blurs into an accumulative white noise "allied to silence," the humming, gathering cacophony of diverse tones, clues, and vocabularies that emerges in such a text results in a white noise of its own. Envisagement of a crisply delineated, coherently unfolding scene proves difficult as conceivable contexts, interests, and perspectives remain not only disparate and discontinuous, but also, as at the overdetermined nodal center of a Freudian dream, disparately gathered together. Here numerous cross lights, throwing an object or event into incongruous forms of relief, are effectually "concealing by their glare whatever object they illuminated" (227). To approach the white "hum" of the "universal" in such a text is to experience not consensus or synthesis but the eclipse of any literal, steadied experience of form.

"My Kinsman, Major Molineux" proffers an extreme example of scenic turbulence. But throughout Hawthorne's fiction, various forms of interplay and perceptual incongruity disturb the settled visibility of forms in space as well as unity of scenic focus. At times, as we have seen, the ostensible coherence of the visualized object or of the unfolding social ritual takes shape only against the accompanying exposure of discordant detail in the background, latently challenging, upon careful scrutiny, closed cultural models of what seems real there. Or unity of scenic focus fractures into incongruous activities that do not really add up – "if you once look closely" – into a unified public occasion. Or moments of still more dramatic incongruity develop wherein contending interpretative possibilities seem to collide, leaving a kind of hermeneutic black hole in the midst of which an enigmatic object in a custom house attic, or a densely suggestive scene such as that at the climax of "My Kinsman, Major Molineux," cannot be definitively contextualized and judged. In fiction where a timeless dimension unequivocally outside the "perverted" compass of "artificial system" no longer seems reachable, culturally meaningful spectacle itself nevertheless becomes sufficiently challenged by a recalcitrant residuum of secondary detail – and sufficiently destabilized by interpretative intermixture and collision – to lose much of its ostensibly "settled" character.

Whether in the "wilderness" or the "settlement," competing claims to name, describe, and determine the most fundamental character of whatever we grasp and see begin to destabilize all mastery over the "neutral territory" developing. As Hawthorne emphasizes in his celebrated passage in "The Custom-House," the shifting aspects of such a "neutral territory" are neither merely "imaginary" (for they often seem at least as persuasively abstracted out of empirical reality as fluctuating aspects of a Rorschach inkblot) nor quite "actual," if by the "actual" we mean a clear-cut standard against which an array of distorted, hallucinatory, or abnormal perspectives can be definitively adjudged to be such (*Scarlet Letter* 36). Volatile and multi-dimensional rather than homogeneously envisaged in a single way, such "neutral territory" remains perceptually unsettled – a landscape of "incongruity" and "sad . . . disturbance" over which no definitive vision prevails.

In disclosing such instability and "disturbance" extending all the way back toward the colonial origins of the Republic, Hawthorne shatters inertly retrospective historical stereotypes to reveal a turbulent, trans-perspectival cultural space that becomes the equivalent of Chillingworth's medicine: "elaborately compounded," observes Hawthorne, of both "the European pharmacopoeia" and "Indian . . . herbs and roots," medicine of this sort, in the very process of becoming "compounded," nevertheless remains too "heterogeneous" and "far-fetched" to solidify into something completely unified, systematically knowable, and stable (*Scarlet Letter* 119–20). In keeping with the latently admixed character of such an adulterated cultural environment, where Puritan theology is ultimately "constrained to avail" itself of "the lore of Rabbis, and monkish erudition" (*Scarlet Letter* 126), and where the pumpkin vine intertwines dissonantly with the English rose bush in Governor Bellingham's garden, fullest perception of the immediate, concrete moment itself becomes "elaborately compounded" and "heterogeneous" in Hawthorne's writing: a matter of shifting lights and incongruous cross-perspectives into what resists inert, stable capture.

Ultimately, everything from the bottom up turns out to be "elaborately compounded" and "heterogeneous": nearby objects and forms, institutions and the public spectacles that they authorize, or broader regional or national entities that otherwise become defined on more stable, homogeneous terms. It is easy, however, to overlook the ubiquity of the heterogeneously "compounded" throughout Hawthorne's writing. In the very act of crediting him with genuine sensitivity to disparate realities, for example, Lauren Berlant proposes that in his negotiation, in the middle of the nineteenth century, of an array of "social and political" affiliations – "national, regional, provincial" – Hawthorne confronts a "competition" for allegiances between "the federal state" and "its internal Others, its rivals."[19] But it is more accurate to emphasize that the "federal state" and "its internal Others, its rivals" all ultimately dissolve into incongruous cross-perspectives in Hawthorne's writing. At various scales of reference and levels of social generalization, that is to say, from an interpretatively dissonant scarlet "A," through ambiguous, perceptually shifting scenes of regional New England life, to the "miscellaneous collection of" Americans – "mostly unknown to one another, and without any common sponsor" – who gather around a "tall, loose-jointed" Lincoln in an impromptu Washington, D.C. ceremony in "Chiefly About War Matters" (1862), resistance to the totalizing, homogeneous perspective prevails.[20]

No doubt in "Chiefly About War Matters," Hawthorne feels a certain "comfort" in contemplating the patriotic frieze currently being painted on the Capitol ceiling by Emmanuel Gottlieb Leutze: "It was delightful to see him so calmly elaborating his design, while other men doubted and feared, or hoped treacherously, and whispered to one another that the nation would exist only a little longer" (307). Earlier in the decade, in *The Life of Franklin Pierce* (1852), Hawthorne extolls "that common country which Providence brought into one nation, through a continued miracle of almost two hundred years, from the first settlement . . . until the revolution."[21] But such phraseology notwithstanding, mechanisms at work in Hawthorne's fiction ultimately challenge a "common" politics of simple consensus and synthesis to suggest the possibility of an alternative public space. That is to say, the underlying elusiveness of the most fundamental cultural "objects," starting "away with almost ghostly indistinctness" upon deepest scrutiny, does not simply arouse a frightening sense of the "impalpable" in Hawthorne's writing. In potentiality, such elusiveness furthermore points vision through the dawning inadequacy of parochialized, reductively inflected forms of cultural presence toward recognition of the way everything remains hazarded into a sort of overflowing and metamorphic trans-subjectivity beyond any particular frame of reference: the ongoing give-and-take of viewpoint and perspective amidst which the judgment of Hester Prynne, or of an enigmatic scarlet "A," remains in indeterminate play. Through recognition of such metamorphic trans-subjectivity, a vast and vital public dimension, transcending the narrowness of any parochial perspective, flickers into possibility in Hawthorne's writing.

This is scarcely to deny the involvement of Hawthorne's characters in the "big, heavy, solid unrealities" of thickly historicized modes of existence. The compelling pressure of what is latently contingent and frail, and yet demands to be taken seriously, comes to the surface (as in the case of a frightening scarlet "A" disappearing over the centuries into a mere "rag of . . . cloth") in works of fiction emphasizing how much that eventually mutates or turns preposterous nevertheless is experienced by historicized creatures as pressing and real. Still, in the very thick of apparent settlement, the possibility of the otherwise abides. At bottom, any orienting environment within which members of a community appear to find themselves remains vulnerable to the mediating transformations of the author of a "Romance," who so manages his "atmospherical medium as to bring out or mellow the lights," or to "deepen and enrich the shadows," in the process to demonstrate the alterability of the existential "picture."

Ultimately, what the romancer throws into relief by changing his "atmospherical medium" so explicitly cannot be directly glimpsed or perceived. It spreads everywhere throughout everything more as an "evanescent flavor" than "as any portion of the actual substance of the dish."[22] This ubiquitous flavor of evanescence, subtly tinging everything that seems static, inert, and solid in the Hawthornesque romance with an underlying frailty, emerges as an indefinitely mutable dimension that in stabilizing into hardened objective entities or into steadily perceived spectacles recedes into deceptive eclipse.

Even when so eclipsed, potential mutation of presence and form lies within the compass of what I earlier termed communal "trans-subjectivity." Wholly in contrast, however, to the tendency of the Hawthornesque romance to throw such shifting and transformative power into relief, the demand remains prevalent throughout the nineteenth century, and well into the twentieth, for American art forms wherein steadiness of point of view ultimately lies grounded in what Van Wyck Brooks terms an underlying national

focal centre – that is the first requisite . . . I mean that national "point of rest," to adopt a phrase in which Coleridge indicated that upon which the harmony of a work of art is founded and to which everything in the composition is more or less unconsciously referred; that secure and unobtrusive element of national character, taken for granted, and providing a certain underlying coherence and background of national understanding.[23]

In place of such "underlying coherence" and "background of . . . understanding," Hawthorne discloses within the compass of the community "which they were here planting in the wilderness" the incalculability and proneness to metamorphosis of its most primordial shaping powers, which emerge as analogous to the metamorphic powers thrown into relief in the "Romance." Wrested from political unconsciousness, and forced into self-acknowledgment, such radically transformative activity proves to be burdened by a sense of ambiguity and existential mystery the terrible indefiniteness of which provides no revelatory closure and no "national 'point of rest'."

CHAPTER 2

Thoreau and the interminable journey of vision
"nearer and nearer here*"*

> The image of undistorted nature arises only in distortion, as its
> opposite.
>
> Theodor Adorno, *Minima Moralia*[1]

In plunging us into a colonial New England *mise-en-scène* of shifting perspectives and situations without a steady intersubjective gloss, Hawthorne's
historical fiction challenges the envisagement of "settlement" as stable,
monologically structured space outside the frontiers of which lurk wild
spaces and a sense of the otherwise. Henry David Thoreau, I am now about
to argue, similarly blurs a longstanding antithesis between culturally organized, accredited space and what lies mysteriously and freely beyond its bor-
ders. If anything, he develops a more aggressive, more explicitly thematized
critique of such dualistic geography in affirming that although "these continents and hemispheres are soon run over, an always unexplored and infinite
region makes off on every side," and "we can make no highway or beaten
track into it, but the grass immediately springs up in the path." In inextrica-
bly intertwined geography of this sort, the relationship between culturally
developed space and extra-cultural potential is too ubiquitous, mercurial,
and open-ended to become exhausted or explained by the logic of a single
edge of ordered space beyond which spreads its unexplored antithesis.

No doubt I am speaking of Thoreau at his most provocative and intriguing. No doubt in contrast to the way I have been reading Hawthorne,
Thoreau often does direct yearning and fascination away from landscapes
that appear compromised by cultural mediation and human history into
differed, alien spaces, as if – in Hester Prynne's words – "there thou art
free!" At such junctures in his writing, much like Hester gazing rapturously
into a forest that seems to transcend the compass of culturally molded,
mediating vision, Thoreau emerges as the celebrant par excellence of the
allure of "the wilderness" beyond "lawns and cultivated fields" into great
primordial vistas where "things are wild and free." "My spirits infallibly

rise," he confesses, "in proportion to outward dreariness."[2] He yearns
to make contact with what he terms "untamed, . . . forever untamable
Nature," transcending all human contexts and frames of reference, such
as the forlorn terrain that seems to spread all around him in the "Burnt
Lands" section of the "Ktaadn" essay in *The Maine Woods*, where he writes
that "I looked with awe at the ground I trod on," and where he insists that
"we have not seen pure Nature, unless we have seen her thus vast and drear
and inhuman."[3] Or if not northward toward Mt. Ktaadn, then "westward
I go free" in pursuit of wild lands stretching "uninterruptably toward the
setting sun." "I wish to speak a word for Nature," Thoreau affirms at the
outset of "Walking," "for absolute freedom and wildness, as contrasted with
a freedom and culture merely civil . . . for there are enough champions of
civilization: the minister and the school-committee and every one of you
will take care of that" ("Walking" 266, 250).

"Nature," however – or at least "nature" conceived as a geographically
distinguishable counter-world of "absolute . . . wildness" falling outside
humanly inhabited, cultivated space – turns out to be a troublesome category throughout a continental American landscape where "there is scarcely
a square rod . . . exposed but you may find on it the stone arrowheads of
an extinct race."[4] Even if one ignores traces of an alternative culture and
history throughout virtually every "square rod . . . exposed," ostensibly
wild, alien space appears to be disappearing from the American continent
at the time that Thoreau writes. "The era of the Wild Apple will soon be
past," he foresees.[5] The "mission" of the lumbering industry, he observes
in *The Maine Woods*, appears to be precisely to "drive the forest all out
of the country, from every solitary beaver-swamp and mountain-side, as
soon as possible" (4). And this lament over the disappearance of wild, alien
space into the past history of the nation, prevalent throughout Thoreau's
writing, proves to be a familiar litany as well in the popular press of the
period. Characteristically, a reviewer writes in the 8 May 1847 issue of *The
Literary World* that

the axe of civilization is busy with our old forests, and artisan ingenuity is fast
sweeping away the relics of our natural infancy. What were once . . . wild and
picturesque haunts . . . where the wild deer roamed in freedom, are becoming
the abodes of commerce and the seats of manufactures . . . Even the primordial
hills, once bristling with shaggy pine and hemlock, like old Titans as they were,
are being shorn of their locks, and . . . made to figure in the shape of deal boards
and rafters for unsightly structures on bare commons. Yankee enterprise has little
sympathy with the picturesque, and it behooves our artists to rescue from its grasp
the little that is left, before it is for ever too late. This is their mission.[6]

To what degree does Thoreau similarly define his own literary "mission" as the compensatory memorialization of otherwise doomed, vanishing spaces? Significantly, Steven Fink observes that to envisage such a memorializing "mission" for "our artists" concedes "a fundamental separation" between the "aesthetic" and the "historical," between a vanishing space of intriguing, mysterious vista now largely available only on canvas or as memorialized in literature and the increasingly settled landscapes of actual history itself.[7] Thoreau at his most provocative, however, scarcely assumes that his role is to memorialize a sense of space that has otherwise vanished in actual history. Although it is true that "these hemispheres and continents" may seem "soon run over," "frontiers" marking the outermost edge of the culturally molded, historically organized world are "not east or west, north or south, but wherever a man *fronts* a fact, though that fact be his neighbor, there is an unsettled wilderness between him and Canada, between him and the setting sun, or, further still, between him and *it*."[8] Wherever an environment of settled shape and steady visual form seems to be, "there . . . unsettled wilderness" still stretches indefinitely on and on, and "not till we are completely lost" do we "realize where we are" amidst "the infinite extent of our relations" with it.[9] In Thoreau's writing at its most provocative, that is to say, the present moment itself, no matter how confidently visualized and persuasively conceived, potentially slips away from known images and interpretative profiles to give rise to wholly unsuspected possibilities of visualization and orientation.[10]

Everywhere throughout Thoreauvian space, "east or west, north or south," confident orientation potentially dwindles into a subtle skepticism – a "negative knowledge" ("Walking" 293) – accompanying and putting pressure on whatever seems to become definitively orienting and immediate. Through searching inquiry into the tenuous emergence of the perceived, organized world from out of latently more ambiguous empirical potential, Thoreau exposes unsuspected volatility of image and underlying fluidity of color wherever stability of objective form may have appeared to be. He proposes in his *Journal* entry for 9 February 1852 that

men tell about the mirage to be seen in certain deserts and in peculiar states of the atmosphere . . . [but a condition of] mirage is constant. The state of the atmosphere is continually varying, and, to a keen observer, objects do not twice present exactly the same appearance . . . The prospect is thus actually a constantly varying mirage . . . I cannot well conceive of greater variety than it produces by its changes from hour to hour of every day.[11]

In this "continually varying" atmosphere detectable to "keen" observation, the image of the object becomes incongruous and unsteady, as when the "intense burning red" of autumn leaves loses

some of its strength . . . with every step you . . . take toward them . . . The focus of their reflected color is in the atmosphere far on this side . . . It is partly borrowed fire . . . It has only some comparatively dull red leaves for a rallying-point, or kindling-stuff, to start it . . . You see a redder tree than exists.[12]

Thoreau similarly notices the way shifting patterns of perceptual emphasis and selection will distill now one version of a scene, now another, from out of indefinitely "unexplored and infinite" topography making off "on every side from the mind" (*A Week* 359). Within one and the same landscape, it is nevertheless possible that

the actual objects which one man will see from a particular hill-top are just as different from those which another will see as the beholders are different . . . I have found that it required a different intention of the eye, in the same locality, to see different plants, even when they were closely allied, as *Juncaceae* and *Gramineae:* when I was looking for the former, I did not see the latter in the midst of them. ("Autumnal Tints" 351–52)

Because fresh, unsuspected reality can develop immediately "in the midst" of whatever we appear to see, apparently palpable, nearby scenery becomes potentially hollowed out by other versions of *there* there, as when "the walker in the familiar fields which stretch around my native town sometimes finds himself in another land . . . [where] the idea which the word Concord suggests ceases to be suggested. These farms which I have myself surveyed, these bounds which I have set up . . . fade from the surface of the glass" ("Walking" 297). For the leisurely afternoon walker, "the idea" of "Concord" – indeed, the whole landscape as named, conceived, and organized through the lens of the map – seems to vanish into "another land." In the collision of shifting experiences of landscape, however, Thoreau essentially traffics in the crumbling of rigidified versions of "here" into what he calls "a constant endeavor to get nearer and nearer *here*."[13] Sense of immediacy deepens, complicates, and turns problematic during his travels into it; it does not recede back into the lost, immutable authority of some unwarped primordial world.

What lurks at the very quick of shifting experiences of landscape cannot be seized upon, patterned, and limned in any one particular way. It is most thoroughly known – like the ambiguously sensuous surface of a particularly elaborate optical illusion or Escher etching – in transformation *between* immediacies, one version taking shape in the perceptual depths of another, every image of landscape less than thoroughly saturated into it. In Thoreauvian space the world of "mirage" does not yield at last to one more deceptively stable mirage, but rather to what remains imagistically volatile.

What is volatile and unstable is both inarguably there and yet outside our full imagistic mastery, becoming, as it were, enigmatically immediate. It is, I think, significant that thawing springtime mud along the railroad cut in *Walden* assumes precisely this condition of enigmatic immediacy. Thoreau emphasizes that what he witnesses seems "truly *grotesque*" (305). What is "grotesque," modern scholarship suggests, hovers and wavers problematically between possible definitions, ages, characteristics, and shapes; it seems to invoke what Geoffrey Galt Harpham terms a cognitively dispersed focal "point in the middle distance, the point of the grotesque," in the depths of which "multiple interpretations" of the immediate object incongruously proliferate. "Opposing processes and assumptions," observes Harpham, seem to "co-exist" together.[14] Thoreau encounters just this phenomenon of contrastive meanings and processes in persuasive yet unsettling convergence when gazing into the liquid mass along the cut. Such a flow of matter, for example, seems exquisitely designed in its movements – almost living – and yet, from another perspective, it remains "excrementitious" (*Walden* 308), muddy, oozing, and inchoate there where it flows. Indeed, even in the way it suggests design, such a flow of matter nevertheless eludes stable image and fixed nomenclature to resemble

sappy leaves or vines, making heaps of pulpy sprays a foot or more in depth, and resembling, as you look down on them, the laciniated lobed and imbricated thalluses of some lichens; or you are reminded of coral, of leopards' paws or birds' feet, of brains or lungs or bowels, and excrements of all kinds. It is a truly *grotesque* vegetation . . . more ancient and typical than acanthus, chiccory, ivy, vine, or any vegetable leaves. (*Walden* 305)

That which in "resembling" such and such a form nevertheless makes you "reminded" of another, visually suggesting "leopards' paws or birds' feet . . . brains or lungs or . . . excrements" recalls ambiguous, equivocal, and tricksome imagery in a painting by Hieronymus Bosch. Thoreau himself suggests that what he glimpses in such a flow of matter remains "truly grotesque" – "more ancient and typical," as he puts it, than any definitive species or type. Are we coming upon the most "ancient" and "typical" envisagement of reality that is possible? In other words, does all clearcut categorization and stabilizing abstraction (alone through which sense of "where we are" normally occurs) inevitably reduce and distill what at the

radical remains too ambiguous, volatile, and obscure to become comprehensively perceived in more stable forms and meanings? Let us remember
that for Thoreau the image of the object, once we look more closely at
it, "continually transcends and translates itself" (*Walden* 306) into still another perspective, still another image, the "intense burning red" of leaves at
a distance, for example, shifting toward "dull" as one walks toward them.
Incongruous aspects and profiles of the densely perceived, immediate thing
begin to accumulate at its site. Even the basic geometric shape of the object turns unstable. For within the most accurately gauged depths of the
sensuous, time cannot be arrested, but continues in subliminal motion
throughout what eyesight more crudely stabilizes and abstracts into overt
dependability of shape. The printed image of Cape Cod, for example, may
assume the static, inert look of an "arm" on the map, but "the Cape" itself
is actually "wasting on both sides," and "in some places it" has "lost many
rods within the last year" while "extending itself on particular points on
the south and west."[15] And what is true of the subliminally changing body
of the landscape is true of the human body as well. The "ball of the human
finger," for example, reemerges in the subliminal stream of growth and
incessant time as a "drop" still altering and changing, and "the fingers and
toes" bear the trace of a

> flow to their extent from the thawing mass of the body . . . The ear may be regarded,
> fancifully, as a lichen, *umbilicaria*, on the side of the head, with its lobe or drop.
> The lip . . . laps or lapses from the sides of the cavernous mouth. The nose is a
> manifest congealed drop or stalactite. The chin is a still larger drop, the confluent
> dripping of the face. The cheeks are a slide from the brows into the valley of the
> face, opposed and diffused by the cheek bones. Each rounded lobe of the vegetable
> leaf, too, is a thick and now loitering drop. (*Walden* 307–08)

The arrested visible image of the human body or vegetable leaf thus becomes a "thick and now loitering" abstraction distilled out of subvisible
motion that "continually . . . transcends itself." The truest image of what
is actual, carnal, and thick emerges as continuously spreading itself *across
fixed form* to become youthful flesh aging, or brilliantly red foliage that is
getting duller at closer range; the truest image is always trans-imagistic deep
down.[16]

The "exceedingly grotesque" objects and sights that Thoreau encounters
on Cape Cod beach similarly resist tidy location within settled category
and image (*Cape Cod* 126). A "singularly masculine woman" (54), detritus
along the shore in which "animal and vegetable kingdoms meet and are
strangely mingled" (78–79), and the "fugacious," tonally mixed song of

seabirds that seems part "dirge" but also "song of rejoicing" (82) are among
the scrambled oddities and mixed phenomena along the beach that occupy
a focal "point in the middle distance" between settled meanings, stages, and
tones. But many phenomena in Thoreauvian space exceed (if often more
subtly) crispness of cognitive category and stability of perceptual image
according to the proposition that, in witnessing the nearby object, "we
discriminate at first only a few features, and we need to reconsider our
experience" of it "from many points of view and in various moods."[17] As
we have seen, such ongoing reconsideration "from many points of view" is
encouraged even to the point of contradiction and incongruity at the site
of the sensuous. Ultimately, what seems the focused, foregrounded thing
deepens, turns more ambiguous, and becomes more imagistically uncertain
in becoming more densely itself.

Thoreau thus puts enormous pressure upon perception through scrutiny
of sights and scenes that disrupt categorization and blur ostensible onto-
logical boundaries. Here it is helpful to recall Mary Douglas's observation,
previously referred to in my discussion of instability of setting and scene in
Hawthorne's fiction, that "as perceivers," we ordinarily

select from all the stimuli falling on our senses only those which interest us, and our
interests are governed by a patternmaking tendency, sometimes called *schema* . . . In
a chaos of shifting impressions, each of us constructs a stable world in which objects
have recognisable shapes, are located in depth, and have permanence. In perceiving
we are building, taking some cues and rejecting others. The most acceptable cues
are those which fit most easily into the pattern that is being built up.[18]

Yet Douglas goes on to emphasize the way societies and civilizations tend to
allow "scope for meditation" upon what "our schematising tendencies have
caused us to miss." Dream life, the ritualistic veneration in primitive societies (if across barriers of taboo and disgust) of incongruous, categorically
scrambled creatures, objects, and visions, and many modern "works of art"
as well encourage us, as Douglas puts it, "to go behind the explicit structures
of our normal experience" (*Purity and Danger* 5–37). Thoreau similarly explores the limitations of stable schemata of perception, if only to locate
outside such perceptual schemata a still more immediate, more volatile
world that in growing increasingly less abstract becomes less easily perceived and conceived. For Thoreau, as for Alexander Gottlieb Baumgarten
struggling with precisely this issue in eighteenth-century epistemology and
aesthetics, "the texture of reality, the concrete or existential moment" itself
ultimately "escapes the philosopher as well as the scientist" and, indeed,

seems to defy the most commonsensical forms of categorization the more alertly we try to reach into it.[19]

The most alert reach into the "concrete or existential moment" in Thoreau's writing – I refer again to his assertion that "not till we are . . . lost . . . do we . . . realize where we are" – threatens to take us completely out of our coherence into what begins to flicker and to waver at closest observational range. Since "where we are" at last becomes the site of blurred categorical boundaries and shifting gestalten, Thoreau proposes that "it is easier to discover another such a new world as Columbus did, than to go within one fold of this which we appear to know so well; the land is lost sight of, the compass varies" (*A Week* 383). Where "land is lost sight of" directly amidst what cannot be absolutely literalized and stabilized, Thoreau enters into the underlying precariousness of the most basic formations of reality, from the way colors are conceived (in American autumn foliage, he finds nuances of color not yet recognized in the English language, but inviting drastic shifts in the whole nomenclature and differential scale of tints and tones) to "varieties" of "wild apples" whose many nuances and fine distinctions, once properly enough recognized, would ultimately "exhaust the Latin and Greek languages" ("Autumnal Tints" 335–36; "Wild Apples" 387). Beyond what languages can discriminate, classify, and gather into broad categorical schemata, Thoreau recalls once glimpsing a "matchless and indescribable light blue, such as watered and changeable silks and sword blades suggest . . . a vitreous greenish blue, as I remember it" (*Walden* 177), the exact verbal nuance proving elusive within a "Nature" so varied that "I doubt if you can ever get" it to "repeat" itself "exactly."[20] Ultimately, one can at best traffic back and forth between mediational abstractions and what they cannot, on closer view, absolutely organize, assess, and explain. In this betwixt-and-between space, envisaged by Thoreau as "the interval between that which *appears*, and that which *is*," where "distance" that can be crossed ultimately "fails to follow" (*A Week* 387), perception encounters a permanent gap or "interval" that cannot be closed – a depth "further than to sunset" (*A Week* 359) between the observer and what he cannot fix definitively in his sights.

In probing into the innermost core of the existential moment, then, Thoreau discovers increasing friction between structures of mediation and a more ambiguous immediacy. He exposes the way the most fundamental formations of reality – perceived colors and shapes, basic categories and conceptual polarities – must be wrested from what remains recalcitrantly trans-imagistic, chronically in motion, and categorically unsettled at closer observational range. The most elementary organizational schemata emerge to him as forms of inevitable phenomenological theater, assuming on close enough view of them the status of "a kind of fiction, a work of the imagination," apart from which "the presence and criticism of a part of me" stands "remote" by virtue of "a certain" skeptical "doubleness" (*Walden* 135). For what is exposed at the core of reality is not the firm foundation of the commonsense world in "nature" ("nature," Thoreau emphasizes, is "so vast . . . that we have never seen one of her features" ["Walking" 297]), but rather the way all coherent feature somewhat falsifies and reduces what remains more ambiguously there.

The ostensibly coherent, commonsensical world assumes carnal shape by virtue of a certain willing suspension of disbelief. Its incarnation remains imperfect. The dream of the perfect "incarnation" of "civilization" in material "nature," explored so thoroughly by Myra Jehlen as fundamental to American thought,[21] is discredited in Thoreau's writing by subtle discrepancies that keep showing up between the coherent interpretative image, on the one hand, and matter in recalcitrant "retreat" from manmade forms of coherence, on the other. Ultimately, Thoreau confesses, "I begin to see . . . an object when I cease to *understand* it . . . but I get no further than this . . . What are these things? . . . [They] keep so aloof! and Nature is so reserved."[22]

Such prevailing discrepancy between interpretative image and interpreted thing, opening up a depth "further than to sunset" between perceptual form and what it tries to localize and stabilize within its sights, emerges most unmistakably for Thoreau in contemplation of the Indian arrowhead:

It is humanity inscribed on the face of the earth . . . the best symbol or letter that could have been transmitted to me.

The Red Man, his mark =⟨⟩

At every step I see it, . . . a footprint – rather a mind-print – left every where, and altogether illegible.[23]

The terms "symbol or letter" and yet "altogether illegible" are meant, however contradictorily, to describe one and the same thing. The "arrowhead" splits, that is to say, into a culturally mediated artifact and yet an immediate, puzzling object that survives (if less starkly than Stonehenge stone) much of its vanished cultural history. Normally, to be sure, the object remains much more thoroughly mediated into and domesticated within a specific historical context. There we see it as familiar, ordinary, and settled. But once to acknowledge the covertly "illegible" otherness of the object – once to recognize the conceivable strangeness, for example, of markings like "q" and "y" (potentially as odd and unfamiliar as cuneiform) or to accept the potential preposterousness of clothing styles that now seem normal – is to grasp the obscure other side of any culturally mediated object or material surface. It is to witness material surfaces becoming somewhat withdrawn from their historically determined values and meanings while still somewhat equivocally supporting them. Within such equivocal depths of vision, immediacy continues to resist (even as it remains resisted by) mediating values and frames of reference, and beyond that tensional condition, no further cultural conquest over, incursion into, or merger with the material basis of civilization seems possible, even along a great American frontier.

A merger between idea and matter thus never quite occurs in Thoreau's writing. The underlying irony remains that while "these continents and hemispheres are soon run over . . . an always unexplored and infinite region makes off on every side from the mind, . . . and we can make no highway or beaten track into it, but the grass immediately springs up in the path" (*A Week* 359). The provisionality of "humanity inscribed on the face of the earth" is emphasized. But the ultimate question remains: why brood with so much intensity and fervor into still unsettled depths where categorization wavers and imagery becomes suspicious? Certainly it is true that the deconstructive vehemence of Thoreau's writing – the insistence that "not till we are lost" do we "realize where we are," the disorienting cry atop Mt. Ktaadn of "*Contact! Contact! . . . where* are we?" (*The Maine Woods* 95) – entails violent subversion of the authoritative shape of the world as prelude to fresh discovery. Thoreau seeks to deprive immediate reality of authoritative structure and settled shape in part because

it is only when we forget all our learning that we begin to know. I do not get nearer by a hair's breadth to any natural object so long as I presume that I have an introduction to it from some learned man. To conceive of it with a total apprehension I must for the thousandth time approach it as something totally strange. If you . . . would fain perceive something . . . you must approach the object totally unprejudiced.[24]

Commentators like Lawrence Buell focus on the "restorative side" of such violent disruption of perceptual habit. To "reperceive the familiar" – or so Buell argues in addressing Thoreau and other writers who "racalibrate" our recognition of familiar places and scenes – entails a "deepening" rather than a fundamental questioning of "sense of place": such a process, Buell proposes, entails "defamiliarization" that serves to "*dis*place in order to *re*place," in effect returning us to where we thought we were already with "new understanding and enthusiasm."[25] I would argue, however, that more is ultimately at stake in Thoreau's recognition of the "strange" lurking in the depths of the familiar than a simple restorative effort to "*dis*place in order to *re*place." Between displacememt and replacement lurks a rupture in the fabric of the real that Buell's vocabulary too easily overshoots. To "forget all our learning," on the one hand, and to "approach" what we thought we knew as "totally strange," on the other, is to break sharply with, rather than to build progressively upon, prior assumption and mental habit. It is to accept what Thoreau calls "steep, and sudden, and . . . unaccountable transition" – transition not to be accounted for in "the common train of my thoughts . . . each implying the next" (*A Week* 386) – at the axis of profound perceptual disruption and metamorphosis. It is to open up fissures rather than to sustain faith in orderly, continuous progress in the depth of drastic perceptual transformation, as when "intense burning red" at a distance nevertheless becomes "dull" closer up, or when what seems to suggest pattern and shape in thawing sand nevertheless seems inchoate and "excrementitious" from another point of view. Ultimately, the site shared by such extreme discontinuities in shifting image and cognitive profile becomes, as in a Picasso painting, a place of paradox and perceptual incongruity rather than of synthesis or of progressively unfolding design. Indeed, back and forth across such cognitive dissonance, "I, on my side, require of every writer . . . some such account as he would send to his kindred from a distant land; for if he has lived sincerely, it must have been in a distant land to me" (*Walden* 3–4). The concept of "land" shifts from what seems stable and in common between writers and observers to what drastically alters – becomes potentially another land, a "distant land to me" – through other voices and different eyes, and "what," then, "shall this great wild tract over which we strolled be called? . . . What shall the whole be called?"[26]

Passages such as this, which suggest an inevitable collision of descriptive vocabularies and aesthetic strategies competing for control of the same turf, no doubt recall numerous other cases of multi-perspectivism in American art and writing, from Melville's interpretatively dissonant gold doubloon in *Moby-Dick* to Jasper Johns's incongruously envisaged *Map* of America itself. But Thoreau's tendency is to locate such collision and perspectival competition directly amidst the most minute empirical impressions of "the natural object" itself, where its color, closely observed, "depends on the position of the beholder in relation to the direction of the wind,"[27] where what seems exquisitely designed in flowing sand nevertheless seems inchoate and "excrementitious" from another point of view.

No universal awareness of the object emerges. Quite the contrary, the proclamation that "I, on my side, require of every writer . . . some such account as he would send" from an entirely alien "land" implies multiplication, not harmonization, of perspective. Perception builds its way, through shifting gestalten and from alternative angles of vision, disparately and somewhat incongruously into awareness of what is present. Thoreau rejects what Thomas Jefferson calls "the common sense" view of the object presented "in terms so plain and firm as to command" the "assent" of all "mankind."[28] Reaching into a more volatile, less harmonious space suppressed by the idea of "common sense," Thoreau is able to accept, for example, that when Joe Polis, his Penobscot guide into the Maine wilderness, "gave me Indian names for things," in "proportion as I understood the language, I saw them from" an altered "point of view." To explore "a dictionary of the Indian language," Thoreau stresses, is to break dramatically with cognitive preconception and to plunge into "a wholly new life to us" – a "life within a life" – "threading the woods . . . still."[29]

"Life within a life" – reality taking altered, foreign shape in the depths of reality still persuasively conceived in a different way – is precisely what occurs as well at the river conflictingly known in different cultures as "Musketaquid" or "Concord" (*A Week* 5), or where the dullness and yet the intensity and colorfulness of the same autumn foliage can be witnessed from shifting angles of vision.[30] In Thoreauvian topography, realities incommensurable with one another neither entirely cancel out nor are entirely nullified and superseded by their alternatives. Rather, as in the case of the pun that proves so important an ingredient in Thoreau's prose,[31] incommensurable realities become incongruous, mutually qualified aspects of what resists direct, definitive capture, and cultivating this dissonant way of seeing and conceiving seems to be about as close as Thoreau can get to a sense of "the whole" of whatever landscape or phenomenon he is witnessing. A less tensional understanding of what is witnessed – knowable more directly through what seems "plain and firm" in category and concept, in perspectival image and hue – ultimately reduces its complexity. Accordingly, at the equivocal convergence of shifting angles of vision, Thoreau locates a sense of reality that is dissonantly present throughout mutually incongruous characteristics and qualities but never directly, steadily, and absolutely seen.

Where what is known as "Concord River" is also known as the river "Musketaquid," or where "excrementitious" sand nevertheless seems designed, Thoreau reaches through stabilized versions of landscape and of topographical "fact" to a kind of inmost, inevitable blind spot – volatile, problematic, shifting – that "cannot be represented on a map, color it as you will" (*Cape Cod* 74). He exposes the slippage of "where we are" away from whatever seems "so plain and firm as to command" the "assent" of all "mankind." Developing a sense of place wherein versions of "mirage" are wrested out of what can always be differently conceived, he tends to juggle, not to synthesize, a number of "flitting perspectives" and "demi-experiences" (*A Week* 8) all at once.

No doubt the historical shift, all but consummated in mid-nineteenth-century Massachusetts, from native tribal to Euro-American culture entails the stabilization of a sense of landscape into localities and regions that seem fixed and firm. The logic of the scale map, with its divisions and subdivisions extending into every nook and cranny of zoned, regulated space, becomes the omnipresent epistemological basis – questioned by few – of farmland boundaries, public preserves, lots for sale, and county limits.[32] On numerous local handbills, Thoreau himself advertises his skills as a specialist in

LAND SURVEYING of all kinds, according to the best methods known; the necessary data supplied, in order that the boundaries of Farms may be accurately described in Deeds; Woods lotted off distinctly and according to a regular plan; Roads laid out, &c., &c. Distinct and accurate Plans of Farms furnished . . . so that the land may be laid out in a winter evening. Areas warranted accurate within almost any degree of exactness . . . Apply to Henry D. Thoreau.[33]

In Thoreau's writing, however, static "areas" start to metamorphose into shifting cognitive profiles and perspectives, and topographical features that seem arrested and fixed remain in subliminal flux. A space of "boundaries . . . accurately described" and of phenomena "distinctly" witnessed is becoming relinquished for a more volatile, at times more incongruous sense of the real.

Contemporary American geography may appear to be stable, but cartographical representation not only artificially arrests the subliminally shifting contours of topographical feature, but furthermore proves to be abstracted out of the ongoing flux of printed geographical history itself. Significantly, Thoreau reaches back in *Cape Cod* toward before the legendary landing at Plymouth Rock – origin of current New England geography – and explores the volatile "Ante-Pilgrim history" of what is now called "New England": a name first emergent in a map by John Smith in the relatively late year of 1616. Reviewing "successive maps" before this period, Thoreau observes the way what is presently known as "Cape Cod" has in the past been "sprinkled

over with French, Dutch, and English names" vying for provisional territorial claim to the same disputed turf. And he notes the way boundaries
and geographical entities have altered over time, "the shore between Race
Point and Wood End" that now simply stretches between these points,
for example, having formerly been designated by the French as an independent territorial entity named "Bevechier" (273–76). To the English and
their successors, moreover, the entire region is called "Cape Cod," a name
derived from the vast amount of cod-fish which "Captain Bartholomew
Gosnold caught there in 1602" (2); but to the French it was "*C. Blan* (i.e.,
Cape White), from the color of its sands" (273).

Such disclosure of the way current New England geography has stabilized itself against an "Ante-Pilgrim" history of prior place names and
fluctuating geographies is illuminating. And in other ways as well, it is the
underlying flux within the depths of the visually and geographically arrested
that Thoreau continually emphasizes in his writing. In space of this sort,
"two or three hours' walking" even within familiar, nearby countryside will
sometimes

carry me to as strange a country as I ever expect to see . . . There is in fact a sort of
harmony discoverable between the capabilities of the landscape within a circle of
ten miles' radius, or the limits of an afternoon walk, and the threescore years and
ten of human life. It will never quite become familiar to you. ("Walking" 259).

What cartographical representation appears to fix and to freeze, or what
the Currier and Ives engraving would stabilize and stereotype into a classic, finished scene universally perceived in the same standard way, Thoreau
would expose as "volatile truth" (*Walden* 325) that so alters and shifts that it
"will never quite become familiar to you." In one case, representative form
serves to codify and to standardize vision, leaving the perceptually volatile
backdrop out of which it inevitably issues in eclipse; in the other, multiple viewpoints and incongruous perspectives wrest shifting possibilities of
immediacy out of a backdrop of "vastness and strangeness" (*Walden* 171)
that "the painter may not daub," whatever "figure we may have made in
the foreground" (*A Week* 392).

Dramatically in contrast, then, to the pursuit of standardized, universally
fixed and framed vision, which characterizes not only the stereotypic portraiture of place and scene in contemporary lithographic prints, but also
the would-be stabilization of sense of landscape into a geography of settled
"boundaries" and "woods lotted off distinctly," Thoreau develops incongruous, perceptually unsettled space. Affirming that he has chosen to dwell

elsewhere than in "Concord," he exposes the heterogeneity and even the discord of the most minute empirical impressions of objects and material forms. Instead of emerging as a conceivable site of objective, steady reference, Thoreauvian landscape at its most radical proves to be irremediably mutable, metaphoric, and given to "sudden . . . unaccountable transition" in visibility and presence.

Ultimately, Thoreau spans the range from minute scrutiny into the underlying frailty of visual categories and schemata to broadly theoretical speculation, his inquiry into the minutiae of the appearance-world resulting in startling metaphors and strange turns of phrase that violently revamp the official schemata of mid-nineteenth-century American geography. The audacity of such metaphors and phrases is a hallmark of Thoreauvian style, from the disclosure of still "unsettled wilderness" – spreading further than the "setting sun" – wherever visibility seems fixed, to the subversion of finite Euclidean measurements of distance in the indefinitely prolonged voyage "nearer and nearer *here.*" What begins to emerge is a perceptually open mode of space that cannot be exhausted. However preliminarily, Thoreau's spadework into the indefinitely alterable depths of empirical presence opens up a much different way of encountering forms in space, and of envisaging the fading edge of cultural order, than that fostered by the official geographic premises of the mid-nineteenth-century United States.

CHAPTER 3

Herman Melville's home cosmography: voyaging into the inscrutable interior of the American Republic

> What does Africa, – what does the West stand for? Is not our own
> interior white on the chart?
> Thoreau, Walden[1]

Like prospects into the wilderness in *The Scarlet Letter*, or like Thoreau's far-off spaces that are "soon run over," the Melvillian ocean ultimately remains overlain with interpretation and suffused with projective fantasy. Even the vast Pacific in *Moby-Dick* scarcely looms up, Ishmael's phraseology notwithstanding, as "unwarped primal" space spreading unequivocally beyond "the miserable warping memories of traditions and of towns."[2] Not only is the Melvillian Pacific freighted with a rich profusion of metaphors and allusions, but also, as a recent reading of *Moby-Dick* suggests, the ocean into which Ishmael voyages has become thickly mapped, charted space by the middle of the nineteenth century. It is gridded by latitudes and longitudes, and even its underlying currents seem open to precise calculation by Captain Ahab with the aid of contemporary oceanographic tables. Far out on the Melvillian ocean, a space of predictable, static constants that can be summed up in tables and charts and registered in exact geometric imagery facilitates – albeit at the expense of a richer experience of the sensuous – precise navigation throughout a precisely oriented world.[3]

In this sense, the Melvillian ocean scarcely falls outside culture and history. What Andrew Delbanco terms Melville's "complex meditations on epistemological imprisonment" do not lead specifically toward the freedom of wild, desolate space.[4] Much more subtly, they disclose the limitation of mechanisms of mediational, organizational power that appear to situate human beings within any well-oriented present, wherever that might be. Precisely as in writing by Hawthorne and Thoreau that we have been considering, the ultimate effect of interrogating such mediational mechanisms is to envisage a relationship between culturally organized space and extra-cultural potential that cannot be reduced to the simple, spatial logic of an expanding (or crossable) frontier-edge where culture ends, and an

extra-cultural dimension begins. Rather, the fading edge of oriented geography and of coherent, mediated spectacle lies everywhere in general
and nowhere in particular. In the very midst of a Wall Street law office,
words can fail, identities can turn fluid and uncertain, and fundamental
distinctions between office-space and domestic space can blur.

Ishmael may begin *Moby-Dick* by distinguishing between the fluidity and
openness of the ocean, on the one hand, and this "turnpike earth," on the
other, "all over dented with the marks of slavish heels and hoofs" (66). But
a long history of colonization and settlement notwithstanding, the well-
surveyed river valleys and richly storied hills of the American Northeast
ultimately prove to be sites of visual mutation and dramatically shifting
perspective in Melville's later fiction. It is true that we are told at the outset
of *Pierre* that "the beautiful country" around Young Master Glendinning

appealed to very proud memories . . . In Pierre's eyes, all its hills . . . seemed
sanctified through their . . . long uninterrupted possession by his race.
   That fond ideality which, in the eyes of affection, hallows the least trinket once
familiar to the person of a departed love; with Pierre that talisman touched the
whole earthy landscape around him; for remembering that on those hills his own
fine fathers had gazed; [that] through those woods, over these lawns . . . many a
grand-dame of his had merrily strolled when a girl; vividly recalling all these things,
Pierre deemed all that part of the earth a love-token; so that his very horizon was
to him as a memorial ring.[5]

"The whole earthly landscape around" Pierre – "long" in "possession by his
race" – may appear saturated with "the proudest patriotic and family associations" (5); all the way out to his furthest conceivable "horizon," he may
seem to gaze into well-mapped, "long-settled" (132) geography steeped in
national and personal memory. But as Melville's seventh novel progresses,
we are made aware that this "settled," culturally stabilized experience of
landscape and place owes its existence not simply to the mediative power
of map, image, and shaping cultural idea, but furthermore to the suppressive
power of violence and brute force, from fierce fighting "in the wilderness
before the Revolutionary war," when Pierre's ancestors waged war on the
"Indian" (29), to the more recent military suppression of "farmer-tenants"
with an alternative agenda for Hudson River plantations owned by a few,
powerful families, but worked by the landless and the poor (11). Against a
backdrop of potentially conflicting economic agendas, varieties of cultural
memory, and relationships to the land, brute force, at bottom, intermit-
tently defends the private property rights, the official "patriotic and family
associations," and the Anglo-Saxon place names of a landscape and sense

of place still troubled from time to time by counter-perspectives and alien envisagements both of its destiny and its past.

Such force notwithstanding, alternative memories and ideas of place simmer subversively in the novel's background, and Pierre's "fond" gaze into the "whole earthly landscape around" him remains limited and edged. Indeed, a major preoccupation throughout Melville's tales, novels, and sketches of the 1850s is the inevitably problematic, parochializing character of human gazing and description within an "ever-shifting Nature" (*Pierre* 9) that cannot quite become arrested and visually pinned down. Recent scholarship in particular emphasizes Melville's critique, in works such as *Pierre* and "The Piazza," of the representative and discursive practices officially shaping sense of natural landscape in antebellum America. In contrast, for example, to the glorified pictorialization of American natural scenery in publications such as *The Home Book of the Picturesque* (1852), Melville, observes Samuel Otter, "does not consecrate American scenery, endow it with legends," elide "its violent past," or pretend that it is the site of "Edenic," unwarped beauty. Rather, Melville, according to Otter, emphasizes "the framings, veilings, animations, and dissolutions of American views," in the process exposing how "control over" such views is ultimately "control over American absences and presences," over the ability to background, foreground, and stage-manage what seems innocently and literally visible to the naked eye.[6]

As Otter and other scholars indicate, it is the underlying *textuality* of American natural scenic spectacle that Melville emphasizes in *Pierre* and in the fiction that follows, according to the proposition advanced in *Pierre* that "Nature is not so much her own ever-sweet interpreter, as the mere supplier of that cunning alphabet, whereby selecting and combining as he pleases, each man reads his own peculiar lesson according to his own peculiar mind and mood" (342). One implication of such textualization of "Nature" into a "mere . . . cunning alphabet" is that just where the "natural" image seems most unwarped and objectively pure is where human manipulation is most cunningly disguised. By way of reaction to such camouflaging of the artificially manipulative within the ostensibly natural, Melville, proposes Barton Levi St. Armand, becomes an out-and-out "mannerist" in his exaggerated, distorted deployment of perspectives and scenic effects elsewhere characteristic of contemporary American landscape art, and nowhere does this "mannerism" emerge more vividly than in "The Piazza" sketch intended to frame and to set the keynote for the entire *Piazza Tales* collection. Whereas American natural spectacle in paintings by Asher B. Durand, for example, is ostensibly hallowed with "God-given" religious significance, such spectacle in "The Piazza" becomes a phantasmagoria of exaggerated "manipulation, invention, and management" in the depth of which lurks a sensed "existential vacuum": a felt "artificial illusionism" operating throughout a plethora of scenic effects.[7] St. Armand at one point quotes Wylie Sypher on manneristic aesthetic technique by way of illuminating what is occurring in Melville. Mannerism, according to Sypher – which he generalizes beyond its origins in sixteenth-century art into a more widespread cultivation of theatrically managed, overtly manneristic visual effects – plunges us into a universe of willfully exaggerated "experiment with . . . techniques of disproportion and disturbed balance"; it entails a "spiral . . . motion" of the eye sweeping through "space" that seems to open "like a vortex or alley" populated by "oblique or mobile points of view and strange – even abnormal – perspectives that yield approximations rather than certainties."[8] Such overt and exaggerated mannerism of "strange . . . perspectives" and "mobile points of view," proposes St. Armand, characterizes many passages in "The Piazza," in which natural spectacle becomes "a freakish combination of shadow and substance," and an almost "Jamesian" syntax of "asides, hesitations, parentheses, convolutions . . . serves to convey the mirage-like quality" of spectacle and scene:[9]

From the piazza, some uncertain object I had caught, mysteriously snugged away, to all appearance, in a sort of purpled breast-pocket, high up in a hopper-like hollow, or sunken angle, among the western mountains – yet, whether, really, it was on the mountain-side, or a mountain-top, could not be determined; because, though, viewed from favorable points, a blue summit, peering up away behind the rest, will, as it were, talk to you over their heads, and plainly tell you . . . that he considers himself – as, to say the truth, he has good right – by several cubits their superior, nevertheless, certain ranges, here and there double-filed, as in platoons, so shoulder and follow up upon one another, with their irregular shapes and heights, that, from the piazza, a higher and lower mountain will, in most states of the atmosphere, effacingly shade itself away into a higher and further one.

A wizard afternoon in autumn – late in autumn – a mad poet's afternoon; when the turned maple woods in the broad basin below me, having lost their first vermilion tint, dully smoked, like smouldering towns, when flames expire upon their prey . . . and the hermit-sun, hutted in an Adullum cave, well towards the south, according to his season, did little else but, by an indirect reflection of narrow rays shot down a Simplon pass among the clouds, just steadily paint one small, round, strawberry mole upon the wan cheek of Northwestern hills.[10]

A "mirage-like," thickly manneristic, excessively theatricalized nature certainly prevails in such passages. And the thrust of the remainder of Melville's story, in which the narrator-observer actually makes a journey into the hills, is precisely to emphasize "mirage-like" perspectival activity in want of solid reference. For what it all comes to, in the end, is the disenchanting collapse of the narrator's grandiose pictures and overwrought illusions as he presses forward into the empirical heart of his vision. Here he discovers the lonely Marianna living in destitution and decay, where the hot sun, no longer easily poeticized, "nearly blinds," and a "rotting" old house of "mended" window panes, deteriorating and in decrepitude, suggests as well the precariousness of human structure, artifact, and shaping image within a crumbling empirical base (447–49).

In Melville's fiction, daily social life as well harbors "mirage-like" forms that prove precarious on closer scrutiny. The frailty of humanly meaningful spectacle is certainly felt throughout the "masquerade" of shimmering, fragile surfaces that comprises the *mise-en-scène* of *The Confidence-Man*. The counterfeit detector proffered to the old man by the boy in the concluding scene of the novel, for example, demonstrates, if anything, how much leeway must actually be accorded to the play of faith and imagination, consent and even gullibility, across what seem solemnly objective material appearances orienting human beings within the present. What, within that present, can be more meaningful, tactile, and solid than *money*, which is clutched in the hand, stuffed in the pocket, and trusted in absolutely even by the most mistrustful of sharpers, barbers, and hucksters on board the riverboat *Fidele*? Yet wherein does this pecuniary confidence that survives all other faiths in Melville's suspicious, pervasively cynical riverboat world actually ground itself? With "something of the air of an officer bringing by the collar a brace of culprits to the bar," the old man begins using his counterfeit detector by placing "two bills" of either authentic – or fake – American money

opposite the Detector, upon which the examination began, lasting some time, prosecuted with no small research and vigilance, the forefinger of the right hand proving of lawyer-like efficacy in tracing out and pointing the evidence, whichever way it might go.

After watching him a while, the cosmopolitan said in a formal voice, "Well, what say you, Mr. Foreman; guilty, or not guilty? – Not guilty, ain't it?"

"I don't know, I don't know," returned the old man, perplexed, "there's so many marks of all sorts to go by, it makes it a kind of uncertain. Here, now, is this bill," touching one, "it looks to be a three dollar bill on the Vicksburgh Trust and Insurance Banking Company. Well, the Detector says – "

"But why, in this case, care what it says? Trust and Insurance! What more would you have?"

"No; but the Detector says, among fifty other things, that, if a good bill, it must have, thickened here and there into the substance of the paper, little wavy spots of red; and it says they must have a kind of silky feel, being made of the lint of a red silk handkerchief stirred up in the paper-maker's vat – the paper being made to order for the company."

"Well, and is – "

"Stay. But then it adds, that sign is not always to be relied on; for some good bills get so worn, the red marks get rubbed out. And that's the case with my bill here – see how old it is – or else it's a counterfeit, or else – I don't see right – or else – dear, dear me – I don't know what else to think."

"What a peck of trouble that Detector makes for you now . . . "

" . . . it's troublesome, but I think I'll keep it. – Stay, now, here's another sign. It says that, if the bill is good, it must have in one corner, mixed in with the vignette, the figure of a goose, very small, indeed, all but microscopic; and, for added precaution, like the figure of Napoleon outlined by the tree, not observable, even if magnified, unless the attention is directed to it. Now, pore over it as I will, I can't see this goose."

"Can't see the goose? why, I can; and a famous goose it is."[11]

Where an "all but microscopic" goose only equivocally emerges, and where individual dollar bills undergo such unique and incalculable vicissitude that it is difficult to trace their apparently missing threads, rubbed out marks, and other lapses of form to simple old age or to an out-and-out counterfeited origin, the line between authentic and inauthentic material appearance begins to blur. Indeed, the more scrupulously one inquires into the immediate material basis of culturally meaningful spectacle in *The Confidence-Man*, the more tenuous it becomes. Socially relevant forms and features may seem – like Goneril's "rather beautiful" face – reasonably certain "at a distance." But closer in, and more alertly scrutinized, Goneril's beauty starts to equivocate, her "rosy" complexion assuming "a certain hardness and bakedness, like that of glazed colors on stone-ware . . . while her mouth would have been pretty but for a trace of moustache" (50). To reach with alertness into the empirical depth of shape, texture, and visible feature is to encounter the residually troubled material core of all culturally meaningful, valued appearance, in scrupulous witness of which the earnest old man, in closely inspecting his "three dollar bill on the Vicksburgh Trust," at last cries out: "I don't see right – or else – dear, dear me – I don't know what else to think" (214).

The visibility of culturally relevant phenomena does not rest, at bottom, upon an absolutely trustworthy and supportive empirical foundation, and Barber Cream's credo announced at the close of the novel – "*No trust*" in humanity; trust only in the hardened, faceless neutrality of dollar bills – obscures the ultimate focal center of such forms in human gazing, gullibility, expediency and desire (194).

Isabel's strange autobiographical reminiscence in *Pierre*, in which she recalls the earliest formation of culturally meaningful appearance in her eyes, emphasizes that the ultimate focal center of phenomena such as the beauty of a human face or the very lettering of her name lies in a precarious visibility that originates strictly in human history and social experience. Haunted by memories of the time when such precarious phenomena took hesitant, provisional shape against "the wide and vacant blurrings of my early life," Isabel remains only marginally adjusted to the world of culturally meaningful appearance and image. "Never wholly have I recovered from the effects of my strange early life," she emphasizes. "Always in me," she concedes, "the solidest things melt into dreams, and dreams into solidities." She still can remember a perceptually more fluid and uncertain era in her early childhood when sensations were not quite capturable through the lens of meaningful contexts and knowable schemata. For example,

> some uncertain, tossing memory have I of being . . . in . . . [a] round, open space . . . Yet often it seems to me that there were three tall, straight things . . . somewhere there nigh to me at times; and that they fearfully shock and snapt . . . And the floors seemed sometimes to droop at the corners . . . and changefully drooped too, so that I would even seem to feel them drooping under me. . .
>
> In thy own mind, thou must now perceive, that most of these dim remembrances . . . hint vaguely of a ship at sea. But all is dim and vague to me. (117)

Haunted by memories of such a marginal, indeterminately grasped proto-universe of vaguely understood impressions, sensations, and forces, Isabel confesses that even now "I feel I am an exile" (119) within the world of commonplace presences and forms, outside of which lettering fades back into visual gibberish, contexts grow confused, and "all visible sights and all audible sounds" grow "stranger and stranger" (116).

Isabel's never more than provisional commitment to what others take to be "solidest things" emerges ambivalently in *Pierre* as a source of horror, wonder, revulsion, and allure: a liberating window out of the imprisoning contingency of culturally mediated, organized vision, but also an appeal for deliverance from a bleakly a-social experience of bewilderment and formlessness. Isabel fascinates Pierre but also evokes a sense of "horrible forlornness" and "desolation" (93). Unlike the desolation of a wilderness landscape, which can, at least, be painted and visualized, turned toward (or turned away from), what Isabel recalls opens up "one infinite, dumb" dimension of "mystery, underlying all the surfaces of visible time and space" (52).

Against such a ubiquitously "infinite, dumb" backdrop "underlying all the surfaces" of the visible, the very appearance of selfhood proves precarious in Melville's fiction. Selfhood, that is to say, emerges as visible, communicable, and tangible only throughout and as the gesticulation and the speech, the writing and facial expression that signal its participatorial self-display in culturally encoded, socially intelligible forms. In "Bartleby," the absence of something more definitively essential within and behind this pageantry of communally intelligible forms is exposed by Bartleby's sudden, scandalous preference *not* to copy: not simply writing, but also, in large measure, the gestures and the facial expressions, the mannerisms and social behaviors that normally display, visualize, and situate human beings within an historically specific social milieu.[12] No doubt "the presence of learned culture in the body," as Elaine Scarry puts it, indicating the body's thick historicization into particularity of place and time, is very powerful and deep. "Learned postures . . . gait, the ease or reluctance with which" a face "breaks into a smile" – all these and countless other attributes localize, historicize, and nationalize.[13] The performative, legible text of human bodily appearance, however, fluctuates markedly from culture to culture, from age to age, and the Wall Street "copyist" who fails to "copy" gestures of eye, lip, and limb – "His face was leanly composed; his grey eye dimly calm. Not a wrinkle of agitation rippled him" – illustrates an unsettling epistemological principle: ostensibly translucent, empathically open forms of humanness, normally mimicked and gestured back and forth between figure and figure, are nevertheless configurations and images of humanness that can wither away, leaving something surviving there that turns out to be opaque, hollow to the knock, and by no means "ordinarily human."[14]

Profoundly influenced, early in his career, by traumatic experiences of culture shock in the South Seas, Melville emphasizes that what emerges as approachable, normal, and translucent in human bodily appearance is, in fact, historically constituted, and inevitably bears a parochial marker. In Melville's first novel, for example, the Typee's tatooed face, however familiar, approachable, and normal to the Typee, proves distancing and estranging to Tommo's Western eyes. Forms of beauty, enticement, and gesture, like forms of writing, are familiar and translucent – or estranging and opaque – depending upon perspective, and Bartleby the non-copying copyist mimics none of these, receding into a bleak, impoverished timelessness beyond

the shifting mimicries of social presence. Again and again, he is pictured
standing mutely "among the ruins" (23), silent and Adamic, like a cryptic
"bit of wreck" (29) in the desert or in the middle of the Atlantic whose
context – and whose determinable meaning – have been lost.

From natural spectacle to cultural spectacle to the meaningful, historicized
legibility of the human body itself, it is the inevitably mediated, latently
precarious text of the coherently visible that Melville exposes. But to what
end? Surely a thickly textualized and mediated visibility, one is tempted
to argue, is legitimate to this degree: it serves complex cultural, psycho-
logical, and economic needs. Just as a "three dollar bill on the Vicksburgh
Trust and Insurance Banking Company" sustains potency and credibility
in continued exchange from hand to hand and through the power of social
assent, so, too, arguably, does a landscape full of Bunyanesque and Greco-
Roman associations – or a riverboat "masquerade" of shimmering textures
and surfaces – lie rooted in social accreditation and assent.

   Yet it is precisely this complex socio-cultural basis for what otherwise
disappears or mutates dramatically over time that grows troubled and confused in Melville's writing. The problematic communal basis for spectacles
and object-forms that do not endure on their own and have no objective,
sensuous guarantee is certainly at issue in *The Confidence-Man*. On the one
hand, Barber William Cream's sign, "*No Trust*," aimed warily into the untrustworthy swirl of humanity on the crowded decks of the riverboat *Fidele*,
but indicating unflagging faith in the hard, faceless objectivity of dollar bills
and material commodities, is, as I have suggested, fraught with irony. For
the basis of what Cream covets and trusts is, if anything, social, human,
historical and perceptual. In Melvillian America, however, an unstable social space of uncertain traditions and colliding interests is threatening to
open up a hole in this accrediting and constitutive power. Significantly,
in the Mississippi riverboat *mise-en-scène* envisaged in Melville's crowded,
transient novel, where everyone is a visitor, remains in passage, and comes
from somewhere else, "Sioux," "Mormon" and "mulatto" passengers, "tee-
totalers and convivialists," "parlor-men and backwoodsmen" are all uneasily
"blended" together in sitting rooms or along crowded decks (6). What does
this multiform swirl of heterogeneous humanity gather into, experience,
and witness in common? How can its commonality or intersubjectivity
become accurately measured and assessed?

   The assessment of monetary behavior – how cash is spent, exchanged,
kept back, or calculated as the registry of services and wares – would appear to emerge as the most trustworthy window into such a world. Where

gregarious words ring hollow, public presentations of self are consistently untrustworthy, and fictive, counterfeited stories abound, money and monetary behavior would appear to emerge as the expressive *ne plus ultra* – the proverbial bottom line – of such a *mise-en-scène*. But money itself assumes shape, as we have already seen in the episode of the old man and the boy, within paper, ink mark, and thread only by virtue of a certain tacit epistemological trust around the edges of which lurks the shadowy world of counterfeiters and unreliable counterfeit detectors. In mid-nineteenth-century riverboat America, moreover, the worth of money itself, showing up at the bottom line of it all, can turn wildly inflationary and mercurial.[15] And as for serving as the registry of communally determined value and worth, cash at the nexus of it all becomes at best the fluctuating mathematical expression of mercurial marketplace swings and moods, one case in point being the exuberant "confidence" followed by sinking "panic" in the precise value of shares in the "Black Rapids Coal Company" (*The Confidence-Man* 18), another involving the "Samaritan Pain Dissuader" huckstered by the "herb-doctor" which is at first utterly ignored – until, that is, someone purchases a bottle, whereupon the "others of the company began a little to wake up as it were; the scales of indifference or prejudice fell from their eyes; now, at last, they seemed to have an inkling that here was something not undesirable which might be had for the buying" (74).[16]

Within the ambiguities of a mercurial social space where the fluctuating passions, fascinations, and interests of "miscellaneous," suddenly formed crowds – just as easily dissolved as they are formed – become "conflictingly spoken or thought" (5), where stock shares inflate or deflate, and where the monetary registry of value is susceptible to wildcard marketplace swings, what is public, communal, and collective fails to focalize in any steady, dependable way. Rather, like the eternally missing face of the central, shape-shifting figure who circulates throughout Melville's novel, what ricochets publically from eye to eye as consciousness and perception, as yearning, indifference, fascination or desire, mutates and evolves. It assumes no steady, public face that can be believed in, trusted, and known.

Although the vagaries of marketplace values are clearly at issue, the mercurial *mise-en-scène* of *The Confidence-Man* raises the specter of an absent communal focal center that for many Americans at midcentury constitutes the especial danger of the West. In characteristic phraseology of the period, for example, Dr. Lyman Beecher warns that in "the great West," an unstable population "from all the States in the Union, and from all the nations of Europe . . . is rushing in like the waters of the flood, demanding for

its moral preservation the immediate and universal action of those institutions which discipline the mind, and arm the conscience." Beecher goes
on to worry that "so various are the opinions and habits, and so recent
and imperfect the acquaintance, and so sparse are the settlements of the
West, that no homogeneous public sentiment can be formed."[17] Melville's
disclosure throughout the transient riverboat world in *The Confidence-Man*
of just such a communal void where "no homogeneous public sentiment
can be formed" seems to speak directly to such fears. The atmosphere of
mutual paranoia troubling all social exchanges just beneath the veneer of
small talk and banter on board the riverboat *Fidele* testifies to how warily "Northern speculators" and "Mississippi cotton-planters," "Quakers,"
"Mormons," "Baptists" and "Jews" (6) covertly eye one another within this
unstable, mixed-and-mingled social space.

The counter-myth at midcentury, as Angela Miller observes, is that this
loose, "polyglot" society is transitory and passing. The assumption in eastern clubrooms and editorial offices is that "the anomalous, potentially disturbing aspects of western society" will by degrees disappear "in the coming
waves of settlement."[18] Certainly from the perspective of the more homogeneous, rigidly stratified northeast society depicted at the outset of *Pierre*,
patterns of public belief and moral consensus, "hereditary forms" and communal "usages" (89) appear considerably more stable. Mississippi riverboat
life seems foreign to this stratified, settled world. Whatever revolutionary
violence and Indian warfare may lurk in its own formative background,
such a time of instability and violence has ostensibly subsided into its tumultuous past. Indian wars and "the Revolutionary flood" (*Pierre* 11) have
receded into its history, leaving behind a finished, post-revolutionary society of apparent consolidation and conservatism in which the memory of
past Indian battle and revolutionary upheaval has retrospectively hardened
into symbols and mementoes, public ceremonies and legends that preserve
the memory of the past – and the meaning of America itself – in a frozen,
elegantly stylized manner.

   Yet this would-be retrospective containment of the turbulent formation
of "America" proves deceptive. The ceremonialized, legendary past that
seems to have hardened into aesthetic forms at the outset of *Pierre* masks
a latently troubled social space whose history of colliding interests and
shifting perspectives still remains unfinished, from a recent Hudson River
Valley uprising of "three thousand farmer-tenants" (11) to "social reformers"
and "indigent philosophers" framing "all manner of heterodoxical tenets" at
the "Church of the Apostles" in lower Manhattan (268). Moreover, however

consolidated midcentury American social life may appear to be, partly under Isabel's tutelage, but also partly through his own morbid curiosity and fascination, Pierre, from his position at the apex of this society, begins to probe in shock and amazement into the latent frailty of premises and schemata that quietly choreograph its confidences and certitudes. From the idealized roles and relationships of bourgeois family life that prove deceptive as Pierre delves, with Freudian-style suspicion, beneath its decorous veneer, to the gap between overtly pious Christian sentiment and shady, behind-the-scenes arrangements whereby illegitimate daughters such as Isabel are shunted off to asylums, Pierre discovers just how delusive the "fair structure of" such a world still remains "from the lowermost corner stone up" (87). Arguably, in working his way in shock and grief toward weaknesses in primary communal paradigms that appear to regulate social action and that govern communal perception, he begins to emerge in many respects as a latter-day, more intellectual, more fiercely iconoclastic revolutionary figure than his elite ancestors of the era of 1776.

No truths held to be self-evident, however, provide Melville's protagonist with a radical basis outside historical vicissitude from which to "gospelize the world anew" (273). Rather, in confronting enigmatic "Silence" – "the only Voice of our God" – Pierre is thrown into endless, Hamlet-like doubt "whether certain vital acts of his were right or wrong" (204–05). In relinquishing prevailing vocabularies and frames of reference, his "mind roams up and down in the ever-elastic regions of" its "evanescent invention," and creates "multitudinous shapes" out of "the incessant dissolvings of its own prior creations" (82). The period of "half-developments and transitions" (76) within which he remains permanently in flux seems attenuated, foreshortened and stalled in the light of the one model of action that he continues to sustain to take the measure of his travail: the eventual fulfillment of all interregnum skepticism and doubt only in the recuperative capacity to "gospelize the world anew."

In his continued use of the verb to "gospelize" to define the ostensibly proper objective of his moral and intellectual "transitions," Pierre continues, in reflection of the official culture that he appears to be repudiating – and in consequent disgust of his own "evanescent," self-critical relativity – to maintain tight mental allegiance to the ideal of the single norm, the universal framework, the sole, over-arching perspective. Certainly elsewhere throughout Melville's writing, continued belief in the standpoint of gospelizing omniscience and in an absolute, universal context within which human history unfolds is shown to dominate official American culture.

Such faith certainly informs Father Mapple's sermon at the outset of *Moby-Dick*. Mapple's sermon focuses on the biblical figure of Jonah, who tries to flee "into countries where God does not reign." But the lesson of the sermon – all the more urgently promoted in a cosmopolitan seaport such as New Bedford where cannibals rub elbows with Christians – is that the great central Christian "God is everywhere," the ubiquity of His gaze penetrating "ten thousand fathoms down" even into the subterranean water-world "beyond the reach of any plummet," and into the most private "depths" as well of any human soul (48–54). In the globalized, totalized space of absolute transparency and omniscience envisaged by Father Mapple on the eve of Ishmael's departure for points remote, no form of sinfulness, private inward rebellion, perversity, or strangeness escapes the ubiquitous surveillance and fixed gaze of a single providential God.

In the light of such a gaze, everything purportedly becomes fixed, positioned, and elucidated in its radically absolute form. And lest Mapple's sermon be approached simply as an archaic throwback to a waning theology, it is important to recognize that such a panoptic, globalizing gaze, which assumes formidable theological power in Mapple's sermon, elsewhere assumes significant social power in the nineteenth century as the ostensible vantage point not only of comprehensive maps of the world, but also of technologies of surveillance in an era increasingly given to bureaucratic centralization and to the colonization of alien spaces. Such a vantage point emerges, for example, as the Foucauldian "eye of power" so infamously available to the occupant of the central tower in Jeremy Bentham's circular prison.[19] In association, as historian Alan Wallach emphasizes, with emerging nineteenth-century ideologies emphasizing "supervision," "surveillance," and "oversight," such a mode of vision is ostensibly "intensive" as well as "extensive": that is to say, it not only covers "the entire lateral circuit of visibility," but also highlights every minute and minuscule "element within the visual field."[20] Arguably, what is at work is the secularization of theological omniscience as social, administrative power, but in either its theological or secular modes (or as the latter ostensibly grounded in the former), such power of surveillance assumes the ultimate transparence of a world that otherwise appears indefinitely hazarded into eternally shifting perspectives and descriptions.

It is precisely such an all-seeing gaze that is affirmed in Father Mapple's sermon, emphasizing a mode of watchfulness, surveillance, and oversight from which there is no escape. Yet even as Mapple's sermon announces the omniscience and inescapability of such an all-mastering mode of vision, the sermon itself, it should be noted, is delivered within a modest, enclosed chapel, however cleverly Mapple's pulpit has been staged within the chapel to suggest a much grander prospect and gaze: such a pulpit, that is to say, is shaped like the prow of a ship, so that when Mapple climbs his ladder and takes his position behind it, he appears, as the far-seeing "pilot of . . . God" (*Moby-Dick* 47), to be peering into vast oceanic vistas – not into the small interior of a New Bedford church where a few morose souls sit while the November rain falls outside.

To make the modestly limited, enclosed prospect seem oceanic and vast: that is the intention of Mapple's ingeniously stage-managed pulpit, even as it is the would-be effect of scalar maps of the world. Conversely, to emphasize that any claim to oceanic, all-diffusive vision is inevitably limited, reductive, and partial – that is the counter-lesson of much of Melville's mature art. Here we might consider the celebrated case in *The Confidence-Man* of the "Drummond light, raying away from itself all around it – everything is lit up by it, everything starts up by it," so that the entire visual field seems illuminated through and through. But we are then told that two such lights would "conflict to chaos" (205), each throwing into relief, sharpening, or backgrounding details and contours within one and the same visual field in dramatically different ways.

Sense of depth in Melville's mature fiction thus becomes other than simply quantitative and spatial. Rather, it is the enigma of the eye itself – of human consciousness and gazing – that ultimately deepens, becomes cryptic, and turns impenetrable to itself as it pours itself into, reshapes, and revises what is directly in front of its gaze. Everywhere the eye turns, it may seek to penetrate, to illuminate, and to grasp what is immediately there. But "no body is there" in the depths of sight – only a precarious visibility that potentially alters and gives way, according to the principle that as

far as any geologist has yet gone down into the world, it is found to consist of nothing but surface stratified on surface. To its axis, the world being nothing but superinduced superficies. By vast pains we mine into the pyramid; by horrible gropings we come to the central room; with joy we espy the sarcophagus; but we lift the lid – and no body is there! – appallingly vacant as vast is the soul . . . (*Pierre* 285)

In such a passage, the journey into the unresolved depths of objective visibility, where "no body is there" as "surface" gives way to "surface," simultaneously becomes a journey into the unresolved depths of "the soul" to disclose "nobody" – as well as "no body" – amidst mutations in human consciousness and perspective.

In a text such as *The Confidence-Man* – which emphasizes the enigma of the gaze and "the mystery of human subjectivity in general" (112) in transit from eye to eye – the totality, or grand public sum, of what is perceived, valued, and publically shareable in common grows as inscrutable as it does in "My Kinsman, Major Molineux," where disparate voices, perspectives, and tones gather together into a "universal hum, nearly allied to silence." In communal space of this sort, no single perspective or voice adequately encompasses the fluid totality of what is most comprehensively shareable by all. Rather, the endlessly abortive, forever incompleted figure of Enceladus the struggling Titan in the final pages of *Pierre*, its coming into focus stalled amidst all the incestuously garbled incongruity of a partly human, rock-like, godlike, "mixed," and "uncertain" condition (347), seems to loom up, in its ambiguity and uncertainty, as kind of anti-statue or non-monument at the heart of it all. Such a non-monument proves more reflective of the problematic, shifting character of communal reality in Melvillian America than monuments and statuary, myths and narratives, purportedly registering the endurance (or progressive coming into focus) of something ageless, timeless, whole, and triumphantly revolutionary.

Young Master Glendinning, legatee to the complex history of America, heir to lands that seem "sanctified through . . . long uninterrupted possession by his race," ends up contemplating, instead, the uncertain lineaments of Enceladus taking provisional shape in his dream within Hudson River Valley rock. In Pierre's dream, Enceladus seems to emerge not only as a figure of irremediably stalled revolutionary potential, powerless to storm the heavens and to "gospelize the world," but also as a reminder of the precariousness of interpretative imagery itself within a more inchoate rocky mass. Yet Pierre's gloomy assessment of the Enceladus-figure is "fateful and foreboding," the narrator suggests, "possibly because Pierre did not leap the final barrier of gloom; possibly because Pierre did not willfully wrest some final comfort" even from the figure of visual uncertainty and stalled incompletion in front of his dreaming eyes (346).

Armless, atrophied, and at best equivocally emergent out of its rocky mass – and a figure, moreover, of permanently unfulfilled revolutionary struggle toward the new gospelizing dispensation – the equivocal shape of Enceladus, I have argued, is a kind of anti-statue or non-monument. It stands in dramatic contrast to the tendency of much public statuary during the antebellum decades to solicit what Robert H. Byer terms "filopietistic" reverence for figures of "idealized authority" carved in hard, polished marble. Such statuary, like "the perfect marble form of his departed father" that

Pierre enshrines in his heart – "without blemish . . . marbleized . . . unchangeable and eternal" (*Pierre* 68) – is meant, Byer observes, to stand out against "the deepening uncertainties of contemporary American society" as a call into a "monumental sublime" of "transgenerational" virtues and values. From out of this "monumental sublime" of "marbleized" gesture and hyper-idealized human figuration, forms such as the imposing equestrian statue of Andrew Jackson sculpted by Clark Mills, or the vast "phallic" monument to George Washington stretching skyward, are meant to project authority, stability, and permanence, and to solicit the "reverence" of the citizen for a timeless national dimension beyond generational change and the "play of cultural differences."[21]

Pierre, in contrast, is left by the end of Melville's novel with shattered icons and blasted forms of figuration, from the "long-cherished image of his father" which lies in ruin in his eyes as he begins to surmise his father's cover-up of an illegitimate daughter, to his fear that his mother will "crumble into nothing" if he informs her of his suspicions. Indeed, the whole "world of solid objects now slidingly displaced itself" all around him into shifting perspectives and endless ambiguities (85–89).

Over and against this loss of well-framed objective realities to an engulfing sense of ambiguity, to be sure, looms the objectification of "America" itself into a trans-generational legacy handed down to Pierre on very concrete terms: in insignia and mementoes such as the "majestic, silver-tipped" staff that Pierre's grandfather, an heroic Revolutionary War general, once wielded (12); ultimately, as the "whole earthly countryside," fraught with "the proudest patriotic and family associations," that in spreading all around Pierre seems "sanctified through . . . long uninterrupted possession by his race." But such "sanctified" countryside ultimately constitutes a call, as we have seen, into "nothing but" the "surface stratified on surface" of changing perspectival forms. Within such a malleable topography of alternative interpretations, allusions, anthropomorphic projections and conflicting interests, what initially appears to loom up in the distance in the gaze of a Baptist farmer as Bunyan's "Delectable Mountain" is later renamed the unassailable "Mount of the Titans" by a "moody . . . bard." What to a "strolling company of young collegian pedestrians" appears to writhe out of the earth as the tragically sculpted figure of Enceladus still remains, from another perspective, only an inert masss of a deaf, dumb, if suggestively physiognomic rock (342–45).

Throughout Melville's fiction, all such landscapes and material formations that seem to arrest the "mystery of human subjectivity" into revelatory objectifications of its capacities and powers prove vulnerable to change. In

Moby-Dick, the celebrated gold doubloon, nailed to the ship's midmost "navel," that serves as the grand prize for whoever first spots the white whale, itself opens into multiple interpretations and gestalten as "I look, you look, he looks; we look, ye look, they look," but "I, you, and he" and "we, ye, and they" are all "bats" (475). In *Pierre*, all shifting meridional readings ultimately converge – and disappear – into a midmost arctic "Pole" where the direction-finding "needle" of the compass indefinitely "respects all points of the horizon alike" (165).

Melville, like Hawthorne and Thoreau, cannot discern an intersubjective focal center in the midst of such differently conceived and perceived realities. And yet "possibly" Pierre might have crossed "the final barrier of gloom" into acceptance of such a condition. This would imply recognition of an indefinitely malleable social space without orienting monuments pointing skyward, as if into the "unchanging" and "eternal," or sermons invoking God as an "eye of power" in whose omniscient gaze a globalized, all-transparent reality is inescapably caught. Melvillian America no doubt remains heavily given over to such monuments and sermons. But in texts ranging from "The Piazza" to *The Confidence-Man*, a massively different understanding develops of the way the "mystery of human subjectivity in general" actually plays across the shifting features and mutating surfaces of America itself, which still remains, from deep within its portraiture and visualization, as indefinite as any shifting, multi-storied sea.

PART II

Historicizing the American vanishing point: Indian removal, slavery, and class

CHAPTER 4

The cultural politics of American literary ambiguity

There must be the Abyss, Nox and Chaos, out of which all come,
and they must never be far off. Cut off the connection between any
of our works and this dread origin, and the work is shallow and
unsatisfying . . .

There is a moment in the history of every nation when, proceeding
out of this brute youth, the perceptive powers reach . . . across the
entire scale, and with . . . feet still planted on the immense forces of
Night, converse . . . with solar and stellar creation. That is the moment
of perfect health, the culmination . . .

Ah, let the twilight linger!   Ralph Waldo Emerson, *Journal*[1]

Even from within the confines of texts such as *Cape Cod* and *Pierre*, it is
apparent that midcentury American authors do not write within a socio-
political vacuum. If they reach into the inchoate "origin" of meaningful
visual forms, of mapped, surveyed landscapes, and of culturally accredited objects, they do so only against the formidable counter-pressure of
complex cultural mechanisms sustaining the power of officially endorsed
environments during the antebellum decades. Having explored such interplay between mediated forms of environmental coherence and a more
inchoate immediacy – "never . . . far off" – within American Renaissance texts themselves, I would like at this point in my study to take a
still closer, more historically textured look at the specific mechanisms of
visualization and spatial representation that midcentury American writing vigorously challenges. On the one hand, such mechanisms entail certain shaping social values and premises. They tacitly endorse particular
aspects of the social moment while hushing up others. On the other
hand, in very specific ways that can be enumerated and explored in depth,
these mechanisms are challenged by the texts that we have been addressing. To fully understand the massive retheorization of space underway
during the American Renaissance, it is helpful to explore these mediating cultural conventions, their ideological implications, and the way

they are challenged, probed, and interrogated by American Renaissance authors.

On the one hand, a very aggressive array of mediating strategies orchestrates a sense of the visible and the spatial during the antebellum decades. Such strategies include: (1) the tendency in lithographs and paintings to envisage cities, towns, and surrounding countryside from a bird's-eye, panoramic perspective, so that the sense of vista and depth, here *positively visualized* as space open to spectatorial penetration as far as the eye can see rather than as space receding enigmatically into the shadows, seems, even as it stretches away, to become sublimely encompassed and mastered by vast spectatorial power; (2) the envisagement of farmlands and prairies, riverboat towns and rural depots, as all caught up in an evolving national history – progressive and coherent – rather than as hazarded into what Thoreau terms "steep, and sudden, and . . . unaccountable transition," not to be conceived as a single "train" of events, whereby expectations are disrupted, and shifting historical frames of reference grow incommensurable with one another over time; (3) heavy reliance, as in Currier and Ives lithography, on the standardized visual sample and the typified human figure in the would-be portraiture of ostensibly stable, easily recognizable scenes of Americana.

In the cultural politics that I am about to explore, the collision of American literary ambiguity with these more assertive, more spectatorially positive processes for envisaging landscapes and figures in space has widespread implications. On the one hand, Angela Miller emphasizes that the endowment of an otherwise "historically thin" nation with defining "images" of itself is vigorously fostered and sought during the antebellum decades.[2] But the critique of such "images" as it develops in notoriously ambiguous American Renaissance writing is equally vigorous and formidable.

To begin with, if American literary ambiguity emphasizes the resistance of the historical moment to firm spectatorial capture, the alternative viewpoint favored by midcentury American artists is often from a great commanding height, with vast prospect and vista extending all around. Popular "bird's-eye" panoramas of burgeoning American cities, for example, such as James T. Palmatary's celebrated *View of Chicago* (1857), combine massive spectatorial sweep with the scrupulous delineation, in fine detail, of public buildings, city parks, railroad depots, and accurately drawn streets. The sweeping spectatorial authority conveyed by such midcentury lithography, in which the eye seems to gather vast distances into a single, all-mastering perspective, goes hand in hand with the recognition throughout this period

Figure 2 J. T. Palmatary, *Bird's-eye View of Chicago*, 1857, drawn on stone by
Charles Inger, published by Braunhold & Sonne.

that railroad and steamship travel is beginning to compress immense distances in still another manner. The commentary accompanying "Rail-road
Scene, Little Falls" in *American Scenery; or, Land, Lake and River Illustrations
of Transatlantic Nature* (1840) is in this respect instructive. "Before the completion of the Rail-road," it is observed, "fifteen miles" of slow, horse-drawn
distance once lay between Little Falls and Utica, but now to "a traveller on
the Rail-road," these towns appear as "nearly . . . together as two drops
on a window-pane. The intermediate distance is, by all the usual measurements of wear and time, annihilated."[3] Where actual localities within the
landscape seem as "nearly . . . together" as "drops on a window-pane," a dramatically diminished sense of scale has obviously begun to spread from the
printed world of the map or the framed picture into physical distance itself,
which can be rushed through and all but "annihilated" by contemporary
modes of conveyance.

Charles Olson's celebrated pronouncement that "I take SPACE to be the
central fact to man born in America" in that "it comes large here" – "large,
and without mercy" – must be qualified in the light of such phraseology.[4]
What is more arguably at work is the transmutation of vast space "without
mercy" into space as the ostensible registry of formidable powers of observation and control. Significantly, the technologically spanned, networked distances of the nineteenth-century United States, open to increasing vehicular mastery, heightened surveillance, and rapid communication,
are punctuated by depots, junctures, and centers of power from which

outlying developments can be controlled, and where records can be gathered, switches thrown, and comprehensive authority administered. The panoramic city views commissioned by midcentury mayors and railroad moguls tend to disclose metropolitan centers of power beyond which spread railroad lines, country roads, telegraph poles, and inland rivers.[5] And even in paintings situated away from urban centers in the countryside, the enormous spectatorial power of central observation seems to extend from apexes and zeniths, mountaintops and heights. A case in point is Thomas Cole's striking painting, *View from Mount Holyoke, Northampton, Massachusetts, after a Thunderstorm (The Oxbow)* (1836), which is "paradigmatic," or so Alan Wallach argues, of the aspiration of perceptual power, in an era of heightened surveillance and new technologies of observation, toward a vantage point that is "both panoramic and telescopic, vast and yet minutely rendered."[6]

Dramatically in contrast, in the writing that we have been considering, the idea of midmost spectatorial power gives way to collisions of reciprocally incommensurable perspective in the midst of which no panoptic gaze is possible. Whatever centralized authority seems registered in bird's-eye views of vast cities, texts such as *Pierre* and "My Kinsman, Major Molineux," in marked contrast, display the shifting, ever-mutable authority of the vocabularies and frames of reference through which landscapes, figures in space, and unfolding social scenes are alternatively perceived. No panoramic bird's-eye view hovers above the indefinite perspectival vicissitude of such texts.

If American literary ambiguity undermines the hallucinatory authority of centralized, panoptic vision, it furthermore challenges a second, prominent feature of the way American space becomes visualized and conceived during the antebellum decades: the tendency to invoke a sense of chronological narrative and evolutionary progress even within the statically rendered spatial prospect. Summing up such temporalization of landscape and scene in his retrospective essay, "The Significance of the Frontier in American History" (1893), Frederick Jackson Turner observes that throughout the long period of American westward expansion now coming to an end, it has traditionally been possible in looking westward to compare the vast continental expanse to "a huge page in the history of society. Line by line as we read this continental page from West to East we find the record of social evolution."[7] In the conversion of "social evolution" into visual perspective, American artists, observes Angela Miller, often exploit the tendency initially made prominent by the French artist Claude Lorraine (1600–82) to usher

Figure 3   Frances F. Palmer, *Across the Continent: Westward the Course of Empire Takes Its Way*, 1868.

the eye into the "illusionistic depth of painted space" through "smooth spatial transitions between foreground, middle ground, and distance." The vertical axis into the "illusionistic" depth of the painting becomes open to an imagined line of "narrative," with "Manifest destiny" – "the nation's passage from desolation to plenitude" – furnishing "the grandest" narrative of all.[8]

Sometimes the narrative of history appears to advance immediately up to the gaze of the viewer from out the depths of the painting, as in the striking Currier and Ives lithograph by Frances F. Palmer, entitled *Across the Continent: Westward the Course of Empire takes its Way* (1868). In Palmer's famous lithograph, the vast western plain in the distance, signifying long aeons of empty primordial time, suddenly gives rise in the attenuated, telescoped foreground first to tents, cattle, and Conestoga wagons, and then, with dizzying rapidity, to a handsome public school and well-dressed men, women, and children greeting the arrival of a train. In Asher B. Durand's *Progress (The Advance of Civilization) (1853)*, on the other hand, history advances gradually away from the shadowy wilderness in the upper left foreground into a middle distance of farmland and telegraph poles; then a train crossing an aqueduct emerges further down range, while in the far distance steamships gather at the wharf of a large settlement, and the sun suffuses the sky with spectacular light.

In still another variation of American history visualized as narrative, a serialized succession of pictorial panels characteristically registers the evolutionary, step-by-step improvement of the same place or scene. The four-stage sequence of illustrations in Orasmus Turner's *Pioneer History of the Holland Purchase of Western New York* (1850), for example, initially features – according to Turner's own accompanying commentary – a "rude log house hastily built" with a "roof of peeled elm bark." This is followed, in the next panel, by a "chimney added to house . . . rail and brush fences; neighbors helping to clear more land." The third panel then features "a comfortable house added to the relic log cabin, surrounded by flourishing garden . . . the whole premises beginning to have a look of thrift, comfort, and even plenty." And, finally, in the fourth panel, "forty-five years since the start in the wilderness, . . . a fully domesticated landscape" surrounds a still more splendid mansion "served by a well-made road and stone bridge."[9] William Sonntag's famous (if now lost) series, *Progress of Civilization* (1847), similarly is meant to register the steady, inexorable evolution of a single American scene toward what is described in an anonymous article, appearing in the December 1858 issue of the *Cosmopolitan Art Journal*, as "the highest state of civilization" in "all its full majesty." The "majesty" of "civilization" is ostensibly fulfilled in the final panel of the series, where a river, "narrow and solitary in the first picture," now teems with commerce, and rude, homey structures have become "spires and towers" over which "the grand temple of Liberty crowns . . . the whole scene"[10]

Such would-be visualization of historical evolution assumes that the flux of history is independently discernible in simple, progressive transformations of landscape and physical feature. Or does the movement of history more subtly involve alterations in perspective and taste that in contravening one another call into question whatever seems independently there? For example, as historical perspective alters across the decades, a spectacle such as Sonntag's grandly baroque "temple of Liberty" – a crowning futuristic achievement to 1847 eyes – becomes antiquated and obsolete. Just such powerful mutation of historical perspective with capacity to overrule the seemingly independent primacy of visual spectacle is highlighted by American literary ambiguity, as in the case of Hawthorne's notoriously metamorphic scarlet "A," which mutates over time from a lurid symbol of sin into a benevolent sign of how "Able" Hester has become, at last to lose its symbolic powers entirely as it flattens into a mere "rag of . . . cloth." What among all these fluctuations *is radically there*? Or do we have alternative possibilities that in surging into notice reciprocally problematize one another? Is the inscrutable potential opened up across the indefiniteness of a shifting historical gaze ultimately too incommensurable with itself to become visualized as a single evolutionary spectacle such as that which unfolds in *Progress (The Advance of Civilization)*? The whole spectatorial logic of Durand's 1853 painting is contradicted by the historically changing textures and meanings of Hawthorne's 1850 novel.

If American literary ambiguity interrogates the persuasiveness of the long, steady, historically projective gaze, it furthermore reveals the way the historical moment itself, taken on its own apparent terms as a slice of passing time, at best assumes hesitant shape against a more mercurial and inscrutable sense of immediacy. Ambiguous literary art raises the specter of an immediacy that is inevitably more fluid and complex than its mediation into coherent form, and, in so doing, it challenges the way popular representations of everyday American life at midcentury effectually flatten the moment into starkly stereotypic shorthand. On the one hand, Elizabeth Johns has observed that precisely in response to "economic and political changes" taking place "in the antebellum United States with dizzying speed," and to a world where "social relationships" are becoming "contested" and are shifting "frequently," ostensible "representations of everyday life" in midcentury America grow noticeably standardized in defensive contrast, and begin to rely heavily on "typing." Within a mercurial social space characterized by increasing immigration, social mobility, and economic flux, "typing" becomes a "mechanism" through which "quick points of reference" can be developed, codified, and exploited in jokes, newspaper editorials, prints, paintings, and syndicated cartoons. Typing becomes a means through which otherwise threatened social "hierarchies" can be visually sustained, or through which immigrants, blacks, women, and all social "others" can be denied power by becoming formulated and contained into images of passivity or simplified into figures of ridicule.[11] But if such typing stereotypes the suffragette, or seems to confirm the passivity of the black father and daughter who sit quietly off to the sidelines while white men heatedly discuss war events in Richard Woodinville's *War News in Mexico* (1848), typing also seems to preserve the cherished contours of an otherwise threatened world. Standardized scenes of village lanes with picket fences or families in open-air coaches provide compensatory stabilization within the picture frame for a world of accelerating change outside it. Especially in the case of popular Currier and Ives engravings such as *Maple Sugaring* (1856) and *Life in the Country, The Morning Ride* (1859), mass-produced, standardized images of Americana, their widespread distribution made possible by the power press and new lithographic techniques, develop into what

Figure 4   Louis Mauer, *Life in the Country, The Morning Ride*, 1859.

Bryan F. Le Beau terms a "common" visual "vocabulary" for imagining the nation.[12]

Through such Currier and Ives lithographs, "large numbers of exactly repeatable pictures" as Le Beau puts it, are "hung on the walls of America's homes, stores, barbershops, firehouses, barrooms, and barns."[13] A mass-produced commodity in and of itself that in turn frames and pictorializes a standardized social space, the Currier and Ives lithograph would seem doubly to epitomize what Philip Fisher refers to as the "unprecedented" means through which a homogeneous America begins to emerge in the nineteenth century. That is to say, within a social space in which "standard-ized products," duplicated "in unlimited numbers," start to become "used not for stratification and differentiation, but as tokens of communality" – in effect constituting a "collection of cheap, everyday objects and experiences" repeated across the range of American society and geography – the Currier and Ives engraving serves both as a referential window into a standardized America and as a mass produced commodity within it.[14] Readily available prints of families in open-air carriages, neighbors gath-ered sociably together, or young skating couples in the park, all form a would-be iconography of the American social ordinary. In the 1860 cat-alogue promoting such prints, a child on "the stoop" of the farm house in *Preparing for Market* is advertised as a "specimen of Young America," and everything around the child is generalized into a "specimen" as well, from the unspecified farmyard somewhere in the countryside, to the farmer himself, his "buxom dame," and the obligatory farmyard dog.[15] By way of enhancing such standardization of scene, visualization in Currier and Ives lithography tends to be aggressively true-to-type and geometrically precise rather than nuanced, quirky, or visually irregular. The gestures of human figures themselves often seem stiff and posed, as if the model for such figuration were not so much everyday life as the daguerreotype, which requires, for proper development, the prolonged, self-conscious posing of all pictured-forth participants.[16]

Dramatically in contrast, the notoriously ambiguous writing that we have been exploring entails violent subversion of such a posed, idealized universe of "specimen" and standardization. Moreover, here the alternative to the syndicated, anywhere-in-America style of popular lithography by no means entails what is commonly explored as the antidote to standardization: "particular, local," and "regional" practices and "knowledges" that are said to provide a rich alternative to the "globalizing discourses" by which modern nations take shape within maps, statistical summaries, and abstract legal systems.[17] However vigorously a negotiation may proceed between federalism and regionalism in midcentury American politics and culture, American regionalism itself, or at least to the degree that it becomes stylized into stable, well-defined entities ("New England," "the South," and so forth), ultimately becomes part and parcel of much the same eagerness for socio-political definition that assumes different form as a "homogeneous" America of "standardized products . . . duplicated in unlimited numbers," or federal monuments perceptible to all citizens alike for miles around. Significantly, Elizabeth Johns notes that many of the regional stereotypes that begin to dot the cultural landscape of America "as early as the 1780's" – the Yankee sharper, the tall Kentuckian, the fieldhand black, the northeastern "urban street urchin" – ultimately entail a "reifying of . . . differences" into an "efficient roster" of convenient social "fictions" for "ordering" the nation.[18] Later local color writing may proffer a more intricately nuanced window into regional perspectives and protocols, folk mores, local legends, and provincial forms of speech. But a text such as Thoreau's *Cape Cod*, in dramatic contrast, ultimately escapes whatever regionalism may be suggested by its name. That is to say, Thoreau reaches in such a text beyond even regional oddities of speech, and beyond local mannerisms and mores that ostensibly define time and place, to focus on weird, untoward objects, washed up along the beach, that in their recalcitrant oddity begin to defy all categorization or tidy placement within history. Indeed, through alert geological observation, as we have seen, he notices the way the Cape itself is actually "wasting . . . on both sides" to escape inert representation on any map whatsoever.

A piece of writing such as *Cape Cod* struggles to preserve a sense of the otherwise from all cultural definition (whether regionalized or nationalized) and from any inert map. In pursuit of the otherwise, such a text turns away from remote wilderness prospects to re-explore one of the easternmost, oldest sites of North American settlement, if only to emphasize that "a man may stand there," in the very thick of where history, its maps, and its customs have long accumulated, and "put all America behind him" (*Cape Cod* 331). Writing of this sort, in its disclosure of incalculable potential lurking within habit and frozen perspective, opens up what Theodor Adorno terms "the immanent difference between phenomena and that which they claim to be in themselves." Such writing emphasizes "the possibility of which their" ostensible "reality has cheated the objects and which is nonetheless visible in each one."[19] However subversively writing of this sort may wedge its way into the ostensibly hardened phenomena of everyday existence, its atmosphere of ambiguity and shifting perspectival latitude does not transcend the immediate precincts of the here and now.

I underscore the ultimate *immanence* of such writing because my next two chapters explore the relevance of its techniques of ambiguity and shifting perspectival interplay to two specific socio-political issues plaguing the antebellum United States: (1) "Indian removal" – the premise that native tribal counter-memory and culture can be removed from an expanding national landscape; (2) the destitution of the enslaved and the industrial-revolution poor as it looms up along the crumbling edges of national life as portrayed in popular lithographs and idealized paintings of the period.

In the case of ostensible Indian "removal," American literary ambiguity, let us recall, implicitly challenges an ostensibly linear, progressive sense of history whereby shifting relationships to the landscape – and accompanying values and perspectives – can become conveniently distinguished as primitive and over-and-done-with, or later and more advanced. Hawthorne's notoriously mutable scarlet "A," for example, ultimately *mixes together* the memory and counter-memory of reciprocally incommensurable frames of reference within the same object. Such perspectives no more necessarily predict, announce, and imply one another than the "duck" is inferable from the "rabbit" within the celebrated optical illusion. Nothing is necessarily "earlier" or "later" within such mixed memory. In my fifth chapter, I will be emphasizing the relevance of such a non-narrativized sense of change to the relationship between Euro-American and native tribal worlds as this relationship becomes envisaged in Margaret Fuller's *Summer on the Lakes* and "Chief Seattle's Speech" (ostensibly delivered in the 1850s, if later hazarded into a troubled – if revealing – textual history). In such texts, a non-progressive envisagement of historical memory opens up powerful possibilities of dialogue and exchange repressed by the cultural narrative of clearcut historical progress.

A history whose vicissitude in perspective is not given a priori, obeys no single, over-arching logic progressively realizing itself over time, but proves fraught with contradiction, paradox, and discontinuity, remains fundamentally inscrutable. In shifting attention, in my sixth chapter, to the representation at midcentury of the American enslaved and the industrial-revolution poor, I explore the way a similar sense of the inscrutable opens up within texts that address the experience of destitution: Frederick Douglass's two antebellum slave narratives and Rebecca Harding Davis's pioneering tale of industrial-revolution poverty, "Life in the Iron Mills." Texts of this sort, in denying any comfortable sense of spectatorial and interpretative mastery over the experience of destitution at their core, disclose – no doubt more reluctantly in Douglass's case than in Davis's – the potential enfeeblement of the frames of reference through which a midcentury bourgeois audience is given to taking the measure of reality.

In an era of increasing surveillance and new technologies of visual power, such texts emphasize the breakdown of spectatorial power amidst shocking scenes which defy literary stage-management and satisfactory framing. Yet from "from the very extremity" ("Life in the Iron Mills" 14), Davis writes, of an outrageous and dismal world which "I can paint nothing of" (23) – or least not satisfactorily, at least not through currently enfranchised vocabularies and aesthetic conventions – "the most solemn prophecy which the world has known of the Hope to come" nevertheless issues, and "I dare make my meaning no clearer" (14). To probe in "solemn prophecy" into the deteriorating recesses, as it were, of the cultural moment, where its interpretative vocabularies and ideological reassurances become enfeebled, and its ultimate *failure* is disclosed in lives without purpose and human misery unredeemed by social institutions, is no doubt to become appalled and shocked. But such a journey into shock, horror, and amazement furthermore reopens the question of the otherwise, which resurrects itself precisely along the troubled edges of what can neither be easily absorbed into current cultural frameworks, nor easily dismissed.

CHAPTER 5

Margaret Fuller's Summer on the Lakes *and "Chief Seattle's Speech": the obliquities of the geographic in-between*

The discontinuous space opened up by the invasion – and redefinition – of places and landscapes whose meaning remains significantly different in the memory of native American populations cannot be directly confronted in and of itself. Rather, as William Boelhower argues, what opens up, at bottom – the settled and inert look of "cartographic representation" notwithstanding – is an irremediably fractured sense of landscape and place, replete with "removed meanings" and alternative place-names, whose history and significance cannot be homogeneously comprehended in a single stable manner.[1] By way of exploring this sense of collision and discontinuity that cannot be entirely eliminated from American history, and that emerges in the depths of monologically portrayed versions of American "settlement" upon careful excavation into the past, I now turn to Margaret Fuller's *Summer on the Lakes* (1844) and Chief Seattle's speech, ostensibly delivered in the early 1850s. Both Fuller's troubled text and what remains, in partially blurred, faded newsprint, of Chief Seattle's ostensible address, bear witness to the limits of any ostensibly homogeneous portraiture of a single, synthesized entity, universally self-evident to all Americans, on whose straightforward terms "America" itself assumes objectification and intelligibility in all eyes.

What resists objectification and stabilization in all eyes, and inflects this way or that according to point of view, no doubt remains as *asymmetrically* inflective as the totality of public reality during the "Election Day" ceremonials in *The Scarlet Letter*. In Hawthorne's novel, we will recall, the official gloss over the meaning of events is clearly vested in those who listen to Dimmesdale's sermon on the destiny of New England inside the little Protestant chapel (notwithstanding visitors from neighboring tribes who circulate among the crowd, brooding upon events with an alternative if largely silenced perspective). In actual history, not all conceivable perspectives are granted an equal voice, and the very collection of texts that I will be exploring in this chapter emphasizes the asymmetry of the collision between

Euro-American and native American modes of cultural power interacting with one another only on specific historical terms. Fuller's text, carefully edited and as true as scholarship can make it to its mid-nineteenth-century origins, is not the secondary echo of, but, rather, the actual realization of the printed, literate culture whose credibility nevertheless becomes tested at certain moments in Fuller's narrative by traces of an alien life-world and alternative field of vision. Chief Seattle's ostensible address, in contrast, survives only as filtered through the memory, the incomplete diary notes, and the evidently doctored, embellished revision published in 1887 by a certain Dr. Henry A. Smith, who claims to have heard the speech in the early 1850s through a third party translating Seattle's remarks on the spot. Such an address at best survives – or in large measure is retrospectively invented – within Smith's newspaper column in the 29 October 1887 issue of the *Seattle Sunday Star*. Instead of a living oral performance, what we have is a single, torn sheet of newspaper preserved for research and study at Suzzallo Library on the University of Washington campus in Seattle.[2]

Even so, both the text of Fuller's *Summer on the Lakes* and the more problematic text of Seattle's address are significant, I would argue, not in how they accurately or imperfectly reflect alternative cultures, but, rather, in how each text discloses, each in its own way, the reciprocally alien pressure exerted by alternative cultures and frames of reference across a midmost blind spot that resists thorough mediation in any stable manner. It is this blind spot itself that I want to address as it shows up within two different texts of admittedly unequal textual authority, each nevertheless calling into question more direct representations of what Americans are said to inhabit, to share, and to pass on across the generations as a single history and sense of place.

I begin with Margaret Fuller, who in the summer of 1843, touring partly with companions and partly alone, traveled westward across the Great Lakes territories toward Milwaukee, kept detailed written impressions of her travels, and, encouraged by Emerson upon her return back to New England in September, began to collect her impressions into a book. The result was the publication early in the following year of *Summer on the Lakes:* Fuller's account of a voyage into freshly incorporated US territory still in the process of assuming shape in the national imagination through maps and lithographs, narratives of travel, diaries of settlers, and letters sent back home to curious relatives and friends.

Widespread curiosity at the time about the American West notwithstanding, Fuller's written account of recently settled western lands remains

tenuous and provisional. A mixture of quoted secondary materials as well as
of first-hand reminiscence, of personal anecdote, picturesque prospects into
the tranquil countryside, abstract philosophical meditation, and informal
jottings and impressions, such a text ultimately entails, as Christina Zwarg
observes, a restlessly "changing movement of . . . perspective" in keeping
with Fuller's earlier recognition, in translating German texts into English,
of entirely different "interpretative possibilities" that are "opened to view"
by a shifting mobility of perspective and of voice.[3]

Such relinquishment of fixed interpretative authority for a "changing
movement" of "perspective" is explicitly endorsed by Fuller in *Summer on
the Lakes*. "Do you climb the snowy peaks," she at one point asks the
reader,"from which you can get a commanding view of the landscape?"
The "disadvantages" of such a "position" include, first and foremost, a
frozen totality of vision oblivious to a more richly dialectical, reciprocally interactive interplay of voices and perspectives.[4] Relinquishing any
claim to authorial omniscience, Fuller instead develops – as James Freeman
Clarke proposes in his 1844 review of *Summer on the Lakes* – a "portfolio
of sketches," many emergent in mere outline, none absolutely definitive,
all exerting pressure and counter-pressure on one another.[5] As a "portfolio"
of tenuously sketched, shifting impressions of landscape and event, *Summer on the Lakes* entails much of the disseminated freeplay of Fuller's
celebrated Boston "conversations" for women, whose "inclusive" and
"searchingly open-ended" logic has been explored so extensively in recent
years.[6]

Still, the open-ended generosity that can be summoned up in Boston
conversation proves more difficult to develop in other contexts. It is not the
generosity of an "inclusive . . . searchingly open-ended" process, but, rather,
violence, mis-communication, and mutual paranoia that Fuller ultimately
encounters as she struggles to grapple with the difference between Euro-
American and native tribal perspectives of a landscape which in its shifting
meaning and visibility eludes authoritative capture. Writing forcibly from
the Euro-American side of such a troubled and melancholy collision between worlds, Fuller can scarcely reach through to the other side; rather,
native tribal counter-consciousness of landscape and surrounding space in
large measure remains, as Jean Paul Sartre writes of the cryptic gaze of the
"Other" in *Being and Nothingness*, an "orientation *which flees from me*," "a
spatiality which is not *my* spatiality," so that it "stands as a" haunting "background of things" which can neither be entirely dismissed nor satisfactorily
known.[7]

Throughout extended sections of *Summer on the Lakes*, no doubt, little sense of an alternative, alien perspective – even if felt largely as a cryptic "background of things" more inferred than directly known – is allowed to disturb Fuller's tranquilly picturesque portraiture of landscape and natural feature. In keeping with *The Home Book of the Picturesque; or American Scenery, Art, and Landscape*, the popular, coffee-table collection of descriptive essays and handsome illustrations published by Putnam in 1852, Fuller frames a series of highly aestheticized views of the continental American landscape intended to cater to the tastes of her eastern seaboard readership. The "fine, park-like woods . . . carpeted with thick grasses and flowers," the "velvet lawns" and "high bluffs" assuming "the forms of buttress, arch, and clustered columns" (*Summer on the Lakes* 95–99) – all contribute to what Angela Miller, as we have seen, emphasizes is a hallmark of much American landscape painting from the 1820s to the 1850s: a "stagelike, choreographed" artificiality such that the stylized portraiture of nature seems to become the aesthetic correlative of the "civilizing mission" itself.[8] At times, nevertheless, Fuller ventures beyond such aestheticized portraiture of "fields, and dells, and stately knolls, of most idyllic beauty" (138). Seeking to encounter "the glow . . . of living presence" betrayed by books that "have a . . . second-hand air" and by "stereotypic . . . scenery . . . only fit to be glanced at from dioramic distance" (88–89), she observes that "happy were the first discoverers" of these lands "who could come unawares upon this view and upon that, whose feelings were entirely their own" (77).

Fuller, then, yearns for pure, unadulterated contact with "living presence," but breakthrough into a radically immanent here and now eludes her, and her impressions are heavily compromised by printed, widely disseminated imagery and travelogue description. Niagara Falls in particular emerges even at first-hand encounter as a site of continually recalled images and memorable quotations. The geographic layout of the whole is so familiarly known ahead of time, for example, that the earliest initial glimpses of the visitor are already situated within a known, firmly established context. "When I first came," confesses Fuller, no fresh impressions seemed possible, for "I found that drawings, the panorama, &c. had given me a clear notion of the position and proportions of all objects here; I knew where to look for everything, and everything looked as I thought it would" (72). Such an experience of place is already compromised and belated even on first arrival. A celebrated site such as Niagara – painted, poeticized, and lithographed again and again – is so standardized in image and print that the New Yorker, the Philadelphian, and the traveling woman from New England all converge on the same place knowing "where to look for everything."[9] The heavy influence of print and visual culture on sense of place in the mid-nineteenth-century United States, moreover, is by no means confined to famous localities like Niagara Falls. An English settler to Geneva, Illinois, for example, "showed us a bookcase filled with books about this country; these he had collected for years, and become so familiar with the localities that, on coming here at last, he sought and found, at once, the very spot he wanted" (91).

In *Summer on the Lakes*, however, the emergence of "localities" through the lens of books and lithographic engravings, so that everything seems "second-hand" and suffused with belatedness, reaches a limit, paradoxi-cally, in one of the paramount conventions shaping sense of landscape in the antebellum United States: the sublime. No doubt from one perspective, the sublime represents a derivative convention of its own with a history ex-tending all the way back to Longinus through Nicolas Boileau's influential French translation of Longinus's treatise (1674), and then through major analytic accounts by Edmund Burke (1757) and Immanuel Kant (1790), and finally through the readiness of numerous Romantic writers and painters to conceive of their relationship to nature through the lens of the sublime. The importation of the vocabulary and aesthetic practices of the sublime into the early Republic, where it becomes eagerly adapted to nationalistic ends, has been widely documented over the years. Entailing an experience of transport, wonder, and amazement in the presence of natural spectacle, the American sublime at its most nationalistic entails not only the chau-vinistic affirmation that more "sublime beauty" exists in the US than in Switzerland or Scotland,[10] but also the assumption that majestic American nature stands at the connecting link between national geography and the divine. As William Cullen Bryant characteristically writes in his preface to *The American Landscape* (1830), "the far-spread wildness" of the American continent, in ushering the mind "up to the idea of a mightier power, and to the great mystery of the origin of things," nevertheless remains part and parcel of "our country."[11] Through one and the same stroke, awesome natu-ral spectacle is nationalized, politicized, and appropriated into the mapped, mediated spaces of culture and history – even to become, as in the case of the Niagara Falls, a familiar visual icon to be found on bond notes, fine dinnerware, and institutional letterheads – while remaining hallowed as a majestic aperture into a dimension of timeless, sacred "mystery." These re-lays from the world of printed mediation and political and cultural interest through sublime natural spectacle toward a sacred, transcendent dimension are assumed to be continuous and smooth.

Such adaptation of the sublime to American nationalism, however, exploits an imported convention that bears within itself latently troublesome potentialities. In an illuminating discussion, Howard Horwitz turns to Immanuel Kant for a more thoroughgoing version of sublime dynamics characteristically elided in "America's Christianized and nationalist sublime." Horwitz focuses on Kant's mid-phase of "dispossession" and lost referential bearings – a stage fundamental to Kant's passage of the mind toward sublime exultation in excess of the senses – that is all but hushed up in the American linkage of tangible, richly accessible natural spectacle with "the idea of a mightier power."[12] In the depths of the dispossessive stage of the sublime emphasized by Kant, an alienated nature, as Kant himself insists, begins to "contravene . . . our power of judgement," to wreak an "outrage on the imagination," and to become bewildering and remote. One is brought to a "point of excess": to an "abyss" in which "the imagination . . . fears to lose itself" as vast, maze-like, indefinite magnitudes defeat the struggle of eyesight for sensuous "comprehension" of "the whole"; or, in the case of the "dynamical sublime," the overwhelming "might" of primordial force arouses fear and wonder in contemplation of "thunderclouds piled up to the vault of heaven, borne along with flashes and peals, volcanoes in all their violence of destruction," and other tumultuous phenomena which "make our power of resistance of trifling moment in comparison with their might."[13]

I emphasize such dispossessive phraseology because in contrast to "America's . . . nationalist sublime," Margaret Fuller's visit to Niagara Falls entails just such a stunned recognition of natural spectacle in alien recession from culturally endorsed meanings and perceptual schemata. Within the geography of the United States in 1843, Niagara Falls looms up at the ostensible intersection of named, nationally appropriated spaces with the divine. Here the grandeur of the Republic seems incarnate in visible natural spectacle that, although part and parcel of national topography, nevertheless ferries the mind "up to the idea of a mightier power." These would-be relays from national frame of reference through visible natural spectacle toward manifestation of "mightier power," however, turn increasingly problematic as Fuller's account proceeds. The degree to which Fuller seems to encounter a familiar natural spectacle, faithful to its representations within lithography and written description, is precisely the degree to which what she encounters fails to become sublime. "Prepared by descriptions and by paintings" of the Falls, she initially walks about the grounds adjacent to her hotel, and as her eyes play over details and assume perspectives that are already, in 1843, becoming part of a familiar national iconography, she confesses that "when I arrived in sight of" Niagara, "I merely felt, 'ah, yes, here is the fall, just as I have seen it in the picture' . . . I expected to be overwhelmed, to retire trembling from this giddy eminence . . . but, some-how or other, I thought only of comparing the effect on my mind" with "descriptions" and "paintings" already encountered (76). Only at the point where an easily pictorialized, familiarly described Niagara begins to give way, at closer range, to a predominantly auditory and kinetic experience of overwhelming sound and "rushing" force does "the full" fury of the tumult so draw "me into itself as to inspire an undefined dread, such as I never knew before, such as may be felt when death" approaches (72).

If visualization of the tumult from afar entails its spectatorial mastery and stable capture within a steady point of view, the fury of watery force at closer range threatens to overwhelm point of view. It is true that "from the British side," the tumult of the Falls in the distance may seem like a "magical," far-off "picture," but "from the boat, as you cross, the effects and contrasts" grow more vivid, striking, and "melodramatic," while "close to the . . . fall," the "power of observing details" is "quite lost" (72–73). Written description as well as visualization from a distance may seem to fix and freeze the Falls in various ways. But "to one who has" entered into "the full life of" Niagara, Fuller confesses, "what thoughts can be recorded about it, seem like commas and semicolons in the paragraph, mere stops" (75).

Ultimately, the "perpetual trampling of waters" at Niagara seems to epit-omize what cannot be fixed, seized upon, and visually arrested into a picture or cultural emblem. From "motion" of this sort, Fuller writes, "there is no escape; . . . all other . . . motions come and go, the tide rises and recedes, the wind . . . moves in gales and gusts, but here is really an incessant, an indefati-gable motion. Awake or sleep, there is no escape, still this rushing round you and through you" (71). No doubt the lesson of nineteenth-century geology is that all natural spectacle is subliminally in "incessant . . . indefatigable motion," and, accordingly, that "escape" into a deceptively settled environ-ment of edged, inert material forms, dependable boundaries, and discretely individuated spectatorial images entails considerable abstraction and sim-plification of perception. Throughout *Summer on the Lakes*, Fuller herself eagerly reaches beyond the bounded, schematized world of frozen entities – beyond images and boundaries that seem inert on maps, beyond painted pictorial forms – into a subliminal but inferable reality of "caves . . . con-tinually forming" in the stone (173), and of "bluffs" ceaselessly "crumbling" and altering on river shores (95). Any inert visualization of landscape re-mains as deceptively fixed as human beings themselves whenever they are boxed into gendered polarities that are, in fact, as Fuller observes in *Woman in the Nineteenth Century*, "perpetually passing into one another" such that "no wholly masculine man" or "purely feminine woman" ever thoroughly emerges.[14] Throughout Fuller's writing, concepts, categories, and shapes that constitute the world of image-making and intellectual analysis make sense only in approximation. They take shape within what on closest observational range begins to overflow and to resist excessively tidy typification. In part this reach through coherent interpretative paradigms into a less easily described, more unbounded sense of reality is heralded as a breakthrough into the sacred and divine. For "what is limitless is alone divine" (108), Fuller writes in *Summer on the Lakes*. Or as she puts it in a series of journal entries and letters in 1840 reflecting upon how "I grow more and more what they call a mystic," "dwelling in the ineffable, the unutterable" – breaking through to a sense of being-in-depth that the mediating, restrictive image or concept never quite contains – ostensibly entails a first-hand taste of "central power" whose limitless potential is "too beautiful to be checked."[15] Still, at Niagara Falls, "undefined dread, such as I never knew before," is the price to be paid for relinquishing all mediating framework and form, and "dread" of such sort begins to resist definition as "beautiful" or "divine."

Fuller's "undefined dread" ultimately remains bereft of what the sublime experience in its totality theoretically leads to and supports: a "meaningful jargon of ultimacy," as Thomas Weiskel puts it – "some credible discourse" of transcendental authority – whereby an otherwise culturally unmediated plunge beyond "clearcut thought" and "determinate perception" can be nevertheless rooted outside history and culture in a larger, vaster, metaphysically reassuring dimension.[16] Growing vulnerable and overwhelmed to the point of "undefined dread," Fuller feels shattered, violated, and vanquished. Nevertheless, she writes that as "the perpetual trampling of the waters seized my senses," and as "these waters were poured down with such absorbing force" that "I felt no other sound . . . could be heard,"

> I [began to] . . . look around me for a foe . . . Continually upon my mind came, unsought and unwelcome, images, such as never haunted it before, of naked savages stealing behind me with uplifted tomahawks; again and again this illusion recurred, and even after I had thought it over, and tried to shake it off, I could not help starting and looking behind me. (72)

Initially devoid of lurid images or any sort of meaningful content, the "absorbing force" of Niagara is most radically experienced as a "rushing round you and through you" that overwhelms the "senses" to the point of "undefined dread." But such excess of onrushing, furious sound – much like the onrush of white noise in an echo chamber that so eludes structure, differentiation, and distinguishability that would-be processes of discrimination and orientation are all but overwhelmed – nevertheless gives way in Fuller's account to a very specific, culturally focused fear of "naked savages with uplifted tomahawks." At work in this episode would appear to be what Martin Heidegger, in accounting for the substitutional psychodynamics of dread without an object – indeed, dread *as* in large measure overwhelming *loss* of the capacity to objectify, to define, and to impose finite limits upon a sudden, dizzying break in perceptual confidence – regards as a characteristic displacement of *angst* or dread into *furcht*. That is to say, whereas in *angst* there is ultimately "nothing to hold on to," *furcht* struggles to focus on "some definite thing."[17] In keeping with Heidegger's proposal that what is afoot in such displacement of *angst* into *furcht* is a would-be substitutional maneuver whereby a sense of unbearable limitlessness in the midst of a rupture in coherent perception is accorded a distracting focus or limit (some definite *thing*, much like Ahab's white whale, to be fled, obsessionalized over, or attacked), Fuller's passage registers just such a substitutional maneuver. It quickly becomes apparent, however, that such an association of so-called "naked savages" with Fuller's experience is not ultimately tenable, and she tries to "shake" such an association "off" (72). Indeed, as she indicates elsewhere in *Summer on the Lakes*, so-called "naked savages" themselves, with their alternative "theory of the history of the globe" (192), ultimately construct and inhabit, organize and situate themselves within, culturally mediated universes of their own. Conversely, what overwhelms Fuller at Niagara is too much in "incessant . . . indefatigable motion," and too indefinitely a rupture in stable, well-oriented perception, to become associated with those who inhabit, shape, and perceive one another within their own humanly mediated worlds.

Still, native peoples prove relevant to Fuller's Niagara experience in this one respect: the absence of a "credible" dimension of transcendental "ultimacy" in the depths of "undefined dread" haunts and troubles Fuller as she grows alert, from across a massive socio-cultural divide, to the "modification of life and mind" (88) and the alternative "theory of the history of the globe" represented by native tribal cultures. What, if anything, transcendentally abides and presides in the depth of reciprocally alien variations of culturally structured truth? Or do shifting ethical assumptions, myths of origin, and frameworks of knowledge simply order and reorder what outside such mutation cannot be directly conceived, perceived, and known?

No doubt mutation in socially mediated truth from one cultural frame of reference into another is itself difficult to trace through in *Summer on the Lakes*. How does one gauge the extent of such mutation when one's own perspectives into alien cultures are themselves severely distorted by historical circumstances? Consider, in this respect, Fuller's remembrance of the band of impoverished Pottawattamies who come into Milwaukee to perform a "begging dance" for the casual entertainment and tossed coins of onlookers. Such a dance – "wild and grotesque," a garish panoply of "paint and feather head-dresses" – has in all likelihood been sensationalized and theatricalized to appeal to onlookers and to solicit their money, according to the notion prevalent throughout the boarding houses and saloons of Milwaukee that "Indians without paint are poor coots." Alert to this process of degraded, willfully sensationalized cultural display, the "chief" – "erect" and "sullen" – "did not join in the dance, but slowly strode about in the streets," looking "unhappy, but listlessly unhappy, as if he felt it was of no use to strive or resist" (142).

The "listlessly unhappy" chief hanging back from this dance seems as compelled by historical circumstances into becoming a dismal figure of helpless melancholy as Fuller herself seems involuntary compelled into protesting that "I have no hope of . . . saving the Indian from . . . degradation" (189). A fatalistic chief and a fatalistic narrator both seem caught within a current historical process heavily delimiting, impoverishing, and distorting the way scenes of ostensible contact between alternative cultural worlds can be played out and experienced. Indeed, a figure like Margaret Fuller, we learn, is likely to become enmeshed in spite of her own best intentions within a dismally scripted choreography of fear and mutual estrangement falling between cultures. History sometimes objectifies oneself involuntarily into dismal theater of this sort, and how to resist this sense of becoming a marionette-figure within it? Fuller, for example, enters a sprawling "Indian encampment" in hopes of finding out more about native peoples, but she notices that wherever she walks, she remains in the eyes of onlookers a white stranger – a source of consternation, aversion, and fear – as those whom she would approach flinch and withdraw from her presence: "They seemed to think [that I] . . . would not like to touch them: a sick girl in the lodge where I was, persisted in moving . . . ; a woman with . . . [a] melancholy eye . . . kept off the children and wet dogs from even the hem of my garment" (141).

Where one's presence takes shape in the eyes of others such that they react to it only by shrinking away, then their own counter-visibility remains defensive and opaque. Breaking through such dismal social choreography is difficult, and it does not help that outside such unsatisfactory empirical contact, all that Fuller finds available is a thickening accumulation of picture, narrative, and description effectually reconstituting native American life in Anglo-American cultural space on distorted terms.[18] This is not simply a matter of lack of factual accuracy in a text such as Catlin's *Manners, Customs, and Condition of the North American Indians.* What Gerald Vizenor terms the "colonization of oral traditions and popular memories" – the tendency of a dominant Western culture to alter and deform in the very process of interpreting and appropriating the myths, artifacts, and idioms of "tribal cultures" – is evident throughout the array of texts and images that Fuller consults with a mingling of curiosity and skepticism to complete, or to try to complete, an otherwise abortive quest to make contact with native peoples.[19] For example, Henry Rowe Schoolcraft, we are told, records "mythological or hunting stories of the Indians" in a suspiciously genteel rhetoric in which native "phraseology" appears to have been "entirely set aside," and "flimsy graces, common to the style of annuals and souvenirs," appear to have been "substituted for . . . Indian speech." In such a case, the printed version of native American experience proves to be a suspicious window into a suspiciously altered reality, and "we can just guess what might have been there" (*Summer on the Lakes* 88).

Printed pictures of native Americans consulted by Fuller prove to be especially insidious forms of erased and banished presence masquerading as face-to-face, original contact. On the one hand, the image, as W. J. T. Mitchell puts it, "is the sign that pretends not to be a sign, masquerading as (or, for the believer, actually achieving) natural immediacy and presence." In contrast, we are far more likely, observes Mitchell, to regard the word as "the artificial, arbitrary production of human will that disrupts natural presence by introducing unnatural elements into the world – time, consciousness, history, and the alienating intervention of symbolic mediation." But in fact images as well as words are performative and interpretative acts of mediation rather than neutral, visual forms of pure "immediacy and presence"; as Mitchell suggests, images are themselves a "kind of language" in their own right.[20] Certainly visual portraits do not speak to us with anything even approximating naked, unmediated presence when they are arranged like so many scientific specimens within the publication (explored at great length by Fuller) entitled *Catalogue of One Hundred and Fifteen Indian Portraits, Representing Eighteen Different Tribes, Accompanied by a Few Brief Remarks on the Character &c. Of Most of Them.* These catalogued, passively inert images involve the placement of "Indian Portraits" on convenient display for those with the means to purchase the large, handsomely bound volume published by Colonel Thomas Loraine McKenney and James Hall in 1836, although it is interesting to note that within this catalogue of "portraits," "Red Jacket's face," as Fuller observes, seems to gaze back with a certain "irony" and reserve "that disdains to flicker where it cannot blaze" (208). Such a gaze marks the limits, even within inert lithography and frozen portraiture, of Native American acquiescence to Anglo-American terms of visibility and display. Still, if what "disdains to flicker where it cannot blaze" seems to constitute a certain "irony" unmastered by catalogue portraiture and arrangement, it nevertheless "disdains" even "to flicker." The limits of such a figure's acquiescence to stiffened, posed portraiture are reached – but along that vanishing point, no further visibility is disclosed.

From within posed and stiffened portraiture, then, Red Jacket remains enigmatic and inaccessible; at Milwaukee, a tribal dance is flattened into mere sensationalized spectacle performed for a few tossed coins; elsewhere the effort to make contact with tribal peoples reaches its limit in the "melancholy eye" of a woman who "kept off the children" from "even the hem of my garment." From Red Jacket's laconic face to printed English translations of oral myth that are so doctored that "we can just guess what might have been there," native American consciousness and vision remain largely eclipsed.

Yet precisely because Fuller can largely "just guess" through imagery, spectacle, and translation toward a more satisfactory sense of tribal existence and experience, landscapes recently depopulated of native tribes (except for the few scattered, lingering remnants left behind) seem tinged by the trace of an occluded dimension. Everywhere, for example, Fuller sees flowers, and she remarks at length on their "flame-like" beauty, which "gemmed and gilt the grass" in the afternoon sun (89). But of some of the "brightest" of these flowers, Fuller remembers, "an Indian girl afterwards told me the medicinal virtues," and Fuller goes on to wonder what other unsuspected properties and characteristics might lie throughout features of this "soil" on "which we could . . . look" only "to admire" their "hues and shape" (108). An explicit cognitive horizon is reached in Fuller's gaze into this landscape precisely where her own cultural assumptions leave off, and some other, scarcely knowable dimension – largely outside her field of vision – begins.

As would-be travelogue into the American continental interior, *Summer on the Lakes* thus remains edged not so much by unexplored Western wilderness as by what cannot quite be seen amidst appearances turned obscurely away toward alternative knowledge and vision. In dramatic contrast to *The Home Book of the Picturesque*, Fuller's "dells, and stately knolls, of most idyllic beauty" and her Gothicized "buttresses of rich rock" (99) harbor an alien sense of landscape – "not long since . . . driven away" – "traces" of which lie everywhere in "troughs" for corn planting, in "caches" for food storage, and in "marks" of "tomahawks" still noticeable in the trees (100). No doubt Fuller's phraseology indicates the enormous difficulty of reaching through what "fragments" merely "indicate" (211) – and what "clues" allow us to "just guess" (88–89) – toward more than a provisional "glimpse" into an indigenous counter-world of "Indian life and . . . character" (211). Still, although one "can only gather" (192), surmise, and "guess" across a massive cultural divide, perception of landscape remains shadowed and disturbed by an alternative dimension, and the effect is somewhat similar to what W. J. T. Mitchell discovers in Augustus Earle's painting, *Distant View of The Bay of Islands, New Zealand* (c. 1827): a space of underlying ambivalence and perceptual hesitancy in which the trace of an indigenous perspective lingers, however vaguely and marginally, within the shadows of Western aesthetic conventions and frames of reference. That is to say, although, in Earle's painting, alternative planes of shadow and light spread off into the distance, as in a conventional picturesque landscape, and although a white man, pausing in mid-foreground, appears to take in the tranquil prospect all around him with a leisurely, contemplative, all-surveying gaze, a hint of "something else" – the alternative "visual field," as Mitchell puts it, "of the Maori" themselves – is suggested by the odd, quirky presence of a carved figure to the side, whose "function . . . in Maori culture is to stand guard over tabooed territory," as well as by the unusually dark, somber color that suffuses the entire prospect, "tinting" and muting everything, however picturesquely rendered.

Such a visual prospect, oriented through familiar picturesque conventions, but suggestive of "something else," locates us neither quite here nor quite there; ultimately, suggests Mitchell, the ambivalent focus of such a painting is upon nothing more particular than upon an "odd, disturbing, liminal space, the threshold between . . . cultures," that is starting to become, in and of itself, the difficult-to-perceive subject of a painter like Earle.[21] Similarly for Margaret Fuller, the "threshold between . . . cultures" is starting to emerge evasively between – and to challenge – more emphatic, culturally stabilized modes of visibility and description. Along such a threshold, everything starts to become relativized and to emerge in mutation, from "the Christ" who reappears in native peoples' eyes as "but a new and more powerful Manito" aiding would-be "conquerors" (*Summer on the Lakes* 187), to alternative accounts of the "genesis" of the universe and alien "moral sympathies" (192). Here one and the same landscape simultaneously becomes an eastwardly abandoned site of "homesickness" (142) and nostalgia – heavily freighted with memory – and yet, to invading newcomers, a "West" of opportunity and promise. And precisely where "Mackinaw" island, "crowned by" a "white fort," seems to loom up like a military "helmet" in the distance, the shape of a "turtle" can alternatively be made out within the "helmet," or at least upon one's tracing the distorted Anglicized word "Mackinaw" back to "Michilimackinac," meaning "the great Turtle" (173–74). All such cases suggest discontinuities rather than the survival of universals in the mutation of cultural power and its shaping, organizational lenses.

As Fuller broods on the significance of places and worlds in the "transition state" (142) where "old landmarks are broken down, and the land, for a season, bears none," however, she shrinks back from the specter of discontinuity, paradox, and incongruity in frame of reference, emphasizing, instead, that "I trust by reverent faith to . . . foresee the law by which a new order, a new poetry is to be evoked from this chaos" (86). For the transitional middle time between mutually incommensurable cultural orders is perplexing and disturbing. What hovers, as it were, in the air between invasive and invaded cultures seems to resist becoming known on stable, satisfactory terms; rather, it results in what Fuller terms a medial "chaos" or "discord" (86) that stands between if only to trouble and haunt what appears to take more settled, unequivocal shape at either end. It may be true, to return once again to Christina Zwarg's illuminating linkage between Fuller's earlier work as a translator and *Summer on the Lakes*, that "the double frame of the translator," with its Janus-faced sensitivity to the mutation of consciousness and sensibility from one language into another, appears to have "prepared" Fuller for "the dynamic of cultural contact" by making "her attentive to interpretative possibilities opened to view by shifting cultural frames."[22] Even so, when Fuller writes, for example, that certain "half-breed" and "half-civilized" human faces look "vulgar" in that they "have the dignity of neither race" (*Summer on the Lakes* 210), or that "mingling" and "amalgamation" lead to inevitable loss of "what is best in either type" (188), she obviously wants to keep categories and typification pure, and to avoid what she terms the "discord" of mixed contexts and frameworks of order.

At issue in this aversion to troublesome mixtures and intersections is the desire not only to keep contexts, categories, and "shifting cultural frames" reciprocally quarantined, but also to preserve, at bottom, a tidily linear sense of history unsettled by memory-bearing peoples who "linger behind" their "proper era" (188) to persist incongruously within an alternative life-world taking shaping around them. The ideology of linear, progressive history converts threatened incommensurability between cultural orders into harmony through the assumption that primitive worlds give way to advanced ones along a single historical scale. Fuller, like so many of her contemporaries, remains heavily invested in such linear history. In meditating on current bloodshed, cultural genocide, and the bewildered, shocked look on the face of Pottawattamies and other peoples caught in a strange middle time of mutation, neither quite one world or another, Fuller nevertheless proposes that

> . . . the Philosopher
> Sees through the clouds a hand which cannot err,
> An unimproving race, with all their graces,
> And all their vices, must resign their places;
> And Human Culture rolls its onward flood
> Over the broad plains steeped in Indian blood.
>
> Such thoughts steady our faith . . .
> *(Summer on the Lakes* 184)

"Faith" of this sort is precisely what grows troubled if one peers too deeply into the moral and cultural "chaos" between worlds, where frames of reference and standards of measure become as mutable and shifting as the watery tumult at Niagara.

On the one hand, Fuller seeks to sustain "steady . . . faith" in universal constants transcending all apparent historical tumult. Yet it is precisely the glaring difference between shifting cultural assumptions and attitudes that surfaces, for example, in Schoolcraft's mistranslation of native tribal myths into urbane, parlor-room English, forcing Fuller to "guess" across a cultural divide separating formal printed English from native oral delivery. To reach toward the "peculiar modification of life and mind" actually registered in such myths – to "throw" oneself, as Fuller at one point puts it, "into the character or position of the Indians" (187) – means seeing across a gulf toward "their own theory of the history of the globe" and their alternative "moral sympathies" (192). At least in part, such phraseology indicates Fuller's acceptance of what James Clifford, in *The Predicament of Culture*, terms "a pervasive condition of off-centeredness in a world of distinct meaning systems" over which no "transcendent regime of authenticity" presides.[23]

Fuller's account of westward settlement, however, is not all of a piece. It wavers between the linear, ubiquitously measurable logic of nineteenth-century imperialism, according to which the doomed habitats and worlds of "unimproving races" must "resign their places" to more advanced ones in the "onward" progress of universal "Human Culture," and an "off-centeredness" too mobile and incalculable to make such a determinative measure. By the shifting light of this second, more mutable logic, Fuller cannot take the definitive measure of the transitional landscape through which she passes.

In the collapse of universal measurement and ubiquitous authority, voided of settled point of view, all is no doubt not lost. Toward the close of *The Predicament of Culture*, Clifford writes:

Stories of cultural contact and change have been structured by a pervasive dichotomy: absorption by the other or resistance to the other. A fear of lost identity, a Puritan taboo on mixing beliefs and bodies, hangs over the process. Yet what if identity is conceived not as a boundary to be maintained but as a nexus of relations and transactions actively engaging a subject? The story or stories of interaction must then be more complex, less linear and teleological . . . How do stories of contact, resistance, and assimilation appear from [a] standpoint . . . in which exchange rather than identity is the fundamental value to be sustained?[24]

In *Summer on the Lakes*, Fuller comes close, at times, to writing a "more complex, less linear and teleological" story of incommensurable worlds in "contact" and "exchange." But her own restrictive position within history keeps forcing her back to a more limited, less transactional perspective. For having traveled into the interior of the continent to where native tribal peoples still wander into cities like Milwaukee, still stand silhouetted in small groups against the sky, or still make camp in the evening along lake shores, Fuller keeps discovering, as we have seen, the way these peoples shrink back both from her and her companions, so that direct, intimate contact with them remains difficult. Yet back in New England, whatever scholarship and pictography, translation and narrative is available to Fuller eclipses far more than it mediates native American experience and culture. The complex "relations and transactions" theoretically open to "a subject" whose very "identity," as scholar and author, might develop at the rich if troubled "nexus" of alternative worlds remain largely inaccessible to the author of *Summer on the Lakes*. Neither actual historical circumstances nor available scholarly materials fortuitously conspire to make such a transactional, across-the-worlds perspective as achievable as it might be in the very text that so powerfully demonstrates its necessity.

By virtue of its very uncertainties of authorship and textual authority, another, more problematically authored text opens up the transactional perspective across cultures and worlds more hesitantly emergent in *Summer on the Lakes.* I turn to the faded newsprint on the damaged sheet of paper that remains our earliest registry of the speech which, according to Dr. Henry A. Smith, Chief Seattle gave in the early 1850s extending cooperation – or at least acquiescence – to the organizers of the Washington Territory. The celebrated speech by the legendary chief who gave his name to the city of Seattle, and who ostensibly legitimated US land claims in a dramatic public address before a new territorial governor as well as before crowds of Suquamish and Dewamish onlookers on the Puget Sound waterfront, is carefully preserved on a single sheet of newsprint at Suzzallo Library on the University of Washington campus. Preserved in such a manner, and accessible only if one fills out an official request form, waits twenty-four hours, returns to the library, and agrees to sit in a designated area, the earliest surviving text of the ostensible speech assumes the status of a relic or rare ancestral document; arguably it can be numbered among the "images, narratives, monuments" and "signs" which, as Lauren Berlant puts it, form specific sites through which the nation and its history assume intelligibility to its citizens.[25] But like so much of this sort of material that emerges in the writing that we have been considering, epitomized by the old Puritan "scarlet A" that promises to link Hawthorne to the past, but that fractures equivocally into a quaint "badge of shame," or beautifully sewn ornament of dress, or neglected "rag of . . . cloth," the text of Chief Seattle's speech ultimately emerges at the problematic nexus of mutually incommensurable worlds, points of view, and frames of reference. It is not even clear whether the earliest printed text that ostensibly preserves the speech is the more or less faithful printed echo – the origin – or, most likely, a skewed, distorted version of what seems to take shape in retrospect as a memorable public address. Yet these very uncertainties of author and text serve to situate Chief Seattle's speech between cultures and worlds.

No doubt from one perspective, the address appears to relinquish one world and to legitimate another one. Chief Seattle, that is to say, refers to a treaty about to be ratified whereby violence between "two distinct" peoples will be foresworn, extensive tribal lands will be purchased by and handed over to US territorial administrators, and the Dewamish and Suquamish tribes will "retire to the reservation you offer them." A municipality and a federal territory seem in the process of undergoing earliest accreditation – and invention – in the minds of contemporary witnesses.[26] The speech is not exactly an officially signed, foundational document, but it does look forward to one. Perhaps more importantly, it seems to emerge at the focal center of a great public ceremony and memorable visual tableau imparting an almost sacred aura to the transfer of territorial claims from native to invading peoples – or at least according to Dr. Smith's retrospective remarks in the *Seattle Sunday Star*:

The bay swarmed with canoes and the shore was lined with a living mass of swaying, writhing, dusky humanity, until
OLD CHIEF SEATTLE'S
trumpet-toned voice rolled over the immense multitude . . . [and] silence became . . . instantaneous . . .
. . . Chief Seattle arose with all the dignity of a senator . . . Placing one hand on the governor's head, and slowly pointing heavenward with the index finger of the other, he commenced his memorable address.[27]

As a "memorable address" (imperfectly remembered at best) at the putative focal center of a vast public ceremony ostensibly gathering native peoples and white settlers together in the early 1850s, "Chief Seattle's Speech" is thereafter translated into English, committed to newsprint, and then over the decades republished in books, quoted at numerous public occasions, and framed by various prefaces and headnotes. By degrees it arguably becomes part of what Berlant regards as the body of narrative, iconography, symbol, and myth – assuming an almost religious luster – granting shape and focalization to the meaning of the nation.

Yet "Chief Seattle's Speech" ultimately resists serving such a focalizing function. Through forms of the "National Symbolic" such as the Statue of Liberty in New York Harbor, an aura of "indivisible . . . wholeness" and timeless "totality," as Berlant puts it, is ostensibly evoked.[28] To a certain degree, Chief Seattle's legendary speech, both in and of itself and as situated within a great waterfront tableau of gathered-together peoples and worlds, seems to aspire to this collectivizing and unifying function. Albert Furtwangler, for example, in his meticulously researched study of the textual history of the speech and of various responses to it, cannot resist approaching the address as a summons to unity in the closing pages of his book. Although the address wavers between emerging as "actual event" or a "fabrication from white men's pens and presses" – the "text printed in 1887" containing signs of authenticity, and yet signs of considerable imaginative doctoring as well – and although the speech registers massive differences in religious and cultural outlook, the address, Furtwangler proposes,

also attempts to reach across this conflict. It is a speech, after all, an act of human communication, and effort at . . . agreement, what we still call a meeting on common ground. As we know it, it is a speech recorded in English – a hybrid of indigenous speech and modern print culture. It somehow seems to connect these disparate realms.[29]

Furtwangler's word "somehow" serves as a reminder that within what
Berlant terms "mechanisms for staging" national "unity," it is the "am-
biguation of the relationship between multiple" frames of reference and a
"simulacrum of wholeness" that actually develops.[30] No doubt "disparate
realms" are brought within one another's compass both within "Chief
Seattle's Speech" and within the overall ceremonial occasion – real or imagined – for which the speech ostensibly serves as a centerpiece. But to inquire
more alertly into what falls uncertainly between native oral and "modern
print" cultures, and emerges as an odd patchwork of voices and rhetorics, is
scarcely to encounter "a meeting on common ground." Quite the contrary,
it is to confront what William Boelhower terms the specter of the "discontinuous" that cannot, at bottom, be "eliminated" upon deepest excavation
into the maps – or, for that matter, the speeches and ceremonies – that seem
to objectify and focalize the meaning of "America" as where all dwell.[31]

A sense of discontiunity certainly troubles the harmonious ceremonial
tableau that Smith attempts to frame in his preface to the speech in the
Seattle Sunday Star. Hawthorne, we will recall, deliberately unsettles homogeneity of official ceremonial perspective in *The Scarlet Letter* by drawing
attention to lurking details and contradictory perspectives that overflow the
official meaning of the gathering. In the preface to "Chief Seattle's Speech"
in the *Seattle Sunday Star,* on the other hand, a sense of difference more
unintentionally leaks into the ceremonial tableau framed by Dr. Smith.
That is to say, the "Bay," we are told, "swarmed with canoes," and the
"shore was lined with a living mass of swaying, writhing, dusky humanity." Smith's would-be envisionment of ceremonial harmony is obviously
conceived through a racializing, culturally inflected voice.[32]

By 1887, an alien counter-world of "writhing, dusky humanity" no longer
troubles the Pacific Northwest; Seattle flourishes as a growing American city
on the Pacific Coast; Smith's preface recalls the early 1850s, when hostilities
still flared up between disparate populations in a far less certain time of
fluid and shifting boundaries, geographies and cultures in collision, and
foundational territorial treaties not yet ratified. Even more compellingly, the
address that follows evokes a troubled and unsettled juncture in American
history that ultimately refracts into many perspectives and voices, much as
the very name "Seattle" (or "Sealth," or "Seathl") ultimately refracts away
from any central norm.[33]

If anything, the multi-focalized capacity of Seattle's (or Sealth's) (or
Seathl's) address to span the range of mutually incongruous moral and
religious universes, and to look, as it were, several ways at once with a mixture of anger, acquiescence, insight, nostalgia, and foreboding, introduces

a moment of ambiguity and hesitation between apparently receding and forthcoming life-worlds. Indeed, from the multi-focalized perspective of such a speech, mutually incommensurable worlds that on the one hand are "distinct," and seem to have "little in common," are nevertheless brought into a rare condition of reciprocal transparency and mutual exposure. In part, no doubt, the address cedes land, acknowledges the futility of opposition to a people who "wax strong every day," and seems to accept the increasing marginalization and even the eventual doom of native populations. But most of the speech is a meditation on shifting cultural realities from a Janus-faced sense of relativity in the midst of historical change. Massive differences are specified between a printed "religion . . . written on tables of stone," on the one hand, and, on the other, a religion handed down through ongoing oral recitation while continually becoming reframed by "the dreams of our old men"; between the Christian dead who rise to heaven and "never return" to the earth, and the "invisible dead of my tribe" who will continue to "swarm" throughout these regions; between an invaded people who stick close to the lands of their ancestors, and invaders who "wander away" from their homes, seemingly "without regret," to build empires and cities. What falls between "distinct" cultural orders in the speech itself is precisely the potential of their reciprocal visibility and intelligibility toward one another, and outside such reciprocity of intelligibility across a divide, neither an enduring metaphysic nor a single envisagement of human society or sense of place in general prevails. "Your God seems to us to be partial," emphasizes Chief Seattle in the address. Conversely, the "sky" or heaven that apparently has been full of "compassion" toward "our fathers" for "centuries untold" only "looks eternal," and may change. Or, in other words, cultures, their environments, and the religious frameworks they orient around themselves, are inevitably parochial, contingent, and passing. Communal tribes are made up of individuals, and, however trans-individual, collective, and timeless they may aspire to be, tribes themselves, at bottom, are "no better than" mortal creatures who "come and go like . . . waves." In the exposure of inevitably parochial and passing cultural orders toward one another lurks the reciprocal revelation of their edged, precarious character and their inevitable doom, and "even the white man . . . is not exempt from the common destiny. We *may* be brothers after all."[34]

National icons and rituals, narratives and speeches, may seem to gather the otherwise mortal participants, the shifting and evanescent life-worlds, and the contradictory interests and emotional investments of a variegated history into a timeless dimension of "ideality and wholeness."[35] But in Chief Seattle's speech, the "common destiny" wherein "we" may be gathered

CHAPTER 6

The power of negative space in Douglass's autobiographies and in Davis's "Life in the Iron Mills"

> This is what I want you do to. I want you to hide your disgust, take no
> heed to your clean clothes, and come right down with me, – here, into
> the thickest of the fog and mud and foul effluvia . . . There is a secret
> down here, in this nightmare fog, that has lain dumb for centuries: I
> want to make it a real thing to you . . . It is not the sentence of death
> we think it, but, from the very extremity of this darkness, the most
> solemn prophecy which the world has known of the Hope to come.
>
> Rebecca Harding Davis, "Life in the Iron Mills"[1]

Having explored the way a "disturbing void" opens up within evanescent cultural realities in *Summer on the Lakes* and Chief Seattle's speech, I now want to address a different set of antebellum American texts in which, in a somewhat different manner, void shows through the schemata and modes of spectatorial authority that seem to situate historicized creatures in the present. In these texts, environments of extreme human destitution spawned both by slavery and by industrial-revolution economics exert extraordinary pressure upon the official portraiture of contemporary "America" during the antebellum decades. My focus will be specifically on Frederick Douglass's reminiscences of American enslavement and on Rebecca Harding Davis's pioneering envisagement of the world of the industrial-revolution poor, "Life in the Iron Mills." Such texts, I will be arguing, ultimately raise the same specter of placelessness and indefiniteness, destabilized visibility and troubled material presence at the mercurial, ever-shifting heart of cultural power that we have been addressing in other texts. And although this possibility is more explicitly endorsed by Davis than by Douglass, a close reading of works by both authors, I will be arguing, suggests that this core of indefiniteness and instability at the heart of cultural power "is not," as Davis puts it, necessarily "the sentence of death we think it" – or at least when properly elucidated and explored.

Before I venture into this discussion, however, let me make a preliminary qualification: my use of the word "destitution" in a broad enough manner to encompass both American enslavement and American working-class poverty no doubt neglects significant differences between a racialized and a more strictly economic, class-based exploitation of labor. I do not mean to minimize the importance of the contemporary discussion of race in American culture and history by opening up an alternative line of inquiry into the significance of destitution per se in works by Douglass and Davis. Still, drawing an analogy between slavery and working-class poverty in the antebellum decades is scarcely without precedent. In his discussion of "Frederick Douglass and Postmodernity," for example, John Carlos Rowe discovers an oppressive "complicity" in language patterns and "metaphors" common to "the ideologies of both Northern capitalism and Southern . . . slaveholding."[2] And Douglass himself, in *My Bondage and My Freedom*, argues that "the poor, laboring white" – ultimately a "white slave" – has "taken from him, by indirection, what the black slave has taken from him, directly, and without ceremony. Both are plundered, and by the same plunderers."[3]

Such statements, however, speak to half the issue. In tracing the commonality of enslavement and working-class poverty to the same oppressive apparatus of ideology, language, and economic exploitation, statements such as these focus on ideas and institutions that seem to constitute and to define an experience of destitution from without. But from profoundly within its own recesses, the specter of destitution kicks back, troubles, fascinates, and appalls, if with an alien counter-power of its own as difficult to measure and to gauge as the weird, ungainly figure of korl, sculpted by the puddler Hugh Wolfe, the significance of which falls outside the aesthetic standards and intellectual horizons of the astonished doctor, factory owner's son, overseer, intellectual dilettante, and newspaper reporter who gather around this strange, enigmatic symbol in Davis's story.

Fundamental modes of representation, basic social, epistemological, and aesthetic assumptions – these begin to break down when literature enters into dismal places where social structure disintegrates, and where the ultimate frailty of the power of culture over the sensuous and the tangible is exposed in "foul smells ranging loose through the air" ("Life in the Iron Mills" 11) and in spectacles of decrepitude and decay. And although this descent into a world of enfeebled cultural structure and presence is far more explicitly thematized in Davis's case than in Douglass's, in both cases, I will be arguing, we are dealing with a literature that marks the dismal limit of culturally mediated form – if precisely to open up what Davis calls a dimension of "solemn prophecy" in such an odd, dark, and unexpected way.

I begin with Frederick Douglass's two pre-Civil War autobiographies: *Narrative of the Life of Frederick Douglass, An American Slave* and *My Bondage and My Freedom.* In exploring these texts in the context of Davis's provocative declaration that "hope" lies in "the very extremity of this darkness," and that "it is not the sentence of death we think it," I no doubt step into a complicated problem. Such an approach seems almost perversely counterintuitive in Douglass's case. Douglass's autobiographies, read in succession, would surely seem to invest "hope," if anywhere, in an ex-slave's increasing agency, stature, and influence within northern liberal American society. Surely the self-taught, self-named "Frederick Douglass" is the proverbial man who came from nowhere to assume a prominent position in the life and times of the American nation.

Still, as numerous commentators have argued, Douglass achieves influence and stature in large measure through mastery of frames of reference, rhetorical strategies, and aesthetic techniques – gothicism, sentimentality, the Franklinesque rags-to-riches odyssey, the Victorian code of "manly dignity"[4] – which in the very process of providing Douglass with strategies and conventions acceptable to his largely white, middle-class readers nevertheless threaten to betray what Jenny Franchot terms the underlying "violence" and "chaos" at the core of his reminiscence.[5] To write along a borderland where the experience of enslavement is invoked precisely to be judged and conceptualized within frames of reference that make sense to Douglass's antebellum audience may be a judicious, politically necessary act, and Douglass himself may manipulate prevailing conventions to his advantage. But at the core of his writing lurks an experience that threatens to destabilize his audience's most fundamental assumptions about the structure of reality and the persuasiveness of mediating conventions.

For example, although Douglass is careful to envision much of his autobiographical material through frameworks, vocabularies, and literary protocols familiar to his readers, recognition of a vast disjuncture in perspective and orientation between slave space and free space demonstrates just how wide a difference can open up in the most fundamental consciousness of environment and milieu. Recognition of such disjuncture in sense of space proves to be especially crucial to an understanding of at least one part of Douglass's reminiscence: the attempted escape northward by "our little band." Douglass emphasizes that his readers would probably not, on the face of it, regard the proposed escape northward from the shore of Maryland as a "formidable undertaking," for "to look at the map" of the United States in 1845 is to observe the close proximity of Maryland to the nearby free states of Delaware and Pennsylvania. But Douglass is careful to contrast the reader's cartographically oriented sense of space with the alternative spatial experience of the enslaved, which is characterized by

> vague and indistinct notions of the geography of the country . . .
>   . . . We had heard of Canada, the real Canaan of the American bondmen, simply as a country to which the wild goose and the swan repaired at the end of winter, to escape the heat of summer, but not as the home of man. I knew something of theology, but nothing of geography. I really did not, at that time, know that there was a state of New York, or . . . of Massachusetts . . . On the one hand, there stood slavery . . . the evil from which to escape. On the other hand, far away, back in the hazy distance, where all forms seemed but shadows . . . stood . . . uncertainty . . . the untrodden road . . . conjecture. (*My Bondage* 310–11)

Is what "our little band" conceives as spreading obscurely all around the more immediately defined spaces of the plantation simply an inaccurate view of the world? Here it is important to recall J. B. Harley's observation that maps, like paintings and prints, are ultimately "rhetorical" rather than "impartial or objective" constructs. "Rhetoric," writes Harley, "permeates all layers of the map. As images of the world, maps are never neutral or value free." They bear the trace of "cultural practices, preferences, and priorities" throughout what appear to be their simple representational images and neutral lines and forms.[6] In keeping with this proposition, to read Douglass closely is to encounter a spatial experience not only falling outside, but furthermore marking the unsuspected ideological and cultural horizon of the maps – and, along with them, of contemporary paintings and prints – through the lens of which the antebellum United States is taking shape in the popular American imagination, although not necessarily in the eyes of American slaves.

   On the one hand, in accordance with the emergence of an increasingly centralized, spectatorially mastered sense of space addressed in chapter 4 of this study, and in consonance with the logic of an inexorably expanding "settlement," mid-nineteenth-century maps, prints, and paintings of "America" implicitly invoke and address a subject whose frame of reference is assumed to be far-reaching and global rather than immediate and local, and whose sense of distance is rapidly becoming compressed by the telegraph, the railroad, the steamship and the turnpike. As Whitman declares in "Song of the Open Road":

> To see nothing anywhere but what you may reach it and pass it,
>   . . .
> To look up or down no road but it stretches and waits for you.[7]

Yet such space remains, in the final analysis, alterable and contingent. It is not what members of Douglass's "little band" experience as they peer out from the plantation into obscure distances of fearful "conjecture" and "uncertainty" all around them. Instead of a well-oriented space of inviting roads and mapped, beckoning prospects, denial of access to the world of print results in "vague and indistinct notions" of a "hazy," far-off geography (*My Bondage* 310), and rapid vehicular conveyance through such distance is precisely what is denied. Contemporary lithographs may celebrate easy vehicular penetration into space and distance, but in 1838, Douglass reports,

the railroad . . . was under regulations so stringent, that . . . colored travelers were almost excluded. They must have . . . papers; they must be measured and carefully examined, before they were allowed to enter the cars . . . The steamboats were under regulations equally stringent. All the great turnpikes . . . were beset with kidnappers, a class of men who watched the newspapers for advertisements for runaway slaves. (*My Bondage* 341–42)

At every gate through which we had to pass [in a contemplated escape from St. Michael's], we saw a watchman; at every bridge, a sentinel; and in every wood, a patrol or slave-hunter. We were hemmed in on every side. (*My Bondage* 311)

Any white man is authorized to stop a man of color, on any road, and examine him, and arrest him . . . (*My Bondage* 314)

Whereas contemporary paintings and engravings seem to echo back to the eye a space of agency, of penetrative vision, and of rapid vehicular potential, the slave or "man of color" inhabits space on drastically altered terms: as vulnerable to search, delay, and impediment "at every gate" and "at every bridge"; as the marked, carefully scrutinized object rather than as the privileged subject of increasing powers of surveillance over well-networked, administratively encompassed territory; at the vulnerable other end of enormous spectatorial and vehicular powers becoming extended to map readers, to railroad travelers, and to those for whom, in Whitman's words, "no road" extends into the distance "but it stretches and waits for you."

It might be argued that we penetrate in Douglass's writing strictly to the inverted other pole of this networked, surveyed space; that we reach through merely to the point where human beings become the targeted objects rather than the subjectively enhanced agents of its expanding powers of surveillance; that we reach the point where recognition of increasingly powerful means of transportation over vast, networked distances emerges not as opportunity but as horror: as involuntary severance from familiar circumstances and loved ones with "no hope of reunion," so that when a slave is transported to far distances by steamship, he feels "like a living man going into the tomb, who, with open eyes, sees himself buried out of sight . . . of wife, children, and friends" (*My Bondage* 239) in some distant corner of a vaguely known geography.

This is ultimately to experience, one might argue, the great American space celebrated in "Song of the Open Road" in inversion: as the controlled object rather than as the controlling, empowered agent of formidable new powers over distance and space. To what degree does this world of expanding surveillance and enormous vehicular potential saturate its way into everything to become the inescapable common denominator of everyone, from empowered agent to victim alike? Or do we reach the horizon of this space – and even begin to cross into something else – in Douglass's writing?

In "Talbot county . . . Maryland, near Easton, the county town of that county" – within what can be very precisely situated, located, and defined in contemporary American geography – Frederick Douglass was born as the slave Frederick Augustus Bailey. But Douglass hastens to add that official cartographical orientation of this "district, or neighborhood," whose official printed name, "Tuckahoe," is "seldom mentioned but with . . . derision," ultimately fails to account for the "worn-out," "desert-like" appearance of a place where names on a map seem irrelevant, and "decay and ruin are everywhere visible" (*My Bondage* 139). It is as if the reader, in approaching the deepest recesses of what American enslavement has opened up within the fabric of American reality, were being ushered out of structured, historically textured space into a dimension of catastrophe, placelessness, and ruin where the power of culture to place and to situate, to contextualize, locate, and define becomes cataclysmically enfeebled.

In large measure this involves failure in the power of descriptive language itself to frame and to formulate Douglass's material in a satisfactory way. As has already been observed, a noticeable gap begins to open up in the autobiographies between the experience of enslavement and the vantage point of its retrospective interpretation, between referent and act of reference, between an autobiography-in-process undergoing successive refinement, development, and change within mainstream American culture and the experience of enslavement that remains at the troubled core of it all. What we encounter in the autobiographies, that is to say, is not the experience of enslavement in and of itself, but the complex mediational process of selection, abstraction, omission, and shifting perspective through which Douglass struggles to frame his difficult subject matter. And this sometimes leads to the observation that "the revisions" in Douglass's remembrance of his mother, or of the scene in which Aunt Esther (or Aunt Hester) is brutally whipped by Aaron Anthony, "attest to a disturbing instability surrounding" the slave past that threatens to expose it as the scene of "malleable narrative convention rather than unique and indelible memory." Jenny Franchot, who makes these observations, goes on to argue that "as the principle antagonist" in Douglass's "quest for identity, slavery generated his famed career as a journalist, lecturer, and autobiographer. Against its chaos, violence, and deprivation, Douglass fashioned his order, rhetorical prowess, and achievement."[8]

No doubt such an argument must be refined. Franchot's use of the very term "against" testifies to the trace of what is purportedly repressed in the inconsistences and incongruities, the telling silences and omissions that signal the limits of Douglass's rhetorical "order." And a more comprehensive treatment of the autobiographies such as Priscilla Wald's demonstrates that even as the more rhetorically complex *My Bondage* departs from the earlier *Narrative* through less "overt chafing" against "narrative conventions and cultural prescriptions," a certain self-conscious recognition of the limitation of "rhetorical prowess" characterizes both narratives. In both texts, Wald argues, Douglass ultimately enacts – and yet "calls attention to" – "the task of authorship" and the adoption of "stylistic conventions" in mediating his charged material to readers.[9]

To a certain degree this would seem to be a matter of mid-Victorian censorship becoming aggressively exposed in the very act of becoming observed. Again and again, certainly, the conventionalized, mid-nineteenth-century voice adopted by Douglass reaches a self-imposed limit that nevertheless becomes quite other than quiet, unobtrusive, and discrete, from "the dark crimes" that are said to be "openly perpetrated" – but in ways that must remain "without a name" (*My Bondage* 219) – to the curious proposal that "I aim . . . to give the reader a truthful impression of my slave life, without unnecessarily afflicting him with harrowing details" (*My Bondage* 270). Along this gingerly negotiated but deliberately emphasized borderland between an audience's inquisitiveness and good will and yet its silences and evasions, we are referred to horrors "beyond expression"; to what "I wish I could commit to paper";[10] or to the lurid scene of Aaron Anthony whipping Aunt Esther in which Captain Anthony's "motives" are precisely what literary language available to Douglass in mid-nineteenth-century America "has no power" to reach into, to illuminate, and to name (*My Bondage* 177).

Emerging as an institutionally spawned, legally sanctioned but nevertheless culturally tabooed experience full of "dark" things "without a name," slavery furthermore entails the blurring together, confusion, and instability of fundamental oppositions and moral and intellectual categories, as when Douglass writes that few slaves "had the virtue" – "or the vice" – "to resist" taking Colonel Lloyd's fruit (*Narrative* 25), or of "men and women . . . leveled . . . with horses, sheep, horned cattle and swine" in the public display of estate property (*My Bondage* 237); and within the precincts of this linguistically blurred, categorically troubled world, we are referred to "sleeping apartments – if they may be called such" (*My Bondage* 187), or to "my home" that "was not home to me" (*Narrative* 34), or to "brothers and sisters" who have become virtual "strangers. I had heard the words brother and sister . . . but slavery had robbed these terms of their true meaning" (*My Bondage* 149).

In close engagement, then, with experiences and situations spawned by slavery, language in some cases would appear capable of shedding potential light on what is occurring (although mid-Victorian censorship would seem to keep it from exercising its "power"); but, in other cases, words are entirely "robbed" of their "meaning," polarities and oppositions begin to blur, and the "power" of language becomes not so much explicitly curbed by censorship as noticeably enfeebled.[11]

The question arises: is mid-Victorian rhetoric a veil of censorship that can be pierced – and definitively replaced – by more accurate, illuminating language, or does language itself become enfeebled in close engagement with slavery? Ultimately, I would argue, to recognize the resistance of slave experience to adequate verbal registry in schemata and concepts such as "father," "home," "sister," "brother," "virtue," and "vice" by no means implies that if we could somehow get outside the horizon of this discourse, we would encounter slavery in some articulate, coherent, crisply knowable form of its own. In addressing this issue, Hortense Spillers writes insightfully – but misses something important – in arguing that in the case of slavery,

we search vainly for a point of absolute and indisputable origin, for a moment . . . that would restore us to the real . . . 'thing' itself before discourse touched it. In that regard, slavery becomes the great 'test case' around which . . . the circle of mystery is reinscribed again and again . . . As many times as we reopen slavery's closure, we are hurtled rapidly forward into the . . . motions of a symbolic enterprise.[12]

The testimony of Douglass's writing, however, is *not* that slavery, as Spillers ultimately concludes, forcibly becomes "*primarily* discursive" – primarily hazarded into the "motions of a symbolic enterprise" destined to reshape the meaning and contours of this experience "again and again." No doubt from outside the experience of the enslaved, the contours of slavery seem to shift and alter as interpretative strategies change, and these shifting interpretative strategies can become quite vigorous and aggressive in their claim to correct, deepen, and clarify what has previously been said. Professional vocabularies now exist, for example, that seem capable of probing far more thoroughly than Douglass's circumscribed, Victorian rhetoric into lurid and shocking scenes such as Aaron Anthony whipping Aunt Esther, there to specify in florid, elaborately learned prose underlying sado-erotic motives, or to suggest the way a figure like Captain Anthony seems to tower, like an ominous father-figure in a grim Oedipal myth, before little Frederick Bailey as he witnesses the scene in amazed, transfixed horror through a peep-hole. A commentator such as Spillers, sensitive to the vicissitudes of language and to shifting scholarly protocols, cautions us against allowing such an aggressively interpretative vocabulary so to fix and to freeze scenes of enslavement that description appears to become commensurate with the thing itself, "before discourse touched it." But to argue that "slavery is *primarily* discursive" in that it lies open to such shifting interpretative stances is to miss the still more fundamental point that the deepest "hell of slavery" (*Narrative* 18), or at least as experienced by those within its existential circle rather than as interpreted by those without, in large measure entails the *enfeeblement* – not the alterability – of interpretative vocabularies and orienting frames of reference.

No doubt this must be phrased very carefully. In any discussion of the *enfeeblement* of mediating system and sign within the world recalled by Douglass, it is important to acknowledge the survival within slavery, so carefully documented over the years, of songs, rituals, folktales, and religious beliefs from various African cultures.[13] Still, even a commentator like Sterling Stuckey, in emphasizing the importance of such surviving cultural forms "as a means of ordering" the slave's world, grants that within this fragile, vulnerably constructed slave-culture – ceaselessly open to violation, to dispersal, and to sudden, brutal rearrangement from without – such surviving cultural forms are at best improvisational and "fluid," given to "taking shape in one place and then disappearing," if only "to reappear . . . elsewhere."[14] Gregory Jay puts this even more strongly. "Had slaves been able to perpetuate their African languages and cultures" in unadulterated, unimpeded form, he argues, they might then have had "a nonwhite rhetoric" and culture to structure "their experience." But on these terms they would not "have had the experience" of African-American slavery per se, for such an experience entails "precisely the cultural expropriation and transformation of a people."[15]

"Cultural . . . transformation," however, suggests a dynamic process of shifting social paradigms and evolving ways of organizing experience, whereas something must be added here – or, perhaps more properly speaking, taken away: taken away in the fundamental *failure* of either the surviving but weakened memory of "African languages and cultures," or of the Western cultural legacy itself, adequately to provide order or solace for those caught in the middle of a prolonged period of nationlessness and disrupted cultural context. It is, I think, significant that throughout the widespread commentary on African-American enslavement, we find continual references to slavery's ultimate "unrepresentability," to its emergence as nothing less than a mode of "social death," to a "black hole" – to something "ineffable" – "at the center of every slave narrative," such that "slavery occupies" an indefinitely provocational if peculiarly evacuative "position in the American national memory . . . ; it is what we think we know, what we can never forget, and what seems continually to elude our understanding."[16]

From one perspective, American enslavement is the prolonged period of socio-political "death" into which Africans of various backgrounds and languages are cast, denied kinship ties, miscegenated by slow degrees, irremediably post-Africanized, while denied inclusion and citizenship within any post-African world. From another perspective, in looking back into this experience from bourgeois, middle-class American culture, we are forced to acknowledge that between such an experience, on the one hand, and its retrospective envisagement within officially accredited vocabularies and mediating terms, on the other, yawns a chasm that in large measure simply *cannot be crossed.* That is to say, such an experience entails the *vanishing point* – scarcely emerges as the conceivable *referent* – of mediating, defining terms and frames of reference whose relevance and significance lie outside this more troubled world, however fundamental such terms might be to the representation of bourgeois social space. Slavery, Douglass emphasizes, "does away" with many of the sorts of realities that can occur only as mediated, recorded, documented, and socially transmitted within bourgeois social space. "No family records," for example, are kept of "marriages, births, and deaths," so that "slave-mothers" are obliged to "measure the ages of their children by spring time, harvest time, planting time, and the like; but these soon become indistinguishable and forgotten. Like other slaves, I cannot tell how old I am. This destitution was among my earliest troubles" (*My Bondage* 140). To the degree that "destitution" of this sort marks the absence not simply of material resources, but, furthermore, of the behavioral origins or mediational frameworks of otherwise missing, unformulated realities – absence of the "records" without whose means one's

exact chronological age becomes "indistinguishable," loss of the very behaviors and relationships that constitute bourgeois, middle-class family
life – slavery's "unrepresentability" entails the sort of vanishing point elsewhere reached in the vanishing, for example, of a once communally accredited, luridly superstitious scarlet "A" into a mere rag of cloth. In all such
cases, a limit is reached in the range and scope of constitutive contexts and
processes outside of which certain culturally accredited realities themselves
dwindle away.

On the face of it, to be sure, an American slave narrative is linear, positive, affirmative, and forward-looking; it recounts a successful flight to
northern freedom; it demonstrates how a slave such as Frederick Bailey
becomes a public figure such as Frederick Douglass who achieves stature
and prominence within the bourgeois Western community. But to tell such
a narrative is to tell an irremediably *haunted* story, much as in the case of
Isabel's remembrance in *Pierre*, of culturally meaningful realities that remain existentially edged. Writing of this sort reaches back toward what Eric
Sundquist terms an "anti-beginning,"[17] and toward what Douglass himself
describes as an experience "that left me without an intelligible beginning
in the world" (*My Bondage* 157). One never quite encounters any specific
moment in Douglass's autobiographies in which this lack of an "intelligible
beginning" is considered to be other than catastrophic: an absence to be
sorrowed over, a vacuum to be filled in. But a voided-out "beginning" of
this sort, destitute of map knowledge, genealogy, Western calendar time,
and one's exact chronological age within it – and largely bereft of alternative, non-Western means for ordering the world – opens up a dark,
inchoate counterpoint to culturally mediated truth that constitutes a negative legacy of its own. This is the negative counterpoint that Ralph Ellison
will later emphasize must never be lost sight of even as "societies as well
as individuals" struggle to "give pattern to the chaos" that lurks within all
socially enfranchised "certainties."[18] And from Douglass's reminiscences of
life in slavery to Ellison's exploration of the anarchic, fluid underside of
culturally patterned experience in writings such as "Harlem is Nowhere"
and *Invisible Man*, this recognition of the underlying frailty of the culturally
constructed universe serves as an inchoate – if potentially liberating – cor-
rective within African-American literature to American foundationalism:
to the myth that somehow in America, forms of social, secular order are
cosmically rooted, metaphysically guaranteed, timeless, and inevitable.[19]
They are no more inevitable and guaranteed to exist than are the strange
shapes – "L," "S," "L.F." and so forth – that young Frederick Bailey
learns to recognize as letters on pieces of lumber in a Baltimore ship

yard (*Narrative* 44), and through which "Frederick Douglass" himself eventually becomes quite other than invisible in the eyes of so many readers.

The communally foregrounded but latently vulnerable visibility of lettering and legible language, of shape, structure, and sign against the "chaos" lurking within the "pattern" of culturally formulated certainties is at issue as well in Rebecca Harding Davis's "Life in the Iron Mills." "This is what I want you to do," Davis's narrator announces to an *Atlantic Monthly* readership about to be ushered into a dismal *mise-en-scène* of broken-down objects, "foul smells," effluvia and decay marking the outermost disintegrative edge of cultural power over the visible and the sensuous:

> I want you to hide your disgust, take no heed of your clean clothes, and come right down with me, – here, into the thickest of the fog and mud and foul effluvia . . . There is a secret down here, in this nightmare fog, that has lain dumb for centuries: I want to make it a real thing to you . . . It is not the sentence of death we think it, but, from the very extremity of its darkness, the most solemn prophecy which the world has known of the Hope to come . . . It will, perhaps, seem to you as foul and dark as this thick vapor about us, and as pregnant with death; but if your eyes are free as mine are to look deeper, no . . . dawn will be so fair with promise . . . (14)

A sense of "promise" alien to the jingoistic, upbeat phraseology of the Republic, falling outside "ponderous Church creeds" and grandiose "schemes" of Christian reform, seems to lurk, rather, in material decay, in abject living conditions, and in "dens of drunkenness and infamy" (12) where the orienting vocabularies and moral frames of reference of contemporary middle-class culture reach a crumbling vanishing point, and where every "foul smell" or spectacle of decay indicates the mutinous recession of the sensuous and the visible out of the world of value, meaning, symbol, and clean, distinguishable form. Still, the constant admonition of the text is to "look deeper" and yet still "deeper into the heart of things" (21), even if this should lead into the "very extremity" of an anarchic, culturally uncontrollable "darkness" where all positive description and tidily arranged presence collapses into a "terrible dumb question" that "men have gone mad . . . trying to answer," but that remains, at the radical, "its own" open-ended, chronically unresolved "reply" (14).

In Davis's story, reaching through to this unresolved existential core within the humanly structured, mediated world leads into the slum world of decrepitude and decay, where the illusion of finished, completed presence gives way to a more unfinished reality of fluid textures and inchoate, overflowing entities as resistant to categorization as the fog that "rolls" in

Figure 5   "Wheeling in Virginia," from *The United States Illustratred; in Views of City and Country*, 1853?

gaseous "folds" throughout the town, or settles into "black . . . pools," or hardens into "greasy soot" on human faces (11). On the one hand, the handsome lithographic engraving of "Wheeling in Virginia" that appears in *The United States Illustrated* in the early 1850s – and that features its own version of the town upon which Davis's story is based – portrays a tidy little settlement of sharply delineated houses, clean lines, and well-edged, geometrically precise forms bespeaking stability and order.[20] Davis's murkier, more equivocal aesthetic, in contrast, reaches into a dismal *mise-en-scène* of ambiguous textures and hard-to-see entities where "here and there the flicker of gas lighted an uncertain space" (19), and where objects lie "broken," "strewed about," "dirty," or in "fragments" (12–13). In this obscure and decaying space, the culturally scripted text of the visible becomes fragmentary, "uncertain," and difficult to scan.

Thus in Davis's aesthetic, in a manner that bears reference to Theodor Adorno's *Minima Moralia*, "waste products" – as Adorno puts it – begin to assume a foregrounded prominence of their own. The focus shifts toward

what Adorno terms "opaque, unassimilated material" whose value lies precisely in that it has "outwitted," as it were, the well-administered world of
socially formulated objectives, coherent frames of reference, and recognized
forms of positive achievement.[21] The challenge to the reader is nevertheless
to "come right down with me, – here, into the thickest of the . . . mud and
foul effluvia," in keeping with the proposition that this "is not the sentence
of death we think it, but, from the very extremity of its darkness," nothing
less than a "solemn prophecy of Hope" (14).[22]

The gravitation of Davis's aesthetic toward the tenuous margins of organized, historically accredited appearance is paralleled by the recession, in
the story, of Hugh Wolfe's own assenting subjectivity and gaze from the
way he, himself, has become positioned, objectified, and visualized within
the historical moment. From one perspective, no doubt, Wolfe, like the
other workers, is very precisely positioned and accounted for, objectified
and efficiently used within the great utilitarian clockwork of schedules and
shifts composing "the vast machinery of system by which the bodies of
workmen are governed." "The hands of each mill," we are told, "are di-
vided into watches that relieve each other as regularly as the sentinels of
an army" (19). These forms of being accounted for, "governed," and instrumentalized within the historical moment, however – and an analogy
could of course be made here to the instrumentalized existence of plantation slaves – are such that the subjectivity of the workers has effectively
withdrawn from daily activities and routines, one case in point being the
deadened, voided-out look on the expressionless faces of the workers as
they absent themselves from themselves in their zombie-like walk to the
mills. The alert and anguished Hugh Wolfe, however, emerges as other
than zombie-like and deadened in his "mad cry of rage against God, man,
whoever it is that has forced this vile . . . life upon him." Looking at himself
in "loathing," as if "in a mirror" and in the third person, as he stands visibly in history with his "filthy body" and abject, working-class mannerisms
and accent, Wolfe, we are told, "gripped the filthy shirt that clung, stiff
with soot, about him, and tore it savagely from his arm. The flesh beneath
was muddy with grease and ashes, – and the heart beneath that! And the
soul?" (40) When at last reached and exposed, the "soul" emerges *in the
interrogative* – in the form of a question: "And the soul?" – at the end of
a series of assertions, visualizations, and identifications becoming stripped
away. If anything, what at last emerges in the depths of the consumptive
body, the "haggard" face, and the stumbling, awkward speech patterns (all
historically contingent markers, however tangible and historically concrete)

is Wolfe's "fierce . . . groping . . . desire to *be* – something, he knows not what, – other than he is" (24–25).

Wolfe's "fierce . . . groping" rejection of his own objectification and embodiment within the historical moment opens up a negative dimension in Davis's story that is not easily addressed and assessed. At the top of the class system, the privileged no doubt tend to define themselves through the lens of credentials and bodily appearances, activities and involvements that more or less situate them meaningfully within a coherent historical present. But among the destitute, where Wolfe rips and tears as if at his very bodily existence "with . . . loathing," an historically uninvested subjectivity begins to loom up outside the degrading, historically imposed terms of its objectification and instrumentalization within the social moment.[23]

Throughout the dismal slum-world of material decrepitude and decay depicted by Davis, then, we reach a series of limits and edges: the limited specular power of mediating imageries and visual forms that disintegrate into filth and debris; the limited range and benefit of the current economic system; ultimately, the limited power of the world of destitution to orient, nourish, and sustain the subjective allegiances of its inhabitants, who either walk in zombie-like withdrawal from their actions and their surroundings on their way to the mills, their despair registered in their "pale, bleared eyes" (22), or, in the case of Hugh Wolfe, betray a "fierce . . . groping . . . desire to *be* – something," one "knows not what, – other than" what they appear to be.

If a slave-narrative is ostensibly pointed toward acquisition of cultural literacy, credential, and agency by way of filling in this "groping" aim, Davis's story, one might assume, is a narrative of would-be rescue and retrieval whereby the alienated inhabitants of the slum-world are to be ushered up the promissory rungs of what Kirby (however cynically) defines as "our American system": in theory, "a ladder" which every person "can scale" (34). According to such a reading of Davis's text, to peer downward toward the "lowest deep" (39) of the community and of the nation at large is to approach not the vanishing point of socio-economic power but the redeemable target of American reformist energy and mid-nineteenth-century idealistic zeal. In Davis's story, however, just as junk and debris represent the recession of the sensuous and the visible out of what is shaped, valued, and accredited by socio-cultural power, Wolfe himself, with his "foreign thoughts and longings breaking out . . . in innumerable curious ways" (24), raises the specter of a socially unabsorbed human dimension that transcends the imaginations and moral sympathies of "many a . . . reformer"

who has ventured into the slum (15). Perhaps such a dimension must remain indefinitely provocational and socially unabsorbed. Significantly, the
"groping" figure of the korl-woman sculpted by Wolfe in reflection of his
"fierce . . . desire to *be* – something, he knows not what" – remains "dumb,"
"rough," and unfinished (35). Such a figure never quite comes into focus. It
raises the question to the perplexed observers who gather around it: "What
does the fellow intend by the figure? I cannot catch the meaning" (32).

The "meaning" of the korl-woman remains enigmatic to the last – long
after Wolfe's own arrest, imprisonment, and suicide. In contrast to the
way the "vast machinery of system" closes remorselessly in upon him, the
suggestive figure that he sculpts and leaves behind seems to loom up outside all systemization and contextualization as a reminder that historically
conditioned, socially contextualized lives take shape only against a vaster
backdrop of possibility. Between such indefinite possibility and more compromised modes of human existence yawns a difference that cannot be
definitively closed. For "something" is inevitably "lost," the narrator ruefully cautions as she concludes her narrative – "something . . . which might
have been, and was not" (64) – that remains in the inchoate background of
whatever is highlighted and accredited, realized and defined by historicized
creatures within formal social space.

This recognition that culturally accredited, mediated reality inevitably con-
stricts possibility helps to illuminate why the trajectory of writing such as
Douglass's slave narratives or Davis's "Life in the Iron Mills" ultimately
remains so equivocal. That is to say, if, in Douglass's case, the aim of the
narrative is toward agency, literacy, and the ability to project onself into
prevailing cultural contexts and vocabularies, it is also retrospectively back
toward a more inchoate, anonymous existence "against which," as Franchot
puts it, Douglass frames "his order, rhetorical prowess, and achievement."
And even as Hugh Wolfe at one point yearns to talk, act, and look like
the well-dressed, smoothly spoken Mitchell, the counter-aim of Davis's
narrative, in dismissal of contemporary aesthetic standards and cultural
norms, is "down with me, – here, into the thickest of the fog and mud
and foul effluvia," where unawakened potential still falls outside whatever
is accredited, highlighted, and framed within culturally prevailing idioms
and socially sanctioned contexts.

At the close of Davis's story, such uncertainty of trajectory into and
yet out of what still remains unformulated in the depths of socio-cultural
power results in the indefinite circularity of the interchange between the
gaze on the korl-woman's face – imploring, inquisitive, bewildered – and the

narrator's return, haunted gaze back toward the korl-woman. On the one hand, although the narrator can speak elegantly, forcefully, and vigorously, she keeps opening up lacunae and blind spots in whatever perspectives and descriptions she develops. She repeatedly refers to what "I dare not put into . . . words" (14), or to what "I can paint nothing of" (23), in keeping with her admonition that throughout all positively framed description and all historicized forms of selfhood, "something is" inevitably "lost." On the other hand, from out of the lost, imploring condition of the korl-woman's bewildered existential hunger on the outskirts of cultural opportunity and context, we are reminded that the free-floating suggestiveness with which such a figure haunts those normally ensconced within more orthodox historical contexts entails all the perplexity of an Isabel Glendinning, whose untutored mercurial openness so appalls – even if it also so intrigues – Pierre.

Whatever boundary of inclusion and/or exclusion we might look for in such texts – there to mark a conceivable entry-point where the destitute might enter into bourgeois social space precisely by becoming bourgeois – remains equivocal and tenuous. In the final analysis, it is not necessarily in the name of what assumes culturally accredited shape on this side of such a conversion-point that the wretched and the destitute are to be redeemed.

Conclusion: a community voided of time and place

Again and again in the texts that we have been exploring, whatever seems to take shape within culturally organized space – a superstitiously lurid scarlet "A" capable of fading back into innocuous cloth, Hugh Wolfe's frustrated projection of himself into heavily accentuated, working-class utterance – becomes manifest against a sense of existential potential that "I can paint nothing of." Existential openness of this sort, quite unlike the expansive spectatorial sweep of Thomas Cole's *The View From Mount Holyoke*, can no more be omnisciently surveyed from any standpoint within it than one figure can be inferred from another within the shifting obscurity of a Rorschach inkblot. Indeed, to reach the midmost pivotal heart of radical change, again to quote from Melville's provocative passage in *Pierre*, is like reaching the arctic "Pole" that is itself *voided* of the shifting compass readings that are conceivable all around it. Within the directionless, indefinitely potential midst of shifting directional readings and conflicting gestalten, everything becomes "dubious, uncertain . . . the most immemorially admitted maxims of men begin to slide and fluctuate, and . . . become wholly inverted . . . [and] the needle indifferently respects all points of the horizon alike" (*Pierre* 165). This sense of directionlessness and bewilderment in the turbulent thick of change (however readjusted everything might again become on its far side) is certainly felt throughout the shifting envisagement of Major Molineux's ordeal in the midst of socio-political crisis; and it surges up as well as the "odd, disturbing, liminal space, the threshold between" alternative "cultures," that itself eludes clearcut descriptive focus in *Summer on the Lakes*. The "disturbing . . . threshold between . . . cul-. tures" also emerges in Chief Seattle's meditation on the cataclysmic change of worlds sweeping across the nineteenth-century Pacific Northwest. Yet Seattle's meditation (itself probably destined to remain neither a definitively native American speech nor a purely ventriloquized one) suggests that the potentially *communalizing* lesson of such a massive socio-cultural shift – that which most comprehensively lurks within a massive mutation in perspective and frame of reference – is precisely the reciprocally disclosed contingency of fluctuating human realities, all prone to decay, whose inevitable parochialism and conditionality, once recognized as such, may make us "brothers."

Such an admittedly obscure definition of brotherhood raises the question: what ultimately constitutes *community?* Does community, for example, necessitate the sort of positively conceived, well-choreographed social theater that in the opening scene in *The Scarlet Letter* seems to gather everyone into itself according to officially prevailing ideas of rank, gender, and behavioral protocol, from Hester Prynne at the heart of the spectacle wearing her "ignominious badge of shame," to the common people gathered below, to Reverend Wilson, Reverend Dimmesdale, and Governor Bellingham magisterially presiding over the scene from high on the balcony? Does such social theater in all its well-arranged pageantry and carefully choreographed detail truly focalize and render intelligible a sense of the communal? Or is it more the case that spectacle of this sort is inevitably too narrow and restrictively conceived, too repressive and artificially arranged, to gather in, subsume, and display the fullest range and depth of the community at large? Ultimately, we will recall, Hawthorne's well-choreographed social spectacle is nevertheless so displayed that it proves to be fraught with what Virgil Nemoianu, in *A Theory of the Secondary*, terms "downtrodden masses of details" and "subordinated events and objects" which inevitably overflow any officially accredited foreground.[1] From Dimmesdale's hand nervously fluttering "over his heart" to the informal gossip of women among themselves, it is precisely amidst "secondary," easily overlooked details of this scene that we catch otherwise neglected (but massively significant) forces at work which the foregrounded social spectacle does not officially incorporate, legitimate as important, dignify, and highlight.

But if overt social spectacle fails to reach all the way into the depth of "downtrodden . . . details" and overlooked tendencies transpiring within the precincts of what it ostensibly absorbs, choreographs, and frames, how, then, does a gathered-together community become coherently intelligible to itself? How does it emerge as that *into* which, for better or ill, human beings are born – or that *into* which they have immigrated – such that it is within that communal space that they are said to be situated and placed? *In* what precisely do they live? What does it look like? How does it become intelligible and defined? Again and again in the texts that we have been addressing, pressure of an extraordinary sort is visited precisely upon whatever threatens to become too concretely visible as shared spectacle and communally organized space. In contrast to all that conspires to take visible, tangible shape as milieu, scene, or spectacle in common, "not till we are lost," Thoreau proposes, "do we begin to find ourselves, and realize where we are," and the effect of such a proposition is to suggest that we "begin to find ourselves" not within – but in *excess* of – any orienting spectacle or communally organized space.

Such phraseology situates an ultimately "lost" communal "we" amidst the sort of uncertainty of spectacle and fluctuation of perspective that a text like "My Kinsman, Major Molineux" broaches to the point of giddy excess, in the thick of which no steady, intersubjective reading of events manages to hold authoritative sway over a tumultuous and transitional moment in American history. Rather, the Major's ordeal, as we have seen, provokes "mirth" – or "terror" – as he looms up equivocally amidst competing lighting effects, interpretative vocabularies, tones, voices, and moods "like some dead potentate, . . . majestic still," while "windows flew open" and "voices hailed each other from house to house, all demanding the explanation, which not a soul could give." At such a transformative, mercurial moment, what precisely is going on cannot be steadied, framed, contextualized, and judged in a single definitive way. Dramatically in contrast to the opening scaffold scene of *The Scarlet Letter*, such a volatile existential moment remains too explicitly up for interpretative grabs – and too much a moving, revolutionary event through which fixed social paradigms are becoming shattered or destabilized on the way to something else – to epitomize the community in some frozen, steady way.

What community collectively enacts at such a tumultuous moment is not a ritual or event through which it becomes intelligible to itself, but, rather, the wildcard possibility of its own radically transformative power that otherwise withdraws into, and becomes congealed and hidden amidst, deceptively independent and neutral environments. In contrast, the texts that we have been exploring tend to focus – again to refer to remarks by W. J. T. Mitchell quoted at the outset of this study – not on what "environment" or "landscape 'is'" but on "what it *does*, how it works . . . as cultural practice," how it becomes "an instrument of cultural power, perhaps even an agent of power that is (or frequently represents itself as) independent of human intentions." "Environment" in this sense, emphasizes Mitchell, "naturalizes . . . cultural and social construction, representing an artificial world as if it were simply given and inevitable, and it also makes that representation operational by interpellating its beholder in some more or less determinate relation to its givenness as sight and site." The alternative, suggests Mitchell, is to "trace" back the "process" by which environment "effaces" its alterability and vulnerability such that this "medium" in "which 'we live and move and have our being'" emerges as "itself in motion," "dynamic" and "transitional."[2]

In midcentury American literature, such probing through false "given-ness" of "environment" into what remains "itself in motion" and irrevocably "transitional" no doubt leads to a crisis of faith in visual spectacle and in stable representation of form. The interior of the visible, structured moment remains, "if you once look closely at it," open to cognitive dissonance, vulnerable to skepticism, volatile and fluid. And yet at times this latently fluid and alterable sense of reality begins to assume – or so Thoreau proposes – a strangely communalizing power, according to the proposition that "not till we are lost . . . do we begin to find ourselves, and realize where we are" amidst the "infinite extent of our relations" with it.

The question remains: must the coming into recognition of "ourselves" entail, as Homi K. Bhabha puts it, the "narcissistic" collectivization of consciousness and will around a well-focused sense of place and a reassuring set of symbols, rituals, and public statuary "upon which the group's *amour propre*" can be "based," and whose desecration or diminution "evokes an archaic anxiety and aggressivity?"[3] In contrast to such would-be focalization of group "*amour propre*" in America around tangible embodiments of communal identity, the writing that we have been addressing calls attention to the underlying vulnerability, vicissitude, and drift into which all culturally constituted presence actually remains hazarded and cast throughout American history, from shifting early maps of what eventually became "New England" to the way a once lurid scarlet "A" dissipates over time into a mere rag of cloth. What emerges is a drift in concrete material possibility through ongoing mutation in the socio-cultural mechanisms whereby it is measured and endowed with value, semioticized into symbol and sign, mapped, categorized, and formulated in the eye.

To recognize such a socio-material drift is by no means to encounter the inevitable breakdown of the cultural process itself. As anthropologist Kathleen Stewart has recently written, "we need . . . repeatedly" to open up the theory of culture "so that we can imagine culture constituted in use and therefore likely to be . . . contradictory, dialectical, dialogic, texted, textured . . . The theory of culture itself must be brought into the gap between signifier and meaning . . . so that we can imagine it" not as everywhere continuous with itself but as "given to digression, deflection, displacement, deferral and difference."[4] Already in the middle of the nineteenth century, American writers are beginning to conceive of the cultural process in this digressive, aleatory manner rather than as what results in forms of spectatorial settlement that situate us definitively in the here and now.

Specific *places*, in contrast, appear to spread away from the eye or to emerge in lithographic prints such as "Wheeling in Virginia" in coherent, settled form; they are what settlers are said to defend, fence in, map, and name this side of the placeless wilderness. But places in this sense are not where the texts that we have been addressing transact their most provocative and illuminating cultural work. Work of this sort throws into relief the way the New England forest, for example, begins to alter and shift in one's gaze as one learns native tribal words for nuances of color and characteristics of foliage that otherwise do not appear there, but fall outside the explicit field of vision of an English-speaking observer. However definitively places may appear to spread all around us, the premise of this study has been that we can keep seeing through their threadbare coherence toward a sense of possibility that is the sole and enigmatic destiny (forever beyond definitive manifestation) of communities and peoples in their endlessly incalculable, nomadic drift.

A final point worth considering is the relationship between fluid sense of landscape and milieu in American Renaissance writing and the underlying placelessness of foundational political documents originating the nation itself: above all the US Constitution and its supplementary Bill of Rights. It is illuminating in this regard to consider phraseology deployed by scholars such as Philip Fisher and Angela Miller to disclose a vacuum in foundational US documents that is ostensibly filled in by latter-day cultural mechanisms apparently compensating for what is missing. Fisher writes that "we might revise Gertrude Stein's phrase about Oakland and say that by 1850, for the United States, there was at last a 'there' there . . . What was there as geography, culture, and political sovereignty was a state of hard fact, very different from what might earlier have been described as the promise or the idea of America." In contrast to what "was at last" emergent as "geography" and socio-political "fact," Fisher suggests that "the earlier idea" of the nation, developed in writing by delegates from mutually suspicious regions of a loose federation, is largely placeless and abstract.[5] Somewhat similarly, Angela Miller emphasizes the absence of what she terms concrete "grounding . . . in time and place" in written documents that initially establish a "United States of America" largely through a series of abstract processes, general rights, checks and balances, protocols of legislation, and unspecified pursuits of happiness. The picturesque "landscape art" later promoted by the midcentury New York art societies, Miller argues, serves to "root" an initially vague "national identity" in tangible scenes of rolling meadows, well-tended farmlands, and families out for a country ride.[6]

But the question arises: is this latter-day "grounding" of American "national identity" in detailed, richly historicized scenes of "time and place" a supplementary phenomenon necessitated by – or an ultimate betrayal of – an origination of nationhood as protocol, process, and legal right rather than as shared sense of place and densely textured social milieu? Ralph Ellison, for example, who explores the dark side of dislocation and placelessness in "Harlem is Nowhere," nevertheless approaches the absence of richly historicized "time and place" in originative US documents as the very sine qua non of their logic. Efforts to localize and to parochialize national identity notwithstanding, the entirety of the history and cultural experience called "America," Ellison emphasizes, always remains "in cacophonic motion." It draws all participants not toward a communal focal point but toward a "vortex of discordant ways of living." It entails the "agonizing mystery" of a free-floating "intergroup" potential that is in principle facilitated, or at least according to Ellison's reading of the Declaration of Independence, the Constitution, and the Bill of Rights, by processes of juridical review, ongoing amendment, and reciprocally exercised checks and balances the fluid, pragmatic logic of which is originally "committed to paper" during a time of "revolutionary break with traditional forms of society." Such a "cacophonic" process, Ellison emphasizes, "offers no easily recognizable points of rest, no facile certainties as to who, what, or where (culturally or historically) we are."[7]

This is not to deny that considerable anxiety accompanies the suspicion that such restless historical flux eludes final, determinative envisagement. No doubt in an initial repression of its own incalculable and dynamic potential, the US Constitution itself as originally framed does seek to delimit a particular American history and communal identity against a specifically differed socio-cultural background. Excluding "Indians not taxed" from "the whole Number of free Persons" to be counted in determining any state's proportion of "Representatives" in Congress, and considering "all other Persons" (or, in other words, slaves) as exactly "three-fifths" of a person in any such census, the infamous Article 1 as originally formulated delimits and racializes the community of citizenship in a very specific manner. It takes later amendments to void the community officially established by the Constitution of all clannish, racist, class-bound, or other inflective or parochialized markers. But although this voiding process occurs only by degrees, the comprehensive concept of community per se – of "We the People" – does indeed end up in principle as radically abstracted from specific contexts and milieus, ancestral ties or ethnic definitions. Such a non-parochialized concept of "the People" differs in kind from the sense of community that ostensibly finds focus and self-intelligibility, for example, in the social hierarchies, sartorial appearances, customs, symbols, and rites of punishment that constitute the opening scaffold scene of *The Scarlet Letter*, outside the closed circuit of which Indians, Catholics, and others are excluded.

Communal theater of this parochial sort, ostensibly "grounding" human beings in "time and place," certainly verifies W. J. T. Mitchell's observation that however "artificial" and evanescent a particular "environment" may be, it tends to draw its participants into an active, involved relationship with its apparent "givenness as sight and site." Again to refer to Mitchell's remarks, such a localized sense of milieu and place tends to become the "medium" not only through which human beings literally see objects and material forms, but also "live and move and have" their very "being" in specific, oriented ways.[8] But what sort of historically mediated selfhood is appealed to and invoked, and what is the socio-cultural "medium" in common, when mutually alien life-worlds are reciprocally exposed toward one another as inevitably contingent and fleeting in a text such as "Chief Seattle's Speech"?

In keeping with the possibility of a mobile and incalculable sense of the communal that spans alternative life-worlds and cannot be pinned down, American Renaissance texts invite readers to confront what Stanley Cavell terms the ultimate "uncanniness of the ordinary." In such texts, the underlying "weirdness" or "surrealism," as Cavell puts it, of whatever "we call, accept, adapt to, as the usual, the real" keeps destabilizing all would-be environmental and spectatorial closure.[9] This is scarcely to deny the way, for example, shifting textures and features of natural foliage become highlighted, named, and preserved in alternative versions of cultural memory and within languages of various sorts, from Penobscot to English. But when it comes to preserving the intriguing if "agonizing mystery" of radically "intergroup" potential, an indefinitely destabilizing counter-pressure, disclosing the limits of culturally foregrounded environments, and revealing the unsuspected fluctuations of visibility itself, properly intrudes into everyday life. Keeping faith with just such an indefinitely disruptive dynamic, the notoriously ambiguous writing of the American Renaissance sustains permanent resistance to inevitably parochialized versions of "time and place," and eschews direct representation of the vast, tumultuous history in which these versions of cultural theater remain immersed. Within such unsettled history, life-worlds do not so much progressively evolve into one another as they mutate, reciprocally problematize any claim to dominance, fail to synthesize, overlap. The blind spot opening up in the midst of such historical turbulence potentially marks where all would-be parochialization of milieu and sense of place seems to revolve, as Ellison puts it, around an "agonizing mystery."

The question arises: can even an "agonizing mystery" in the depth of cultural vicissitude somehow be orchestrated and choreographed? In space of this sort, that is to say, can such absence of a communal focal center nevertheless become equitably regulated by mechanisms of exchange and free debate, by legal protections of socio-cultural diversity, and by ongoing, pragmatically self-amending legislation as voided over the long run of privileged cultural content as the legislative and legal mechanisms of the US Constitution, which in accounts by Fisher, Miller, and Ellison remain, in and of themselves, devoid of localized, parochialized inflection?

No doubt from Currier and Ives engravings to *Saturday Evening Post* covers by Norman Rockwell, the American yearning for stereotypic self-portraiture prevails. But another alternative, emergent in the ambiguous writing that we have looked at, is to force into recognition a social process that offers "no easily recognized points of rest," no "facile certainties" defining "who, what, or where we" ultimately "are." Such writing might even be said to mark the conversion of closed, homogeneous envisagements of American history and sense of place into the disclosure, at bottom, of what turns out to be a cross-cultural, meta-national history of collisions, discontinuities, and mutations as resistant to finite perceptual capture as shifting characteristics of the wilderness highlighted in the English or Penobscot languages. Such fluctuating space ultimately escapes all inert visualization as landscape, milieu, or definitive national scene in common. And the fundamental question posed by this study is whether the idea of community itself can survive and even flourish in this ever-shifting, potentially discontinuous space, which in its Rorschach-inkblot fluidity cannot ultimately be seen, encountered, and inhabited in any stable and comprehensive way. Indefinitely unmoored from any "givenness" as "site and sight," can what then turns radically fluid and a-specular nevertheless remain publically shareable as process, as transformation, and as the reciprocal exposure of alien life-worlds and milieus toward one another? Does the idea of community *at its most humanly comprehensive* fulfill itself precisely on these a-specular, un-grounded terms? Is it ultimately betrayed, in its fullest prospect and range, by whatever seems to reduce it into a local habitation and a name?

Notes

INTRODUCTION: THE UBIQUITY OF NEGATIVE GEOGRAPHY

1. Henry David Thoreau, *A Week on the Concord and Merrimack Rivers*, ed. Carl F. Hovde et al. (Princeton: Princeton University Press, 1980), p. 359.

2. The phrase "American Renaissance" was originated by F. O. Matthiessen in *The American Renaissance: Art and Expression in the Age of Emerson and Whitman* (London: Oxford University Press, 1941). Although Matthiessen limited himself to the period between 1850 and 1855, and although he focused primarily on the subject of democracy across a range of canonized American writings, the meaning of the "American Renaissance" has predictably been altered, tweaked, and amplified over the decades. See, for example, "Slavery, Revolution, and the American Renaissance," in *The American Renaissance Reconsidered*, ed. Walter Benn Michaels and Donald E. Pease (Baltimore: Johns Hopkins University Press, 1985), p. 6, where Eric Sundquist expands the years covered by the "American Renaissance" to encompass the period "from the 1830s through the Civil War," and where he amplifies the significance of a would-be "renaissance" in national purpose and self-comprehension to include "anxious meditation" on "the national crisis over slavery." Also see David S. Reynolds, *Beneath the American Renaissance: The Subversive Imagination in the Age of Emerson and Melville* (Cambridge, MA: Harvard University Press, 1989), in which canonized American authors are studied within a much broader matrix of lesser-known works and popular art forms. For a still more recent recontextualization of Matthiessen's original phrase, see Timothy B. Powell, *Ruthless Democracy: A Multicultural Interpretation of the American Renaissance* (Princeton: Princeton University Press, 2000), where Powell's development of a "multicultural" approach to the "American Renaissance" includes not only "Hawthorne, Thoreau, and Melville" but also "women, black, and Native American writers" (7). Throughout these and other studies, the term "American Renaissance" is generally used to indicate a second-wave, mid-nineteenth-century reconsideration of the meaning of the nation and its history: a revisitation of unfinished cultural business. It is in this sense that I once again invoke Matthiessen's much-discussed phrase.

3. William Bradford, *Of Plymouth Plantation, 1620–1647*, ed. Samuel Eliot Morison (New York: Knopf, 1952), p. 62.

4. *Ibid.*, p. 62.

5. See William Cronon, *Changes in the Land: Indians, Colonists, and the Ecology of New England* (New York: Hill and Wang, 1983), pp. 82–91. For primary accounts by the initial explorers themselves, see Giovanni da Verrazzano, "Transcription of the Cellere Codex" (1524), trans. Susan Tarrow, in *The Voyages of Giovanni da Verrazzano, 1524–1528*, collected and with supplementary commentary by Lawrence C. Wroth (New Haven: Yale University Press, 1970), especially pp. 137–39; Samuel de Champlain, *Voyages of Samuel de Champlain*, trans. Charles Pomeroy Otis (Boston: Prince Society, 1880), rpt. as vols. I–IV of Prince Society Publications (New York: Franklin, 1966), especially pp. 63–89 and 109–39; and John Smith, *A Description of New England* (London: 1616), rpt. in *Tracts and Other Papers Relating to the Origin, Settlement, and Progress of the Colonies in North America, from the Discovery of the Country to the Year 1776*, collected by Peter Force, 3 vols. (Gloucester, MA: Peter Smith, 1963), vol. II. For an excellent summary of all this material and of how it problematizes early Puritan accounts of a "desolate" pre-New England "wilderness," see David Laurence, "William Bradford's American Sublime," *PMLA* 102 (1987), 63.

6. Cole comments extensively on his compositional processes and techniques throughout his letters. See especially Cole's letter to Robert Gilmore, Jr., 25 Dec. 1826, as printed in "Correspondence between Thomas Cole and Robert Gilmore, Jr.," Appendix 1 to Howard S. Merritt, " 'A Wild Scene': Genesis of a Painting," in *Studies in Thomas Cole, an American Romanticist, Annual 2* (Baltimore: Baltimore Museum of Art, 1967), p. 47, where Cole writes that the artist must "make selections, and combine them" such that "parts of Nature may be brought together, and combined in a whole that shall surpass in . . . effect any picture painted from a single view." I should add that Cole ultimately spans – and illustrates – a wide gamut of contradictory attitudes and aesthetic possibilities. For example, in his painting *Desolation* (1836), the fifth in his celebrated *The Course of Empire* series (1833–36), which appears on my book jacket, Cole's imagery of ruin suggests an equivocal margin, neither quite inside nor quite outside humanly structured space, which other paintings of his, such as *Snow Squall, Winter Landscape in the Catskills* (c. 1825–26), appear, however improbably, to have broken through toward what is both expertly painted and yet radically outside history.

7. Laurence, "Bradford's American Sublime," 63.

8. See Howard Horwitz, *By the Law of Nature: Form and Value in Nineteenth-Century America* (Oxford: Oxford University Press, 1991), p. 21.

9. See, for example, Annette Kolodny, *The Lay of the Land: Metaphor as Experience and History in American Life and Letters* (Chapel Hill: University of North Carolina Press, 1975) and Roderick Nash, *Wilderness and the American Mind* (New Haven: Yale University Press, 1967).

10. Lawrence Buell, *The Environmental Imagination: Thoreau, Nature Writing, and the Formation of American Culture* (Cambridge, MA: Harvard University Press, 1995), pp. 60, 77–81, and 86.

11. John W. McCoubrey, *American Tradition in Painting*, new edn. (Philadelphia: University of Pennsylvania Press, 2000), pp. 1–38.

12. See, for example, Angela Miller, "The Mechanisms of the Market and the Invention of Western Regionalism: The Example of George Caleb Bingham," in *American Iconology: New Approaches to Nineteenth-Century Art and Literature*, ed. David C. Miller (New Haven: Yale University Press, 1993), pp. 112–34. Miller proposes that in a painting, for example, such as *Fur Traders Descending the Missouri* (1845), a "dreamlike, self-contained world" does not so much bespeak the vulnerability of human presence against a vast, mysterious backdrop as it "taps a . . . fantasy of the West exempt from the pressures visibly transforming the East throughout the nineteenth century" (114).

13. McCoubrey, *American Tradition*, p. 121.

14. Entry for 1 Jan. 1858 in *The Journal of Henry David Thoreau*, ed. Bradford Torrey and Francis H. Allen, 14 vols. (1906; rpt. New York: Dover, 1962), vol. x, p. 233.

15. Thoreau, entry for 6 March 1858, in *ibid.*, p. 295.

16. Thoreau, entry for 5 March 1858, in *ibid.*, p. 294.

17. See W. J. T. Mitchell's Introduction to his edition of collected essays, *Landscape and Power* (Chicago: University of Chicago Press, 1994), pp. 1–2.

18. See J. B. Harley, "Text and Contexts in the Interpretation of Early Maps," in *From Sea Charts to Satellite Images: Interpreting North American History through Maps* (Chicago: University of Chicago Press, 1990), pp. 4–5. Harley's influential work in the contemporary field of cultural geography, which exploits both Marxist and poststructuralist theory to lay bare the ideological underpinnings of ostensibly neutral representations of geography and space, includes "Deconstructing the Map," in *Writing Worlds: Discourse, Text and Metaphor in the Representation of Landscape*, ed. Trevor J. Barnes and James S. Duncan (London: Routledge, 1992) and "Silences and Secrecy: The Hidden Agenda of Cartography in Early Modern Europe," *Imago Mundi* 40 (1988), 57–76. For a specific look at how poststructuralist theory has influenced contemporary geography, see Derek Gregory, *Geographical Imaginations* (Cambridge, MA: Blackwell, 1994).

19. Edmundo O'Gorman, *The Invention of America: An Inquiry into the Historical Nature of the New World and the Meaning of its History* (Bloomington: Indiana University Press, 1961), p. 4. Perhaps "invention" is not quite the term for this process. For an intricate study of ongoing give-and-take between empiricism and aggressive interpretation "during the centuries immediately following Columbus's voyages," see Richard White, "Discovering Nature in North America," *The Journal of American History* 79 (1992), 874–91.

20. For detailed discussion of Columbus's accounts of New World discovery, see Tzvetan Todorov, *The Conquest of America: The Question of the Other*, trans. Richard Howard (New York: Harper and Row, 1984), pp. 3–33.

21. William Boelhower, *Through a Glass Darkly: Ethnic Semiosis in American Literature* (Oxford University Press, 1987), pp. 47–48. Also see J. B. Harley, "Silences," for an excellent discussion of such standardized cartographical envisagement of landscape, and of the way this new cartographic language reflects emerging "scientific" belief in an ostensibly objective, neutral order of space while

also answering to the requirements of capitalistic economics and of centralized administrative control.

22. For a persuasive argument that such dismal counter-space – fearful, wild, nightmarish – looms up primarily in the eyes of English rather than French or Spanish settlers, see White, "Discovering Nature," 884.

23. Bradford, *Of Plymanth Plantation*, p. 62.

24. John R. Stilgoe, *Common Landscape of America, 1580–1845* (New Haven: Yale University Press, 1982), pp. 7–21.

25. William Cullen Bryant, Preface to *The American Landscape* (1830), as quoted in Merritt, "'A Wild Scene'," p. 17.

26. Angela Miller, *The Empire of the Eye: Landscape Representation and American Cultural Politics, 1825–1875* (Ithaca: Cornell University Press, 1993), p. 82.

27. Theodore Dwight, *Sketches of Scenery and Manners in the United States* (1829; rpt. Delmar, NY: Scholars' Facsimiles and Reprints, 1983), p. 63.

28. Angela Miller, *Empire of the Eye*, pp. 10–13, 72–82.

29. Bryan Jay Wolf, *Romantic Re-Vision: Culture and Consciousness in Nineteenth-Century American Painting and Literature* (Chicago: University of Chicago Press, 1982), pp. 177–86.

30. David C. Miller, *Dark Eden: The Swamp in Nineteenth-Century American Culture* (Cambridge: Cambridge University Press, 1989), pp. 1–19.

31. For nineteenth-century criticism of the latently "false," fabricated note in Bierstadt, see James Jackson Jarves, *The Art-Idea* (1864; rpt. Cambridge, MA: Harvard University Press, 1960), p. 191. Also see McCoubrey, *American Tradition*, p. 25, where it is proposed that even as Bierstadt's "pursuit of untouched" prospects and vistas led him "farther and farther afield," the spectatorial "grandiloquence" of his canvases proves replete, on closer view, with "techniques polished by European study," and also entails "dramatic topographical generalities culled from a variety" of different field "sketches."

32. Thomas Cole, "Essay on American Scenery" (1836), rpt. in *Thomas Cole: The Collected Essays and Prose Sketches*, ed. Marshall Tymn (Saint Paul, MN: The John Colet Press, 1980), pp. 3–19.

33. Ralph Waldo Emerson, "Experience," in *The Portable Emerson* (New York: Viking, 1981), p. 284.

34. Nathaniel Hawthorne, "The New Adam and Eve," in *The Centenary Edition of the Works of Nathaniel Hawthorne*, ed. William Charvat et al., 23 vols. (Columbus: Ohio State University Press, 1962–94), vol. x, *Mosses from an Old Manse* (1974), p. 247.

35. Margaret Fuller, *Summer on the Lakes*, in *The Essential Margaret Fuller*, ed. Jeffrey Steele (New Brunswick, NJ: Rutgers University Press, 1992), p. 76. The full title, *Summer on the Lakes, in 1843*, is compressed by Steele in his edition, and I follow this practice throughout the remainder of my study.

36. Phrases such as "woods lotted off distinctly" and "boundaries . . . accurately described" are used by Thoreau to advertise his skills as a surveyor; see the text of Thoreau's handbill as quoted in Walter Harding, *The Days of Henry Thoreau* (New York: Knopf, 1965), p. 235. But for the idea that lots and boundaries

potentially "fade from" the countryside, see Thoreau's critique of the abstractions of surveyed topography in "Walking," in *The Writings of Henry David Thoreau*, Riverside Edition, 11 vols. (Boston and New York: Houghton Mifflin, and Company, 1884–94), vol. IX, *Excursions* (1893), p. 297. Most readers will be familiar with the episode in which the Puritan scarlet "A" has become a "rag of . . . cloth" in Hawthorne's "The Custom House," in *The Scarlet Letter*, vol. I of *The Centenary Edition* (1962), p. 31.

37. For excellent analysis of such conversion of cultural difference into linear, progressive sequence, see Wai Chee Dimock, *Empire for Liberty: Melville and the Poetics of Individualism* (Princeton: Princeton University Press, 1989), pp. 16–18.

38. Rebecca Harding Davis, "Life in the Iron Mills," in *Life in the Iron Mills and Other Stories* (New York: Feminist Press, 1985), p. 14.

39. As quoted in Neil Harris, *The Artist in American Society: The Formative Years, 1790–1860* (New York: George Braziller, 1966), p. 194.

40. Wayne Franklin, *Discoverers, Explorers, Settlers: The Diligent Writers of Early America* (Chicago: University of Chicago Press, 1979), pp. 179–203.

41. Powell, *Ruthless Democracy*, pp. 3–22, 68–73.

42. Raymond Williams, *Marxism and Literature* (Oxford University Press, 1977), pp. 108–14.

43. Hawthorne, "My Kinsman, Major Molineux," in *The Snow-Image and Uncollected Tales*, vol. XI of *The Centenary Edition* (1974), pp. 227–28.

44. *Scarlet Letter*, p. 197.

45. Mitchell, Introduction to *Landscape and Power*, p. 2. For the source of Mitchell's quotation, see Thoreau, "Life Without Principle," (1863), in vol. IV of *The Writings of Henry David Thoreau*, p. 472. Thoreau writes that "if you chance to live and move and have your being" in the world of daily affairs, then it is this world that will tend to mold and shape your sense of possibility.

46. Krista Comer, *Landscapes of the New West: Gender and Geography in Contemporary Women's Writing* (Chapel Hill: University of North Carolina Press, 1999), p. 11.

47. Homi K. Bhabha, "DissemiNation: Time, Narrative, and the Margins of the Modern Nation," in *Nation and Narration*, ed. Bhabha (New York: Routledge, 1990), pp. 293–313.

48. Lauren Berlant, *The Anatomy of National Fantasy: Hawthorne, Utopia, and Everyday Life* (Chicago: University of Chicago Press, 1991), p. 7.

49. *Ibid.*, p. 24.

50. See Hawthorne, "My Kinsman, Major Molineux," p. 228; Melville, *Pierre; or the Ambiguities*, ed. Harrison Hayford et al. (Evanston: Northwestern University Press, 1971), p. 165; and Dr. Henry A. Smith's ostensible translation – based on "scraps from a diary" – of "Chief Seattle's Speech" (1854?), initially printed in the *Seattle Sunday Star*, 29 October 1887, and rpt. by Albert Furtwangler in *Answering Chief Seattle* (Seattle: University of Washington Press, 1997), p. 16.

51. Giles Gunn, *Thinking Across the American Grain: Ideology, Intellect, and the New Pragmatism* (Chicago: University of Chicago Press, 1992), p. 167.

52. Sacvan Bercovitch, *The Office of the Scarlet Letter* (Baltimore: Johns Hopkins University Press, 1991), pp. 1–33.
53. See Melville's letter to Sarah Morewood (Sept. ? 1851), in *The Portable Melville*, ed. Jay Leyda (New York: Viking, 1952), p. 450.
54. Readers with a long historical perspective will notice affinities between my treatment of midcentury American writers and Charles Feidelson's landmark discussion of loss of static point of view in *Symbolism and American Literature* (Chicago: University of Chicago Press, 1953). Although by now a half-century old, and although focused much more exclusively on aesthetic and epistemological issues than contemporary discussion tends to be, Feidelson's approach, I believe, remains enormously helpful in addressing the more fluid sense of forms and figures in space that emerges in mid-nineteenth-century American writing.

1 CRITIQUING COLONIAL AMERICAN GEOGRAPHY: HAWTHORNE'S
LANDSCAPE OF BEWILDERMENT

1. Nathaniel Hawthorne, "My Kinsman, Major Molineux," pp. 221–28.
2. See especially Sacvan Bercovitch, *The Office of the Scarlet Letter*, where it is argued that Hawthorne's historical novel entails the retrospective projection into seventeenth-century New England of the interpretative dynamics of a "liberalism" whose ostensible liberality is ultimately designed to control cognitive dissonance and interpretative conflict. That is to say, with the threat of Civil War haunting the immediate historical context in which the novel is being written, Hawthorne, according to Bercovitch, cultivates shifting perspectives of Puritan scenes only in order to foster a "hermeneutics" of mutual "tolerance, accommodation, pluralism" – and endless "patience" – designed to defer "conflict" by holding out "faith" in "some ultimate hermeneutical complementarity," some "ideal" if indefinitely receding "prospect" of "ever-larger truth," equated with the ongoing enterprise of American culture itself from its earliest colonial origins down through the troubled antebellum present (8–23). The alternative possibility of "multiple meanings dissolving into irreconcilability" (90), Bercovitch argues, is largely repressed in Hawthorne's fiction.

  For an account stressing what is assumed to be Hawthorne's productive rather than repressive faith in "complementarity," see Donald E. Pease, *Visionary Compacts: American Renaissance Writings in Cultural Context* (Madison: University of Wisconsin Press, 1987). Pease argues that "in the troubled years preceding the Civil War," Hawthorne, along with his American Renaissance contemporaries, seeks to cultivate "cultural agreement" as an ongoing communal "process" dynamically evolving from out of the colonial past toward the future. Incongruities and inconsistencies in value, frame of reference, and meaning, Pease argues, are potentially adjudicated in such fiction by the prospect of a "collective heterogeneity" productively sustaining itself through "varying agreements" and "continuing negotiations of . . . the people" (ix–72).

Also see *The Anatomy of National Fantasy*, where Lauren Berlant emphasizes Hawthorne's tendency to "splice the political and the utopian" in the
"collective," integrative ideal of the American nation, although it is true that
such a tendency is qualified in Berlant's account by Hawthorne's mixed allegiances to the federal state and yet to more local New England customs and
mores, and, furthermore, by a "set of inchoate theoretical gestures" that begin
to imagine possibilities of "collective" life outside the state (6–7).

3. Closest to my reading are studies such as Sharon Cameron's *The Corporeal Self:
   Allegories of the Body in Melville and Hawthorne* (Baltimore: Johns Hopkins
   University Press, 1981), which emphasize what Cameron terms Hawthorne's
   awareness of the frailty of "categorical givens" (86) against "excruciatingly unclear" experiences that at bottom prove "lacking" in "coherent shape" (113).
   Space precludes a complete summary of criticism emphasizing Hawthorne's
   sense of the frailty of mediated knowledge against the backdrop of the
   "excruciatingly unclear," and stressing his recognition of the way such knowledge fractures into multiple and dissonant perspectives. A representative sample of such commentary, from 1980 to the present, includes John T. Irwin's
   chapter on Hawthorne and Melville in *American Hieroglyphics: The Symbol of the Egyptian Hieroglyphics in the American Renaissance* (New Haven:
   Yale University Press, 1980), where Irwin argues that for both writers, "the
   hieroglyphics" are "the linguistic analogue of an enigmatic external world,"
   into the "indeterminate ground" of which conflicting "perspectives" are
   projected (239–41); Edgar A. Dryden's *The Form of American Romance*
   (Baltimore: Johns Hopkins University Press, 1988), where Dryden emphasizes
   that the Hawthornesque romance is "haunted by enigmas" and "unanswered
   riddles" (32–60); Charles Swann's *Nathaniel Hawthorne: Tradition and Revolution* (Cambridge: Cambridge University Press, 1991), where it is proposed that
   "revolutionary turmoil" in Hawthorne's historical fiction potentially opens up
   "radical epistemological doubt" (219–59); and, finally, G. R. Thompson's *The
   Art of Authorial Presence: Hawthorne's Provincial Tales* (Durham, NC: Duke University Press, 1993), which explores the way point of view in such fiction is best
   thought of as "dialogical" rather than "biographical" and "personal": indefinitely
   dispersed throughout multiple positions, perspectives, and interpretations that
   resist interpretative closure (1–22).

   What bears still greater emphasis, however, is the way this endless deferral of a definitive point of view, as it occurs throughout Hawthorne's colonial New England landscape, opens up a receding sense of depth, wherever
   the eye turns, that massively alters the major premises not only of colonial New England geography, but also of landscape and space in general in
   America.

4. Hawthorne, *Our Old Home* (Columbus: Ohio State University Press, 1968), vol.
   v of *The Centenary Edition*, p. 4.
5. J. B. Harley, "Deconstructing the Map," in *Writing Worlds*, pp. 234–25.
6. Hawthorne, *The House of the Seven Gables* (Columbus: Ohio State University
   Press, 1965), vol. II of *The Centenary Edition*, p. 149.

7. Hawthorne, *The Elixir of Life Manuscripts* (Columbus: Ohio State University Press, 1977), vol. XIII of *The Centenary Edition* p. 447.

8. This may seem like a characteristically mid-nineteenth-century, Romantic posture toward the wilderness, scarcely a late seventeenth-century one. But in retracing the European origins of colonial American concepts of space in *Wilderness and the American Mind*, pp. 44–48, Roderick Nash observes that from medieval monastic accounts of meditative reclusion in the forest through seventeenth-century texts such as Thomas Burnet's *The Theory of the Earth: Containing an Account of the Original of the Earth, & of All the General Changes Which It Hath Already Undergone, Till the Comsumtion of All Things* (London: W. Kettilby, 1684), antipathy toward the wilderness by no means completely dominates Western attitudes. It is fitting, then, as James McIntosh emphasizes in "Nature and Frontier in 'Roger Malvin's Burial'," *American Literature* 60 (1988), 188–204, that "perspectives" of the "wilderness" assumed by Hawthorne's early colonial characters, in spanning the full range of Western cultural attitudes, should ultimately fluctuate and invert, leaving what seems to lurk on the far side of an edge segregating civilized from wild space in a condition of "cognitive dissonance."

9. Hawthorne, "Roger Malvin's Burial," in *Mosses from an Old Manse* (Columbus: Ohio State University Press, 1974), vol. X of *The Centenary Edition*, p. 359.

10. Michael J. Colacurcio, *The Province of Piety: Moral History in Hawthorne's Early Tales* (Cambridge, MA: Harvard University Press, 1984), pp. 283–313.

11. Hawthorne, "The New Adam and Eve," in *Mosses from an Old Manse*, p. 237.

12. For an alternative reading of Hawthorne, see Edgar A. Dryden, *Nathaniel Hawthorne: The Poetics of Enchantment* (Ithaca: Cornell University Press, 1977), pp. 12–43. Dryden proposes that "for Hawthorne . . . nature and culture" remain "warring opposites" (the wilderness becoming the site where "culture suddenly loses its authenticity"). But such an envisagement of "wilderness" as the place where culturally legitimated forms and values threaten fully to evaporate is not, I believe, confirmed by a tale such as "Young Goodman Brown," in which a primordial, unadulterated space never completely disentangles itself from the "interpolation of the perverted mind and heart of man."

13. Hawthorne, "Young Goodman Brown," in *Mosses from an Old Manse*, pp. 82, 75.

14. Hawthorne, *The Marble Faun* (Columbus: Ohio State University Press, 1968), vol. IV of *The Centenary Edition*, p. 168.

15. Hawthorne, *The American Notebooks* (Columbus: Ohio State University Press, 1972), vol. VIII of *The Centenary Edition*, pp. 185, 247.

16. Mary Douglas, *Purity and Danger: An Analysis of Concepts of Pollution and Taboo* (London: Routledge and Kegan Paul, 1966), p. 36.

17. Susan Stewart, *Nonsense: Aspects of Intertextuality in Folklore and Literature* (Baltimore: Johns Hopkins University Press, 1979), pp. 85, 9.

18. Over the years, a number of studies have emphasized Hawthorne's development of a significantly more complex, more multi-faceted sense of the American past than that provided by the "providential" envisagement of American

history: the tendency, that is to say, to view American history as a single, divinely orchestrated, communally assented to process headed toward millennial fulfillment, as in George Bancroft's influential *A History of the United States, From the Discovery of the American Continent*, 10 vols. (Boston: Little, Brown, and Company, 1834–75). See especially the discussion of Hawthorne's complex envisagement of American history in John P. McWilliams, Jr., *Hawthorne, Melville, and the American Character: A Looking-Glass Business* (Cambridge: Cambridge University Press, 1984); George Dekker, *The American Historical Romance* (Cambridge: Cambridge University Press, 1987); and G. R. Thompson, *The Art of Authorial Presence*. No doubt as Dekker cautions, Hawthorne seems ambivalently "committed to" as well as "critical of the patriotic myths which figure so prominently" in providential history such as that developed by Bancroft (149). Or, as Lauren Berlant less flatteringly argues in *The Anatomy of National Fantasy*, Hawthorne's "racial and gendered" (209) entitlements as white male American citizen impede his willingness utterly to relinquish myths fusing "the political and the utopian" in the ostensibly continuous, providential development of the American nation from colonialism down through the present (7). Certainly in the notorious *The Life of Franklin Pierce* (1852; rpt. New York: Garrett, 1970), Hawthorne appeals to "that common country which Providence" has "brought into one nation, through a continued miracle" (111). In his most provocative fiction, however, as in a tale like "My Kinsman, Major Molineux," Hawthorne broaches the possibility of ambiguous moments in American history voided of a "common" reading that might legitimate and interpret what is transpiring in the name of a truly collective national consciousness and mission.

19. Berlant, *Anatomy of National Fantasy*, p. 193.
20. Hawthorne, "Chiefly About War Matters," in *Tales, Sketches, and Other Papers*, in *The Works of Nathaniel Hawthorne*, Standard Library Edition, 15 vols. (Cambridge, MA: Houghton, Mifflin and Company, 1882–96), vol. XII (1883), p. 309.
21. Hawthorne, *Life of Pierce*, p. 111.
22. Hawthorne, Preface to *The House of the Seven Gables*, p. 1.
23. Van Wyck Brooks, "The Precipitant," in *Three Essays on America* (New York: E. P. Dutton, 1934), pp. 83–84.

2　THOREAU AND THE INTERMINABLE JOURNEY OF VISION "NEARER AND NEARER *HERE*"

1. Theodor Adorno, *Minima Moralia: Reflections from Damaged Life*, trans. E. F. N. Jephcott (London: Verso, 1978), p. 95.
2. Henry David Thoreau, "Walking," in *Excursions*, vol. IX of *The Writings of Henry David Thoreau*, pp. 278–87.
3. Thoreau, *The Maine Woods*, vol. III of *The Writings of Henry David Thoreau*, pp. 93–94.
4. October 22, 1857 in Thoreau, *Journal*, vol. X, p. 120.

5. Thoreau, "Wild Apples," in *Excursions*, p. 394.
6. As quoted in Perry Miller, *Nature's Nation* (Cambridge, MA: Harvard University Press, 1967), p. 197.
7. Steven Fink, *Prophet in the Marketplace: Thoreau's Development as a Professional Writer* (Princeton: Princeton University Press, 1992), pp. 164–65.
8. Thoreau, *A Week on the Concord and Merrimack Rivers*, pp. 359, 304.
9. Thoreau, *Walden*, ed. J. Lyndon Shanley (Princeton: Princeton University Press, 1971), p. 171.
10. This by no means is meant to deny a powerful counter-tendency in Thoreau's writing, and especially in the *Journal* that increasingly occupies his attention throughout the 1850s, to take precise scientific measurement, to discover underlying pattern, and to develop detailed observations of eccentric varieties of wild apples or of the numerous ingenious ways in which seeds are dispersed throughout a forest. Over the years, scholarship has remained attentive to this aspect of Thoreau's writing. If anything, recent studies such as Lawrence Buell's *The Environmental Imagination* and Robert Kuhn McGregor's *A Wider View of the Universe: Henry Thoreau's Study of Nature* (Urbana: University of Illinois Press, 1997), along with the much-discussed publication of selections of four of Thoreau's late nature manuscripts under the title, *Faith in a Seed: The Dispersion of Seeds and Other Late Natural History Writings*, ed. Bradley P. Dean (Washington, D.C.: Island Press, 1993), highlight the seriousness and care with which Thoreau undertakes the scientific measurement and investigation of natural phenomena. But I would go on to emphasize that critical studies such as Joan Burbick's *Thoreau's Alternative History: Changing Perspectives on Nature, Culture, and Language* (Philadelphia: University of Pennsylvania Press, 1987), and H. Daniel Peck's *Thoreau's Morning Work: Memory and Perception in A Week on the Concord and Merrimack Rivers, the Journal, and Walden* (New Haven: Yale University Press, 1990), are careful to acknowledge, as Peck puts it, that Thoreau's pursuit of precise measurement and observation ultimately "awaits closure," the "complete" picture "always receding before the endless work of observation" (75). Or, as Burbick observes, "anxiety and doubt filtered throughout Thoreau's work," haunting "moments" of ostensible "epiphany" that would appear to entail "the apprehension of" natural "beauty and design" (*Thoreau's Alternative History* 9–10). Also see Laura Dassow Walls, *Seeing New Worlds: Henry David Thoreau and Nineteenth-Century Natural Science* (Madison: University of Wisconsin Press, 1995), where it is proposed that for Thoreau, as for Alexander von Humboldt, although empirical "pattern" gradually emerges through scientific "measurement, collection, and connection" (225), the development of such knowledge is nevertheless dynamic and in motion; the "empirical whole" remains "indeterminate . . . ; no 'totality' is possible. We are thus in no danger of exhausting it or reaching the 'end' of knowledge or of nature" (85).

Throughout this ongoing process that cannot be exhausted, a Janus-faced Thoreau ultimately emerges: a writer at least as committed to disruption, to perceptual crisis, and to the deconstruction of confidence in tidily descriptive form as he is to the discovery of pattern and to precise, meticulous description. Dassow, for example, observes that even in "his last decade, Thoreau repeatedly invoked chaos and contingency, the "saving 'wild,' which alone could redeem an encrusted, static, and alienated civilization" (*Seeing New Worlds* 13). Recent studies focusing still more exclusively on the redemptive character of the "wild" in Thoreau's writing include James P. O'Grady, "Henry David Thoreau: Sauntering Along the Edge," in *Pilgrims to the Wild* (Salt Lake City: University of Utah Press, 1993), pp. 23–46, and Jane Bennett, *Thoreau's Nature: Ethics, Politics, and the Wild* (Thousand Oaks, CA: Sage Publications, 1994), where it is argued that "the Wild speaks to the idea that there always remains a surplus that escapes our categories and organizational practices," and that this "surplus" is meant to keep challenging "powerful pressures toward uniformity" and toward "excessively regulated" social life and thought (xxi–xxiii). Also see Stanley Cavell's commentary on Thoreau in such studies as *In Quest of the Ordinary: Lines of Skepticism and Romanticism* (Chicago: University of Chicago Press, 1988), where it is argued that Thoreau emerges among writers and thinkers who cultivate an estranging sense of "the weirdness, or surrealism, of what we call, accept, adapt to, as the usual, the real: a vision captured in the opening pages of *Walden* when its writer speaks of his townsmen as appearing to be absorbed" in "false necessities" that seem immutable and fixed only by virtue of perceptual "habit" (9).

   Commentary by Bennett and Cavell is especially helpful in disengaging the Thoreauvian idea of "the Wild" from "wilderness" per se so that it more ubiquitously emerges, as Thoreau puts it, "wherever" one "*fronts* a fact," be that "east or west, north or south." If anything, my chapter on Thoreau explores this line of thinking still further and investigates the way it challenges the cartographical and geographical premises of American "manifest destiny."

11. Thoreau, *Journal*, vol. III, pp. 290–91.
12. Thoreau, "Autumnal Tints," in *Excursions*, pp. 347–48.
13. Thoreau, entry for 1 November 1858, in *Journal*, vol. XI, p. 274.
14. Geoffrey Galt Harpham, *On the Grotesque: Strategies of Contradiction in Art and Literature* (Princeton: Princeton University Press, 1982), pp. 3–14.
15. Thoreau, *Cape Cod*, vol. IV of *The Writings of Henry David Thoreau*, pp. 2, 180–81.
16. While the grotesquely trans-imagistic is apparent in most of the examples from Thoreau that I have selected, the celebrated meditation in *Walden* on thawing springtime matter is often interpreted differently. See, for example, *Thoreau's Alternative History*, p. 75, where Burbick takes the more standard position that since the "correspondence" discovered by Thoreau between thawing formations of "sand" and the growth of "leaves, vines and thalluses" seems to be "in matter" itself, Thoreau envisages underlying "design" at the root of diverse forms. But missing in this account – and emphasized in Thoreau's own comprehension of what he sees as "truly grotesque" – is something more unsettling: that is to say, the suggestion of different characteristics and processes in the same thawing flow, to the degree that it seems lifelike, dead, mammalian,

reptilian, vegetative, and excremental all at once, entails, as the very consequence of such wholistic vision, the collapse of primary categories and visual boundaries within one and the same "sort of hybrid" flux (*Walden* 305). Whatever unity emerges at the heart of this passage, I would suggest, is surely a great disorder as well: a "truly grotesque" insight, in keeping with the way modern scholarship views this term, into what is avoided, I think, in meditations on Thoreau's passage evading the epistemologically disruptive character of a thawing, ambiguous flow that scrambles contrastive processes and qualities together.

17. Thoreau, entry for 24 March 1857, in *Journal*, vol. IX, p. 301.
18. Douglas, *Purity and Danger*, p. 36.
19. For a good summary of Baumgarten's observations, see Karsten Harries, *The Meaning of Modern Art: A Philosophical Interpretation* (Evanston, IL.: Northwestern University Press, 1968), pp. 18–19, from which I am quoting.
20. Thoreau, entry for 14 October 1857, in *Journal*, vol. X, p. 97.
21. See Myra Jehlen, *American Incarnation: The Individual, the Nation, and the Continent* (Cambridge, MA: Harvard University Press, 1986), especially pp. 1–21.
22. Thoreau, entry for 20 November 1850, in *Journal*, vol. II, p. 107.
23. Thoreau, entry for 28 March 1859, in *Journal*, vol. XII, p. 91.
24. Thoreau, entry for 4 October 1859, in *Journal*, vol. XII, p. 371.
25. Buell, *Environmental Imagination*, pp. 261–66.
26. Thoreau, entry for 10 June 1853, in *Journal*, vol. V, p. 239.
27. Thoreau, entry for 28 March 1852, in *Journal*, vol. III, p. 361.
28. Letter from Jefferson to Henry Lee, 8 May 1825, in *Thomas Jefferson: Writings*, ed. Merrill D. Peterson (New York: Library of America, 1984), p. 1501.
29. Thoreau, entry for 8 March 1858, in *Journal*, vol. X, p. 295.
30. For evidence suggesting that Joe Polis, Thoreau's Penobscot guide to the Maine woods, himself managed quite successfully to negotiate alternative cultural realities, and, in essence, to live a "life within a life," see Linda Frost, "'The Red Face of Man,' the Penobscot Indian, and a Conflict of Interest in Thoreau's *Maine Woods*," *ESQ* 39 (1993), 38–39.
31. See Michael West, "Scatology and Eschatology: The Heroic Dimensions of Thoreau's Wordplay," in *Transcendental Wordplay: America's Romantic Punsters and the Search for the Language of Nature* (Athens, OH: Ohio University Press, 2000), pp. 445–79.
32. For excellent commentary on the importance of the scale map in the stabilization of American sense of landscape into "a single bounded juridical space," see William Boelhower, *Through a Glass Darkly*, pp. 41–79. Also see Philip Fisher, "Democratic Social Space," in *Still the New World: American Literature in a Culture of Creative Destruction* (Cambridge, MA: Harvard University Press, 1999), pp. 33–55. But also see, in contrast, *Common Landscape of America*, pp. 99–107, where historian Stilgoe paints a more complex picture of difficulties encountered in the stabilization and mapping of American sense of landscape. For example, since "meridians . . . converge at the poles," the

surveying of planar longitudinal boundaries based upon strict meridian read-ings produces irregularities in areas and zones that are supposed to be equiv-alent, forcing later adjustment of the celebrated Land Ordinance of 1785 and its tidy design for the western territories. Moreover, areas laid out prior to the Enlightenment are often determined by "natural" topographical features – water frontage, for example, or sudden topographical elevation – whereas the ideal of perfect "squareness" governs later, so that what emerges, in totality, is a mixture of cartographical systems, criteria, adjustments, and traditions from different historical eras and enforced with different degrees of accuracy.

33. Cited by Walter Harding in *The Days of Henry Thoreau*, p. 235.

3 HERMAN MELVILLE'S HOME COSMOGRAPHY: VOYAGING INTO THE
INSCRUTABLE INTERIOR OF THE AMERICAN REPUBLIC

1. Thoreau, *Walden*, p. 321.
2. Herman Melville, *Moby-Dick or, The Whale* (New York: Penguin Books, 1992), pp. 453, 206.
3. See T. Hugh Crawford, "Captain Deleuze and the White Whale: Melville, Moby-Dick, and the Cartographic Inclination," *Social Semiotics* 7 (1997), 219–32.
4. See Andrew Delbanco, "Melville in the 80s," *American Literary History* 4 (1992), 722.
5. Melville, *Pierre; or, The Ambiguities*, ed. Harrison Hayford et al. (Evanston, IL: Northwestern University Press, 1971), p. 8. Once the indisputably standard edition of *Pierre*, its claim to exclusive legitimacy has been challenged in re-cent years by Hershel Parker, whose much-discussed Kraken Edition of *Pierre, or, the Ambiguities* (New York: HarperCollins, 1995), replete with illustrations by Maurice Sendak, is based on Parker's meticulously researched if still nec-essarily speculative reconstruction of the text that Melville appears to have submitted to "Harper & Brothers . . . a hundred and forty-three years ago, in early January, 1852, before Melville added many wholly unplanned pages on his hero as a juvenile author and then as a young man immaturely at-tempting to write a mature book." Parker, however, is careful to empha-size that his Kraken Edition is ultimately "intended to supplement (not to rival) . . . the standard Northwestern–Newberry edition of *Pierre*" by provid-ing the reader with "the original design" for a book later augmented by much that is "bitter" and "overwrought," although some of this later writing, Parker confesses, "contains splendid prose" (xi–xli). My own selection of the larger Northwestern–Newberry edition assumes that much of the added material not only illuminates motifs and themes implicit in the "original design" of Melville's novel, but deservedly remains included in any comprehensive read-ing of Melville that seeks to work within – but also beyond – the particular confines of the novel *Pierre* toward larger issues.
6. Samuel Otter, *Melville's Anatomies* (Berkeley: University of California Press, 1999), pp. 177–78.

7. Barton Levi St. Armand, "Melville, Malaise, and Mannerism: The Originality of 'The Piazza'," *Bucknell Review* 30 (1986), 78–81. Also see Edgar Dryden, "From the Piazza to the Enchanted Isles: Melville's Textual Rovings," in *After Strange Texts: The Role of Theory in the Study of Literature*, ed. Gregory S. Jay and David L. Miller (University: University of Alabama Press, 1985), pp. 46–68, where Dryden emphasizes the way landscape in *The Piazza Tales* is "troubled by . . . ocular delusions, mirages, and sinister enchantments" such that "nature" becomes in large measure a matter of "social and literary myth." For further commentary on the textualization of landscape in "The Piazza," see, in addition, Mark Slouka, "Herman Melville's Journey to 'The Piazza,'" *American Transcendental Quarterly* 61 (1986), 3–14, and Darryl Hattenhauer, "Space and Place in Melville's 'The Piazza,'" *American Studies in Scandanavia* 20 (1988), 69–81.

8. See Wylie Sypher, *Four Stages of Renaissance Style: Transformation in Art and Literature, 1400–1700* (Garden City, NY: Doubleday and Co., 1955), p. 117.

9. St. Armand, "Melville, Malaise, and Mannerism," 83–84.

10. Melville, "The Piazza," in *Selected Writings of Herman Melville* (New York: Random House, 1952), pp. 440–42.

11. Melville, *The Confidence-Man: His Masquerade*, ed. Hershel Parker (New York: W. W. Norton, 1971), pp. 213–14.

12. Melville's exploration of the textualization of selfhood and his loss of confidence in the would-be essentalization of self, to be sure, are widely explored topics throughout Melville studies. Space precludes a mention of all of such cases, but see, in particular, *No Mysteries out of Ourselves: Identity and Textual Form in the Novels of Herman Melville* (Philadelphia: University of Pennsylvania Press, 1990), where Peter J. Bellis proposes that "in Melville's work of the mid-1850s, selves remain either inaccessible . . . or 'knowable' only through ironized or alienated *mis*representation . . ., precisely the alternatives elaborated at greater length in . . . *The Confidence-Man*" (12). Bellis proposes that "the only conclusion Melville offers is a set of paradoxes: the fictionality of the real self and the reality of the fictional self" (190). Other studies of the problematics of selfhood and human identity in Melville's writing include Warwick Wadlington's chapters on Melville in *The Confidence Game in American Literature* (Princeton: Princeton University Press, 1975); and Arnold Weinstein, "Melville: Knowing Bartleby," in *Nobody's Home: Speech, Self, and Place in American Fiction from Hawthorne to DeLillo* (Oxford: Oxford University Press, 1993), pp. 27–43.

13. Elaine Scarry, *The Body in Pain: The Making and Unmaking of the World* (Oxford: Oxford University Press, 1985), p. 109.

14. Melville, "Bartleby," in *Selected Writings of Herman Melville*, p. 13.

15. See, in this respect, Neil Schmitz's interesting assessment of Joseph G. Baldwin's *The Flush Times of Mississippi and Alabama* (1853) in "Tall Tale, Tall Talk: Pursuing the Lie in Jacksonian Literature," *American Literature* 48 (1977), 474–75, where Schmitz proposes that "Baldwin pursues the same issue that Herman Melville would examine in *The Confidence-Man*": the analogy

between exuberant "tall talk" – freed of its moorings in ostensibly hard, empirical "fact" – and wildly inflationary "paper money" which during the Jacksonian period (1831–1861) at times becomes divorced from gold bullion backing.

16. See *Subversive Genealogy: The Politics and Art of Herman Melville* (New York: Knopf, 1983), pp. 238–39, where Michael Paul Rogin writes that Melville "exposes the absent core of marketplace reality itself" in a world where other measurements and communal forms – family ties, "historically rooted relationship," and formerly dependable, class-based "insignias of dress" – have become unreliable and unstable.

17. Lyman Beecher, *A Plea for the West* (Cincinnati: Truman and Smith, 1835), pp. 15–16.

18. Angela Miller, "The Mechanisms of the Market," in *American Iconology*, pp. 112–13.

19. See Michel Foucault, "The Eye of Power," in *Power/Knowledge: Selected Interviews and Other Writings 1972–1977*, ed. Colin Gordan, trans. Colin Gordan et al. (New York: Pantheon Books, 1980), pp. 146–65; also see Robin Evans, "Bentham's Panopticon, An Incident in the Social History of Architecture," *Architectural Association Quarterly* 3 (1971), 21–37.

20. Alan Wallach, "Making a Picture of the View from Mount Holyoke," in *American Iconology*, p. 83.

21. See Robert H. Byer, "Words, Monuments, Beholders: The Visual Arts in Hawthorne's *The Marble Faun*," in *American Iconology*, pp. 163–71.

4 THE CULTURAL POLITICS OF AMERICAN LITERARY AMBIGUITY

1. Journal entry for November ? 1845, in *Selections from Ralph Waldo Emerson*, ed. Stephen E. Whicher (Boston: Houghton Mifflin, 1972), p. 283.

2. Angela Miller, *Empire of the Eye*, pp. 6–8.

3. N. P. Willis, *American Scenery; or, Land, Lake and River Illustrations of Transatlantic Nature*, 2 vols. (London: George Virtue, 1840), vol. 1, p. 93.

4. Charles Olson, *Call Me Ishmael* (San Francisco: City Lights Books, 1947), p. 11.

5. See Gerald Danzer, "Bird's-Eye Views of Towns and Cities," in *From Sea Charts to Satellite Images: Interpreting North American History through Maps*, ed. David Buisseret (Chicago: University of Chicago Press, 1990), pp. 143–63.

6. Alan Wallach, "Making a Picture of the View from Mount Holyoke," in *American Iconology*, pp. 80, 90.

7. Frederick Jackson Turner, "The Significance of the Frontier in American History," in *The Frontier in American History* (New York: Henry Holt and Company, 1920), p. 11.

8. Angela Miller, *Empire of the Eye*, pp. 82–87, 139.

9. Orasmus Turner, *Pioneer History of the Holland Purchase of Western New York* (Buffalo: Jetwett, Thomas and Company and George H. Derby and Company, 1850), pp. 562–67.

10. "William Louis Sonntag," *Cosmopolitan Art Journal* 3 (1858), 27.

11. Elizabeth Johns, *American Genre Painting: The Politics of Everyday Life* (New Haven: Yale University Press, 1991), pp. xiii–23.
12. Bryan F. Le Beau, *Currier and Ives: America Imagined* (Washington: Smithsonian Institution Press, 2001), p. 7.
13. *Ibid.*, pp. 1–4.
14. Philip Fisher, *Still the New World*, p. 46. For further treatment of the significance of such standardized products in American life well into the twentieth century, see Daniel J. Boorstin, *The Americans: The Democratic Experience* (New York: Random House, 1973).
15. As quoted in Le Beau, *Currier and Ives*, p. 172.
16. See, in this respect, Fisher's interesting comment in *Still the New World*, p. 57: "Because the first photographs required the subjects to remain still for several moments, they appear to us a century later . . . like monumentalized statuary."
17. See Michel Foucault, *Power/Knowledge*, pp. 82–83, from which I am quoting.
18. Johns, *Genre Painting*, p. 12.
19. Theodor W. Adorno, *Negative Dialectics*, trans. E. B. Ashton (New York: Continuum, 1973), pp. 38, 52.

5 MARGARET FULLER'S *SUMMER ON THE LAKES* AND "CHIEF SEATTLE'S SPEECH": THE OBLIQUITIES OF THE GEOGRAPHIC IN-BETWEEN

1. William Boelhower, *Through a Glass Darkly*, pp. 68–73.
2. For a thorough, meticulously researched account of the complex textual and interpretive history of the speech ostensibly made by Chief Seattle on the Puget Sound waterfront in the 1850s, see Albert Furtwangler's detailed study, *Answering Chief Seattle*. All my quotations from "Chief Seattle's Speech" are from Furtwangler's reprint of the earliest surviving appearance of the address in the *Seattle Sunday Star*, 29 October 1887. Furtwangler points out, it should be noted, that the surviving 1887 text of the speech is marred by "missing or half-legible lines in some places" (12). The speech, however, was reprinted shortly thereafter by Frederick James Grant in *History of Seattle, Washington* (New York: American Publishing and Engraving Company, 1891), pp. 433–36, and Furtwangler accordingly offers the 1887 text as supplemented by phrases in brackets from Grant's *History* to clarify otherwise missing or indecipherable copy. Furtwangler's careful research indicates that later versions of what from the outset is a problematic text alter it in large and small ways. For example, a paragraph is added in Clarence B. Bagley's version of the address, included in his article, "Chief Seattle and Angeline," *Washington Historical Quarterly* 22 (1931), 243–75; also see William B. Arrowsmith's embellished and altered version of the speech in *Arion* 8 (1969), 461–64; and, finally, see Ted Perry's highly controversial and massively adulterated version, initially prepared for a television film on ecology, as quoted in full by Rudolph Kaiser in "Chief Seattle's Speech(es): American Origins and European Reception," in *Recovering the Word: Essays on Native American Literature*, ed. Brian Swann and Arnold Krupat (Berkeley: University of California Press, 1987), pp. 497–536.

3. Christina Zwarg, *Feminist Conversations: Fuller, Emerson, and the Play of Reading* (Ithaca: Cornell University Press, 1995), pp. 98–103. Also see "'That Tidiness We Always Look for in Woman': Fuller's *Summer on the Lakes* and Romantic Aesthetics," in *Studies in the American Renaissance, 1987* (Charlottesville: University Press of Virginia, 1987), pp. 250–51, where Stephen Adams attributes "Fuller's loose, fragmented, heterogeneous travel narrative" to "Romantic experimentation with new forms and aesthetic principles. To convey their sense of complex, unstable, manifold reality, the Romantics developed a dramatic, explorative literature of process – an art that generates moments of insight caught from fleeting, often contradictory perspectives."

4. Margaret Fuller, *Summer on the Lakes*, pp. 148–49.

5. James Freeman Clarke, Review of *Summer on the Lakes*, in *Christian World* 2 (1844), rpt. in *Critical Essays on Margaret Fuller*, ed. Joel Myerson (Boston: C. K. Hall, 1980), p. 2.

6. See Annette Kolodny, "Inventing a Feminist Discourse: Rhetoric and Resistance in Margaret Fuller's *Woman in the Nineteenth Century*," *New Literary History* 25 (1994), 378.

7. Jean Paul Sartre, *Being and Nothingness: A Phenomenological Essay on Ontology*, trans. Hazel E. Barnes (New York: Pocket Books, 1966), p. 342.

8. Angela Miller, *Empire of the Eye* pp. 11–13.

9. For detailed discussion of the prominence of Niagara Falls in mid-nineteenth-century American writing and visual culture, see especially Elizabeth R. Mckinsey, *Niagara Falls: Icon of the American Sublime* (Cambridge: Cambridge University Press, 1985), and John F. Sears, "'Doing' Niagara Falls in the Nineteenth Century," in *Sacred Places: American Tourist Attractions in the Nineteenth Century* (Oxford: Oxford University Press, 1989), pp. 12–30.

10. Oliver Oldschool (Joseph Dennie), "American Scenery," in *The Port Folio* 3 (23 May 1807), 331.

11. See Bryant's remarks as quoted in Howard S. Merritt, "'A Wild Scene': Genesis of a Painting," p. 17.

12. Horwitz, *By the Law of Nature*, pp. 32–38.

13. Immanuel Kant, *The Critique of Judgement*, trans. James Creed Meredith (Oxford: Oxford University Press, 1952), pp. 90–130.

14. Fuller, *Woman in the Nineteenth Century*, in *Essential Fuller*, p. 310.

15. Fuller, journal entries from 1840 and letter to Caroline Sturgis, 22 October 1840, in *Essential Fuller*, pp. 11–14.

16. See Thomas Weiskel's still highly regarded study, *The Romantic Sublime: Studies in the Structure and Psychology of Transcendence* (Baltimore: Johns Hopkins University Press, 1976), pp. 3–36.

17. Martin Heidegger, "What is Metaphysics?" trans. R.F.C. Hull and Alan Crick, in *Existence and Being* (Chicago: H. Regnery, 1949), pp. 335–36. For an illuminating article that explores the Heideggerian displacement of *angst* into *furcht* in much greater detail than my analysis, and to which I am indebted, see William V. Spanos, "Breaking the Circle: Hermeneutics as Dis-closure," *Boundary 2* 5 (1977), 421–60.

18. See, in this respect, Susan Gilmore, "Margaret Fuller 'Receiving' the 'Indians,'" in *Margaret Fuller's Cultural Critique: Her Age and Legacy*, ed. Fritz Fleischmann (New York: Peter Lang, 2000), pp. 191–227, where Gilmore notes that Fuller is obliged to pursue the "elusive subject" of native tribal "authenticity" through "a fragmentary clutter" of "hackneyed caricatures" and "delusions."
19. Gerald Vizenor, "Socioacupuncture: Mythic Reversals and the Striptease in Four Scenes," in *The American Indian and the Problem of History*, ed. Calvin Martin (Oxford: Oxford University Press, 1987), pp. 181–83.
20. W. J. T. Mitchell, "What is an Image?" in *Iconology: Image, Text, Ideology* (Chicago: University of Chicago Press, 1986), pp. 7–46.
21. Mitchell's study of Earle's complex painting appears in his chapter on "Imperial Landscape" in *Landscape and Power*, pp. 24–27.
22. Zwarg, *Feminist Conversations*, p. 98.
23. James Clifford, *The Predicament of Culture: Twentieth-Century Ethnography, Literature and Art* (Cambridge, MA: Harvard University Press, 1988), pp. 9–10.
24. *Ibid.*, p. 344.
25. Lauren Berlant, *Anatomy of National Fantasy*, pp. 5–9.
26. All references to the text of Chief Seattle's speech – here to pp. 14–15 – are to Furtwangler, *Answering Chief Seattle*.
27. For the text of Smith's remarks, see Furtwangler, p. 11.
28. Berlant, *Anatomy of National Fantasy*, 22–25.
29. Furtwangler, *Answering Chief Seattle*, pp. vii–viii, 147–48.
30. Berlant, *Anatomy of National Fantasy*, pp. 23–34.
31. Boelhower, *Through a Glass Darkly*, pp. 70–71.
32. Furtwangler, *Answering Chief Seattle*, p. 11.
33. See *ibid.*, p. 66: "There are still arguments over the correct spelling or pronunciation of Seattle's original name. Another common version is Sealth." For still another version, see David Rothenberg, "Will the Real Chief Seattle Speak Up?: An Interview with Ted Perry," in *The New Earth Reader: The Best of Terra Nova*, ed. David Rothenberg and Marta Ulvaeus (Cambridge, MA: MIT Press, 1999), p. 37: "In 1854, Seattle (more correctly Seathl) made his speech . . ."
34. Furtwangler, *Answering Chief Seattle*, pp. 12–17.
35. Berlant, *Anatomy of National Fantasy*, p. 24.
36. Furtwangler, *Answering Chief Seattle*, p. 155.

6 THE POWER OF NEGATIVE SPACE IN DOUGLASS'S AUTOBIOGRAPHIES AND IN DAVIS'S "LIFE IN THE IRON MILLS"

1. Rebecca Harding Davis, *Life in the Iron Mills and Other Stories*, pp. 13–14.
2. John Carlos Rowe, "Between Politics and Poetics: Frederick Douglass and Postmodernity," in *Reconstructing American Literary and Historical Studies*, ed. Günter H. Lenz et al. (New York: St. Martin's Press, 1990), pp. 194–201.
3. Frederick Douglass, *My Bondage and My Freedom*, in *Autobiographies* (New York: The Library of America, 1994), p. 330.

4. For fullest treatment of Douglass's exploitation – and transformation – of gothic motifs and techniques, see Teresa A. Goddu, *Gothic America: Narrative, History, and Nation* (New York: Columbia University Press, 1997), especially pp. 133–40. Henry Louis Gates, Jr., among numerous others, notes the influence of the "sentimental novel," with its "florid asides, severe piety, stilted rhetoric, [and] melodramatic conversation," upon the language of Douglass's *Narrative* in particular; see *Figures in Black: Words, Signs, and the 'Racial' Self* (Oxford: Oxford University Press, 1987), p. 82. For studies locating Douglass's autobiographies in the tradition of Franklin's *Autobiography*, see, for example, Peter F. Walker, *Moral Choices: Memory, Desire, and Imagination in Nineteenth-Century American Abolition* (Baton Rouge: Louisiana State University Press, 1978), p. 213, and Rafia Zafar, "Franklinian Douglass: The Afro-American as Representative Man," in *Frederick Douglass: New Literary and Historical Essays*, ed. Eric J. Sundquist (Cambridge: Cambridge University Press, 1990), pp. 99–117. For an extensive study of the influence of paradigms of Victorian manhood upon Douglass's choice of language and "presentation of self" in *My Bondage and My Freedom*, see David Leverenz, "Frederick Douglass's Self-Refashioning," *Criticism* 29 (1987), 341–70.

5. See Jenny Franchot, "The Punishment of Esther: Frederick Douglass and the Construction of the Feminine," in *Frederick Douglass: New Literary and Historical Essays*, p. 156. Franchot's approach by no means denies Douglass's own active transformation and manipulation of prevailing vocabularies and techniques. As Henry Louis Gates, Jr. emphasizes in *Figures in Black*, Douglass provides one of our "clearest examples" of "the will to power as the will to write" (107–08). Also see "American Literature and the New Historicism: The Example of Frederick Douglass," *Boundary 2* 17 (1990), where Gregory Jay credits Douglass with putting "an alien discourse . . . to work for the black experience," and where he emphasizes that "Douglass's mastery of the master's tongue transforms him from the dictated subject of ideology into the agent of historical (and literary) change" (224). In keeping with such a proposition, Eric Sundquist argues in *To Wake the Nations: Race in the Making of American Literature* (Cambridge, MA: Harvard University Press, 1993) that although many "modern readers" have been "quick to regret" that Douglass's second autobiography, *My Bondage and My Freedom* (1855), is considerably more influenced by prevailing "literary conventions" than the earlier *Narrative* (1845), with its "spare" language ostensibly closer to the bare, bleak facticity of enslavement, in *My Bondage*, Douglass forges a "position" of considerable rhetorical "power," as when he manages to "manipulate the ideology" of the American Revolution "in compelling ways" to sanction and legitimate the current struggle against American enslavement (89–94).

Although criticism of this sort provides a considerably more nuanced approach to Douglass's exploitation of available conventions than the stark, simple assertion that he becomes circumscribed within the prisonhouse of white language and ideology, a case can still be made that the power of language – and, by extension, the power of culture itself – becomes profoundly troubled at many crisis-points in his autobiographies.

6. See J. B. Harley, "Text and Contexts in the Interpretation of Early Maps," pp. 4–5.
7. Walt Whitman, "Song of the Open Road," in *Complete Poetry and Selected Prose*, ed. James E. Miller, Jr. (Cambridge, MA: Riverside, 1959), p. 113.
8. See Jenny Franchot, "The Punishment of Esther," p. 157.
9. Priscilla Wald, *Constituting Americans: Cultural Anxiety and Narrative Form* (Durham, NC: Duke University Press, 1995), pp. 100, 79, and 96.
10. Douglass, *Narrative of the Life of Frederick Douglass, An American Slave*, in *Autobiographies*, pp. 89, 22.
11. For still more extensive discussion of the way "inverted . . . terms" and blurred "oppositions" proliferate in specific episodes in Douglass's *Narrative*, see Gates, *Figures in Black*, pp. 80–97.
12. Hortense J. Spillers, "Changing the Letter: The Yokes, The Jokes of Discourse, or, Mrs. Stowe, Mr. Reed," in *Slavery and the Literary Imagination*, ed. Deborah E. McDowell and Arnold Rampersad (Baltimore: Johns Hopkins University Press, 1989), p. 29.
13. See, for example, John W. Blassingame, *The Slave Community: Plantation Life in the Antebellum South* (Oxford: Oxford University Press, 1973), and William D. Piersen, "Puttin' Down Ole Massa: African Satire in the New World," *Research in African Literature* 7 (1976), 166–80.
14. See Sterling Stuckey, "'Ironic Tenacity': Frederick Douglass's Seizure of the Dialectic," in *Frederick Douglass: New Literary and Historical Essays*, pp. 23–45.
15. Jay, "The Example of Frederick Douglass," p. 224.
16. See, respectively, Teresa Goddu, *Gothic America*, p. 138; Orlando Patterson's description of slavery in general as "social death" – widely quoted throughout commentary on American slavery – in *Slavery and Social Death: A Comparative Study* (Cambridge, MA: Harvard University Press, 1982), especially p. 322; Leonard Cassuto, *The Inhuman Race: The Racial Grotesque in American Literature and Culture* (New York: Columbia University Press, 1997), p. 124; and W. J. T. Mitchell, "Narrative, Memory, and Slavery," in *Cultural Artifacts and the Production of Meaning: The Page, the Image, and the Body*, ed. Margaret J. M. Ezell and Katherine O'Brien O'Keeffe (Ann Arbor: University of Michigan Press, 1994), p. 200.
17. Sundquist, *To Wake the Nations*, p. 90.
18. Ralph Ellison, *Invisible Man* (New York: Vintage Books, 1990), p. 580.
19. To the degree that such a legacy of antifoundationalism persists in exerting pressure on all would-be settlement of culturally mediated truth – including the mediating racial categories that Douglass frequently challenges, as in his remembrance of the "black, brown, copper colored, and nearly white . . . children" all enslaved on the plantation (*My Bondage* 148) – such an antifoundationalist legacy helps to keep open what Gregory Stephens has recently defined as the "interracial and potentially transracial 'third space'" which Douglass tends to occupy in his "life, writing, and oratory." See Stephens's discussion of Douglass, "Frederick Douglass as Integrative Ancestor: The Consequences of Interracial Co-Creation," in *On Racial Frontiers: The New Culture of Frederick*

Douglass, Ralph Ellison, and Bob Marley (Cambridge: Cambridge University Press, 1999), p. 55.

20. This engraving was first published in *The United States Illustrated; in Views of City and Country*, ed. Charles A. Dana, 2 vols. (New York: H. J. Meyer, 1853?), vol. II, p. 30b.

21. See Theodor Adorno, *Minima Moralia*, p. 151.

22. To read Davis's story as a solicitation of the gaze into where culturally organized reality disintegrates and decays raises the question of what sort of "realism" such an aesthetic is drawing us into. Although "no genre," cautions Eric Sundquist, "is more difficult to define than realism" – see Sundquist's introduction to *American Realism: New Essays* (Baltimore: Johns Hopkins University Press, 1982) – commentary over the years repeatedly approaches "Life in the Iron Mills" either as out-and-out "realism," or as "realism" mixed with other aesthetic modes, or in transition from vocabularies and attitudes associated with romanticism and America transcendentalism into the sort of "realism" later emergent in writing by Howells, Garland, and others. See, for example, Arthur Hobson Quinn, *American Fiction: An Historical and Critical Survey* (New York: D. Appleton-Century, 1936), pp. 181–90; Jay Martin, *Harvest of Change: American Literature 1865–1914* (Englewood Cliffs, NJ: Prentice-Hall, 1967), p. 53; Sharon M. Harris, *Rebecca Harding Davis and American Realism* (Philadelphia: University of Pennsylvania Press, 1991), pp. 1–59; and Jean Pfaelzer, *Parlor Radical: Rebecca Harding Davis and the Origins of American Social Realism* (Pittsburgh: University of Pittsburgh Press, 1996), pp. 1–53.

Certainly a number of traits and characteristics invite us to define Davis as in large measure a participant in an American "realistic" movement: her impatience with overly romanticized accounts of past American history; her interest in vernacular speech patterns and her sharp ear for regionalisms of accent and voice; her sensitivity to momentous economic and social changes; and her focus – as Harris puts it – on "plain women, oppressed workers, drunk and brutish men and women, prostitution" and other neglected aspects of "vulgar American life" (13).

Even so, the proposal, as Pfaelzer puts it, that Davis strives for "mimetic accuracy" (21) must be qualified – and especially so in the case of "Life in the Iron Mills." Significantly, in reaction to the evocation of the "monstrous" in Davis's fiction, a three-column review in the 21 November issue of *The Nation* 5 (1867), 410–11, proposes somewhat paradoxically that Davis's art is "disfigured by an injudicious striving after realistic effects" which in very pursuit of the "realistic" nevertheless seems to "leave nature and reality at an infinite distance behind"; or, in other words, such "realistic effects" seem to "leave . . . reality . . . behind" in that their "monstrous" realism violates a more normative understanding of "nature and reality." Certainly in the foggy and lurid *mise-en-scène* of "Life in the Iron Mills," the sort of "realism" ostensibly proffered by the engraving, "Wheeling in Virginia," in Dana, ed., *The United States Illustrated* is subverted by what Mikhail Bakhtin would term an aesthetic of "grotesque realism," whereby what we encounter seems "ugly, monstrous," and "hideous" precisely "from the point of view of 'classic' aesthetics," with its emphasis on abstract purity of pattern, visual definition, and "completed, self-sufficient individuality of form" (see M. M. Bakhtin, *Rabelais and His World*, trans. Helene Iswolsky [Cambridge, MA: MIT Press, 1968], pp. 18–29). This more audacious aspect of Davis's aesthetic – especially prominent in "Life in the Iron Mills" – is certainly implied in Pfaelzer's own alert observation that the concern of such a text is at least in part epistemological: a "critique of nineteenth-century ways of knowing" that explodes "self-protective assumptions about truth and language" associated by Pfaelzer with the nineteenth-century "middle class" sensibility and with the art forms that reflect it (31).

23. To speak of the *uninvested subjectivity* of the poor in Davis's text is to suggest that they cannot be ontologically reduced to forms of visibility, embodiment, and activity that seem objectively to sum them up within the historical moment. For good discussion of the way Deborah, as well as Wolfe, transcends the terms of such objectification in a narrative which "imagines persons to be other than their bodies" – and, in the process, which puts pressure on the proposal, initially introduced yet quickly discarded, that by virtue of the way she looks, Deborah seems "fit to be a type of class" ("Life in the Iron Mills" 21) – see Wai Chee Dimock, "Class, Gender, and the History of Metonymy," in *Rethinking Class; Literary Studies and Social Formations*, ed. Wai Chee Dimock and Michael T. Gilmore (New York: Columbia University Press,, 1994), pp. 94–96. Also see the editorial introduction to *Rethinking Class*, pp. 1–11, where Dimock and Michael T. Gilmore explore "the tremendous difficulties now facing the concept of class" as "a category of analysis" such that it cannot simply be asserted as a "privileged analytic category" without itself becoming "scrutinized, contextualized," and "critiqued for its commissions and omissions."

CONCLUSION: A COMMUNITY VOIDED OF TIME AND PLACE

1. See Virgil Nemoianu, *A Theory of the Secondary: Literature, Progress, and Reaction* (Baltimore: Johns Hopkins University Press, 1989), p. xii.
2. Mitchell, *Landscape and Power*, p. 2.
3. See Bhabha's essay, "DissemiNation," p. 316.
4. Kathleen Stewart, *A Space on the Side of the Road: Cultural Poetics in an "Other" America* (Princeton: Princeton University Press, 1996), p. 5.
5. Philip Fisher, *Hard Facts: Setting and Form in the American Novel* (Oxford: Oxford University Press, 1985), p. 22.
6. Angela Miller, *Empire of the Eye*, pp. 4–7.
7. Ralph Ellison, "The Little Man at Chehaw Station: The American Artist and His Audience," in *Going to the Territory* (New York: Random House, 1986), pp. 17–20. By way of supplementing Ellison's remarks, my graduate student, Boon Leong Goh, has emphasized to me that the US Constitution in particular is actually voided of any grandiose millennial rhetoric grounding the nation in a single historical narrative or in a priori, metaphysical foundations. The Declaration of Independence, to be sure, is somewhat different in that it invokes

Bibliography

Anon, Review of *Waiting for the Verdict*, *The Nation* 5 (1867), 410–11.

Adams, Stephen, "'That Tidiness We Always Look for in Woman': Fuller's *Summer on the Lakes* and Romantic Aesthetics," in *Studies in the American Renaissance, 1987*, Charlottesville: University Press of Virginia, 1987, pp. 247–64.

Adorno, Theodor, *Negative Dialectics*, trans. E. B. Ashton, New York: Continuum, 1973.

  Minima Moralia: Reflections from Damaged Life, trans. E. F. N. Jephcott, London: Verso, 1978.

Arrowsmith, William B., "Speech of Chief Seattle, January 9, 1855," *Arion* 8 (1969), 461–64.

Bagley, Clarence B., "Chief Seattle and Angeline," *Washington Historical Quarterly* 22 (1931), 243–75.

Bakhtin, M. M., *Rabelais and His World*, trans. Helene Iswolsky, Cambridge, MA: M.I.T. Press, 1968.

Bancroft, George, *A History of the United States, From the Discovery of the America Continent*, 10 vols., Boston: Little, Brown, and Company, 1834–75.

Beecher, Lyman, *A Plea for the West*, Cincinnati: Truman and Smith, 1835.

Bellis, Peter J., *No Mysteries out of Ourselves: Identity and Textual Form in the Novels of Herman Melville*, Philadelphia: University of Pennsylvania Press, 1990.

Bennett, Jane, *Thoreau's Nature: Ethics, Politics, and the Wild*, Thousand Oaks, CA: Sage Publications, 1994.

Bercovitch, Sacvan, *The Office of the Scarlet Letter*, Baltimore: Johns Hopkins University Press, 1991.

Berlant, Lauren, *The Anatomy of National Fantasy: Hawthorne, Utopia, and Everyday Life*, Chicago: University of Chicago Press, 1991.

Bhabha, Homi K., "DissemiNation: Time, Narrative, and the Margins of the Modern Nation," in *Nation and Narration*, ed. Bhabha, New York: Routledge, 1990, pp. 291–322.

Blassingame, John W., *The Slave Community: Plantation Life in the Antebellum South*, Oxford: Oxford University Press, 1973.

Boelhower, William, *Through a Glass Darkly: Ethnic Semiosis in American Literature*, Oxford: Oxford University Press, 1987.

Boorstin, Daniel J., *The Americans: The Democratic Experience*, New York: Random House, 1973.

Bradford, William, *Of Plymouth Plantation, 1620–1647*, ed. Samuel Eliot Morison, New York: Knopf, 1952.

Brooks, Van Wyck, *Three Essays on America*, New York: E. P. Dutton, 1934.

Bryant, William Cullen, Preface to *The American Landscape* (1830), as quoted in Howard S. Merritt, "'A Wild Scene': Genesis of a Painting," in *Studies in Thomas Cole, an American Romanticist, Annual 2*, Baltimore: Baltimore Museum of Art, 1967, pp. 7–40.

Buell, Lawrence, *The Environmental Imagination: Thoreau, Nature Writing, and the Formation of American Culture*, Cambridge, MA: Harvard University Press, 1995.

Burbick, Joan, *Thoreau's Alternative History: Changing Perspectives on Nature, Culture, and Language*, Philadelphia: University of Pennsylvania Press, 1987.

Burnet, Thomas, *The Theory of the Earth: Containing an Account of the Original of the Earth, & of All the General Changes Which It Hath Already Undergone, Till the Consummation of All Things*, London: W. Kettilby, 1684.

Byer, Robert H., "Words, Monuments, Beholders: The Visual Arts in Hawthorne's *The Marble Faun*," in *American Iconology: New Approaches to Nineteenth-Century Art and Literature*, ed. David C. Miller (New Haven: Yale University Press, 1993), pp. 163–85.

Cameron, Sharon, *The Corporeal Self: Allegories of the Body in Melville and Hawthorne*, Baltimore: Johns Hopkins University Press, 1981.

Casuto, Leonard, *The Inhuman Race: The Racial Grotesque in American Literature and Culture*, New York: Columbia University Press, 1997.

Cavell, Stanley, *In Quest of the Ordinary: Lines of Skepticism and Romanticism*, Chicago: University of Chicago Press, 1988.

Champlain, Samuel de, *Voyages of Samuel de Champlain*, trans. Charles Pomeroy Otis, Boston: Prince Society, 1880, rpt. as vols. I–IV of Prince Society Publications, New York: Franklin, 1966.

Clarke, James Freeman, Review of *Summer on the Lakes*, in *Christian World* 2 (1844), rpt. in *Critical Essays on Margaret Fuller*, ed. Joel Myerson, Boston: C. K. Hall, 1980, p. 2.

Clifford, James, *The Predicament of Culture: Twentieth-Century Ethnography, Literature and Art*, Cambridge, MA: Harvard University Press, 1988.

Colacurcio, Michael J., *The Province of Piety: Moral History in Hawthorne's Early Tales*, Cambridge, MA: Harvard University Press, 1984.

Cole, Thomas, "Correspondence between Thomas Cole and Robert Gilmore, Jr.," Appendix 1 to Howard S. Merritt, "'A Wild Scene': Genesis of a Painting," in *Studies in Thomas Cole, an American Romanticist, Annual 2* (Baltimore: Baltimore Museum of Art, 1967), pp. 41–81.

"Essay on American Scenery" (1836), rpt. in *Thomas Cole: The Collected Essays and Prose Sketches*, ed. Marshall Tymn, Saint Paul, MN: The John Colet Press, 1980, pp. 3–19.

Comer, Krista, *Landscapes of the New West: Gender and Geography in Contemporary Women's Writing*, Chapel Hill: University of North Carolina Press, 1999.

Crawford, T. Hugh, "Captain Deleuze and the White Whale: Melville, Moby-Dick, and the Cartographic Inclination," *Social Semiotics* 7 (1997), 219–32.

Cronon, William, *Changes in the Land: Indians, Colonists, and the Ecology of New England*, New York: Hill and Wang, 1983.

Dana, Charles A., *The United States Illustrated; in Views of City and Country*, 2 vols., New York: H. J. Meyer, 1853?

Danzer, Gerald, "Bird's-Eye Views of Towns and Cities," in *From Sea Charts to Satellite Images: Interpreting North American History through Maps*, ed. David Buisseret, Chicago: University of Chicago Press, 1990, pp. 165–85.

Davis, Rebecca Harding, *Life in the Iron Mills and Other Stories*, ed. Tillie Olsen, New York: The Feminist Press of the City University of New York, 1985.

Dekker, George, *The American Historical Romance*, Cambridge: Cambridge University Press, 1987.

Delbanco, Andrew, "Melville in the 80s," *American Literary History* 4 (1992), 722.

Dimock, Wai Chee, *Empire for Liberty: Melville and the Poetics of Individualism*, Princeton: Princeton University Press, 1989.

"Class, Gender, and the History of Metonymy," in *Rethinking Class; Literary Studies and Social Formations*, ed. Dimock and Michael T. Gilmore, New York: Columbia University Press, 1994, pp. 57–105.

Dimock, Wai Chee and Gilmore, Michael T., Introduction to *Rethinking Class: Literary Studies and Social Formations*, pp. 1–11.

Douglas, Mary, *Purity and Danger: An Analysis of Concepts of Pollution and Taboo*, London: Routledge and Kegan Paul, 1966.

Douglass, Frederick, *My Bondage and My Freedom* and *Narrative of the Life of Frederick Douglass, an American Slave*, in *Autobiographies*, New York: The Library of America, 1994.

Dryden, Edgar A., *Nathaniel Hawthorne: The Poetics of Enchantment*, Ithaca: Cornell University Press, 1977.

"From the Piazza to the Enchanted Isles: Melville's Textual Rovings," in *After Strange Texts: The Role of Theory in the Study of Literature*, ed. Gregory S. Jay and David L. Miller, University: University of Alabama Press, 1986, pp. 46–68.

The Form of American Romance, Baltimore: Johns Hopkins University Press, 1988.

Dwight, Theodore, *Sketches of Scenery and Manners in the United States* (1829), rpt. Delmar, NY: Scholars' Facsimiles and Reprints, 1983.

Ellison, Ralph, *Going to the Territory*, New York: Random House, 1986.

Invisible Man, New York: Vintage Books, 1990.

Emerson, Ralph Waldo, *Selections from Ralph Waldo Emerson*, ed. Stephen E. Whicher, Boston: Houghton Mifflin, 1972.

The Portable Emerson, New York: Viking, 1981.

Evans, Robin, "Bentham's Panopticon, An Incident in the Social History of Architecture," *Architectural Association Quarterly* 3 (1971), 21–37.

Feidelson, Charles, Jr., *Symbolism and American Literature* (Chicago: University of Chicago Press, 1953).

Fink, Steven, *Prophet in the Marketplace: Thoreau's Development as a Professional Writer*, Princeton: Princeton University Press, 1992.

Fisher, Philip, *Hard Facts: Setting and Form in the American Novel*, Oxford: Oxford University Press, 1985.

 Still the New World: American Literature in a Culture of Creative Destruction, Cambridge, MA: Harvard University Press, 1999.

Foucault, Michel, *Power/Knowledge, Selected Interviews and Other Writings 1972–1977*, ed. Colin Gordan, trans. Colin Gordan et al., New York: Pantheon Books, 1980.

Franchot, Jenny, "The Punishment of Esther: Frederick Douglass and the Construction of the Feminine," in *Frederick Douglass: New Literary and Historical Essays*, ed. Eric J. Sundquist, Cambridge: Cambridge University Press, 1990, pp. 141–65.

Franklin, Wayne, *Discoverers, Explorers, Settlers: The Diligent Writers of Early America*, Chicago: University of Chicago Press, 1979.

Frost, Linda, "'The Red Face of Man,' the Penobscot Indian, and a Conflict of Interest in Thoreau's *Maine Woods*," *ESQ* 39 (1993), 38–39.

Fuller, Margaret, *Summer on the Lakes* and *Woman in the Nineteenth Century*, in *The Essential Margaret Fuller*, ed. Jeffrey Steele, New Brunswick, NJ: Rutgers University Press, 1992.

Furtwangler, Albert, *Answering Chief Seattle*, Seattle: University of Washington Press, 1997.

Gates, Henry Louis, Jr., *Figures in Black: Words, Signs, and the 'Racial' Self*, Oxford: Oxford University Press, 1987.

Gilmore, Susan, "Margaret Fuller 'Receiving' the 'Indians,'" in *Margaret Fuller's Cultural Critique: Her Age and Legacy*, ed. Fritz Fleischmann, New York: Peter Lang, 2000, pp, 191–227.

Goddu, Teresa A., *Gothic America: Narrative, History, and Nation*, New York: Columbia University Press, 1997.

Grant, Frederick James, *History of Seattle, Washington*, New York: American Publishing and Engraving Company, 1891.

Gregory, Derek, *Geographical Imaginations*, Cambridge, MA: Blackwell, 1994.

Gunn, Giles, *Thinking Across the American Grain: Ideology, Intellect, and the New Pragmatism* (Chicago: University of Chicago Press, 1992).

Harding, Walter, *The Days of Henry Thoreau*, New York: Knopf, 1965.

Harley, J. B., "Silences and Secrecy: The Hidden Agenda of Cartography in Early Modern Europe," *Imago Mundi* 40 (1988), 57–76.

 "Text and Contexts in the Interpretation of Early Maps," in *From Sea Charts to Satellite Images: Interpreting North American History through Maps*, Chicago: University of Chicago Press, 1990.

 "Deconstructing the Map," in *Writing Worlds: Discourse, Text and Metaphor in the Representation of Landscape*, ed. Trevor J. Barnes and James S. Duncan, London: Routlege, 1992.

Harpham, Geoffrey Galt, *On the Grotesque: Strategies of Contradiction in Art and Literature*, Princeton: Princeton University Press, 1982.

Harries, Karsten, *The Meaning of Modern Art: A Philosophical Intepretation*, Evanston, IL: Northwestern University Press, 1968.

Harris, Neil, *The Artist in American Society: The Formative Years, 1790–1860*, New York: George Braziller, 1966.

Harris, Sharon M., *Rebecca Harding Davis and American Realism*, Philadelphia: University of Pennsylvania Press, 1991.

Hattenhauer, Darryl, "Space and Place in Melville's 'The Piazza,'" *American Studies in Scandanavia* 20 (1988), 69–81.

Hawthorne, Nathaniel, "Chiefly About War Matters," in *Tales, Sketches, and Other Papers*, *The Works of Nathaniel Hawthorne*, Standard Library Edition, 15 vols., Cambridge, MA: Houghton, Mifflin and Company, 1882–96, vol. xii, 1883.

 The Scarlet Letter, *The Centenary Edition of the Works of Nathaniel Hawthorne*, ed. William Charvat et al., 23 vols., Columbus: Ohio State University Press, 1962–94, vol. i, 1962.

 The House of the Seven Gables, vol. ii of *The Centenary Edition of the Works*, 1965.

 The Marble Faun, vol. iv of *The Centenary Edition of the Works*, 1968.

 Our Old Home, vol. v of *The Centenary Edition of the Works*, 1968.

 The Life of Franklin Pierce (1852), rpt. New York: Garrett, 1970.

 The American Notebooks, vol. viii of *The Centenary Edition of the Works*, 1972.

 "The New Adam and Eve," "Roger Malvin's Burial," and "Young Goodman Brown," in *Mosses from an Old Manse*, vol. x of *The Centenary Edition of the Works*, 1974.

 "My Kinsman, Major Molineux," in *The Snow-Image and Uncollected Tales*, vol. xi of *The Centenary Edition of The Works*, 1974.

 The Elixir of Life Manuscripts, vol. xiii of *The Centenary Edition of the Works*, 1977.

Heidegger, Martin, "What is Metaphysics?" trans. R. F. C. Hull and Alan Crick, in *Existence and Being*, Chicago: H. Regnery, 1949.

Horwitz, Howard, *By the Law of Nature: Form and Value in Nineteenth-Century America*, Oxford: Oxford University Press, 1991.

Irwin, John, *American Hieroglyphics: The Symbol of the Egyptian Hieroglyphics in the American Renaissance*, New Haven: Yale University Press, 1980.

Jarves, James Jackson, *The Art-Idea* (1864), rpt. Cambridge, MA: Harvard University Press, 1960.

Jay, Gregory S., "American Literature and the New Historicism: The Example of Frederick Douglass," *Boundary 2.* 17 (1990), 211–42.

Jefferson, Thomas, *Thomas Jefferson: Writings*, ed. Merrill D. Peterson, New York: Library of America, 1984.

Jehlen, Myra, *American Incarnation: The Individual, the Nation, and the Continent*, Cambridge, MA: Harvard University Press, 1986.

Johns, Elizabeth, *American Genre Painting: The Politics of Everyday Life*, New Haven: Yale University Press, 1991.

Kaiser, Rudolph, "Chief Seattle's Speech(es): American Origins and European Reception," in *Recovering the Word: Essays on Native American Literature*, ed.

Brian Swann and Arnold Krupat, Berkeley: University of California Press, 1987, pp. 497–536.

Kant, Immanuel, *The Critique of Judgement*, trans. James Creed Meredith, Oxford: Oxford University Press, 1952.

Kolodny, Annette, "Inventing a Feminist Discourse: Rhetoric and Resistance in Margaret Fuller's *Woman in the Nineteenth Century*," *New Literary History* 25 (1994), 355–82.

 The Lay of the Land: Metaphor as Experience and History in American Life and Letters, Chapel Hill: University of North Carolina Press, 1975.

Laurence, David, "William Bradford's American Sublime," *PMLA* 102 (1987), 55–65.

Le Beau, Bryan F., *Currier and Ives: America Imagined*, Washington: Smithsonian Institution Press, 2001.

Leverenz, David, "Frederick Douglass's Self-Refashioning," *Criticism* 29 (1987), 341–70.

Martin, Jay, *Harvests of Change: American Literature 1865–1914*, Englewood Cliffs, NJ: Prentice-Hall, 1967.

Matthiessen, F.O., *The American Renaissance: Art and Expression in the Age of Emerson and Whitman*, London: Oxford University Press, 1941.

McCoubrey, John, *American Tradition in Painting*, new edn., Philadelphia: University of Pennsylvania Press, 2000.

McGregor, Robert Kuhn, *A Wider View of the Universe: Henry Thoreau's Study of Nature*, Urbana: University of Illinois Press, 1997.

McIntosh, James, "Nature and Frontier in 'Roger Malvin's Burial'," *American Literature* 60 (1988), 188–204.

McKinsey, Elizabeth R., *Niagara Falls: Icon of the American Sublime*, Cambridge: Cambridge University Press, 1985.

McWilliams, John P., Jr., *Hawthorne, Melville, and the American Character: A Looking-Glass Business*, Cambridge: Cambridge University Press, 1984.

Melville, Herman, "Bartleby" and "The Piazza," in *Selected Writings of Herman Melville*, New York: Random House, 1952, pp. 3–47, 437–53.

 The Portable Melville, ed. Jay Leyda, New York: Viking, 1952.

 The Confidence-Man: His Masquerade, ed. Hershel Parker, New York: W. W. Norton, 1971.

 Pierre; or, The Ambiguities, ed. Harrison Hayford et al., Evanston, IL: Northwestern University Press, 1971.

 Moby-Dick or, The Whale, New York: Penguin Books, 1992.

 Pierre, or the Ambiguities, ed. Hershel Parker, Kraken Edition, New York: Harper Collins, 1995.

Miller, Angela, *The Empire of the Eye: Landscape Representation and American Cultural Politics, 1825–1875*, Ithaca: Cornell University Press, 1993.

 "The Mechanisms of the Market and the Invention of Western Regionalism: The Example of George Caleb Bingham," in *American Iconology: New Approaches to Nineteenth-Century Art and Literature*, ed. David C. Miller, New Haven: Yale University Press, 1993, pp. 112–34.

Miller, David C., *Dark Eden: The Swamp in Nineteenth-Century American Culture*, Cambridge University Press, 1989.

Miller, Perry, *Nature's Nation*, Cambridge, MA: Harvard University Press, 1967.

Mitchell, W. J. T., *Iconology: Image, Text, Ideology*, Chicago: University of Chicago Press, 1986.

"Narrative, Memory, and Slavery," in *Cultural Artifacts and the Production of Meaning: The Page, the Image, and the Body*, ed. Margaret J. M. Ezell and Katherine O'Brien O'Keeffe, Ann Arbor: University of Michigan Press, 1994, pp. 199–222.

Mitchell, W. J. T. (ed.), *Landscape and Power*, Chicago: University of Chicago Press, 1994.

Nash, Roderick, *Wilderness and the American Mind*, New Haven: Yale University Press, 1967.

Nemoianu, Virgil, *A Theory of the Secondary: Literature, Progress, and Reaction*, Baltimore: Johns Hopkins University Press, 1989.

O'Gorman, Edmundo, *The Invention of America: An Inquiry into the Historical Nature of the New World and the Meaning of its History*, Bloomington: Indiana University Press, 1961.

O'Grady, James P., *Pilgrims to the Wild*, Salt Lake City: University of Utah Press, 1993.

Oldschool, Oliver (Joseph Dennie), "American Scenery," *The Port Folio* 3 (23 May 1807), 331.

Olson, Charles, *Call Me Ishmael*, San Francisco: City Lights Books, 1947.

Otter, Samuel, *Melville's Anatomies*, Berkeley: University of California Press, 1999.

Patterson, Orlando, *Slavery and Social Death: A Comparative Study*, Cambridge, MA: Harvard University Press, 1982.

Pease, Donald E. *Visionary Compacts: American Renaissance Writing in Cultural Context*, Madison: University of Wisconsin Press, 1987.

Peck, H. Daniel, *Thoreau's Morning Work: Memory and Perception in A Week on the Concord and Merrimack Rivers, the Journal, and Walden*, New Haven: Yale University Press, 1990.

Pfaelzer, Jean, *Parlor Radical: Rebecca Harding Davis and the Origins of American Social Realism*, Pittsburgh: University of Pittsburgh Press, 1996.

Piersen, William D., "Puttin' Down Ole Massa: African Satire in the New World," *Research in African Literature* 7 (1976) 166–80.

Powell, Timothy B., *Ruthless Democracy: A Multicultural Interpretation of the American Renaissance*, Princeton: Princeton University Press, 2000.

Quinn, Arthur Hobson, *American Fiction: An Historical and Critical Survey*, New York: D. Appleton-Century, 1936.

Reynolds, David S., *Beneath the American Renaissance: The Subversive Imagination in the Age of Emerson and Melville*, Cambridge, MA: Harvard University Press, 1989.

Rogin, Michael Paul, *Subversive Genealogy: The Politics and Art of Herman Melville*, New York: Knopf, 1983.

Rothenberg, David, "Will the Real Chief Seattle Speak Up?: An Interview with Ted Perry," in *The New Earth Reader: The Best of Terra Nova*, ed. Rothenberg and Marta Ulvaeus, Cambridge, MA: MIT Press, 1999, pp. 36–51.

Rowe, John Carlos, "Between Politics and Poetics: Frederick Douglass and Post-modernity," in *Reconstructing American Literary and Historical Studies*, ed. Günter H. Lenz et al., New York: St. Martin's Press, 1990, pp. 192–210.

St. Armand, Barton Levi, "Melville, Malaise, and Mannerism: The Originality of 'The Piazza'," *Bucknell Review* 30 (1986), 72–101.

Sartre, Jean Paul, *Being and Nothingness: A Phenomenological Essay on Ontology*, trans. Hazel E. Barnes, New York: Pocket Books, 1966.

Scarry, Elaine, *The Body in Pain: The Making and Unmaking of the World*, Oxford: Oxford University Press, 1985.

Schmitz, Neil, "Tall Tale, Tall Talk: Pursuing the Lie in Jacksonian Literature," *American Literature* 48 (1977), 474–75.

Sears, John F., *Sacred Places: American Tourist Attractions in the Nineteenth Century*, Oxford: Oxford University Press, 1989.

Slouka, Mark, "Herman Melville's Journey to 'The Piazza'," *American Transcendental Quarterly* 61 (1986), 3–14.

Smith, John, *A Description of New England* (1616), rpt. in *Tracts and Other Papers Relating to the Origin, Settlement, and Progress of the Colonies in North America, from the Discovery of the Country to the year 1776*, 3 vols., collected by Peter Force, vol. II, Gloucester, MA: Peter Smith, 1963.

Spanos, William V., "Breaking the Circle: Hermeneutics as Dis-closure," *Boundary 2* 5 (1977), 421–60.

Spillers, Hortense J., "Changing the Letter: The Yokes, The Jokes of Discourse, or, Mrs. Stowe, Mr. Reed," in *Slavery and the Literary Imagination*, ed. Deborah E. McDowell and Arnold Rampersad, Baltimore: Johns Hopkins University Press, 1989, pp. 25–61.

Stephens, Gregory, *On Racial Frontiers: The New Culture of Frederick Douglass, Ralph Ellison, and Bob Marley*, Cambridge: Cambridge University Press, 1999.

Stewart, Kathleen, *A Space on the Side of the Road: Cultural Poetics in an "Other" America*, Princeton: Princeton University Press, 1996.

Stewart, Susan, *Nonsense: Aspects of Intertextuality in Folklore and Literature*, Baltimore: Johns Hopkins University Press, 1979.

Stilgoe, John R., *Common Landscape of America, 1580–1845*, New Haven: Yale University Press, 1982.

Stuckey, Sterling, "'Ironic Tenacity': Frederick Douglass's Seizure of the Dialectic," in *Frederick Douglass: New Literary and Historical Essays*, ed. Eric J. Sundquist, Cambridge: Cambridge University Press, 1990, pp. 23–45.

Sundquist, Eric, "Slavery, Revolution, and the American Renaissance," in *The American Renaissance Reconsidered*, ed. Walter Benn Michaels and Donald E. Pease, Baltimore: Johns Hopkins University Press, 1985, pp. 1–33.

   To Wake the Nations: Race in the Making of American Literature, Cambridge, MA: Harvard University Press, 1993.

Sundquist, Eric (ed.), *American Realism: New Essays*, Baltimore: Johns Hopkins University Press, 1982.

Swann, Charles, *Nathaniel Hawthorne: Tradition and Revolution*, Cambridge: Cambridge University Press, 1991.

Sypher, Wylie, *Four Stages of Renaissance Style: Transformation in Art and Literature, 1400–1700*, Garden City, NY: Doubleday and Co., 1955.

Thompson, G. R., *The Art of Authorial Presence: Hawthorne's Provincial Tales*, Durham, NC: Duke University Press, 1993.

Thoreau, Henry David, *The Maine Woods, The Writings of Henry David Thoreau*, Riverside Edition, 11 vols., Boston and New York: Houghton Mifflin, and Company, 1884–94, vol. III, 1892.

Cape Cod, "Life Without Principle," vol. IV of *The Writings*, 1893.

"Autumnal Tints," "Walking," and "Wild Apples," vol. IX of *The Writings*, 1893.

The Journal of Henry David Thoreau, ed. Bradford Torrey and Francis H. Allen, 14 vols. (1906), rpt. New York: Dover, 1962.

Walden, ed. J. Lyndon Shanley, Princeton: Princeton University Press, 1971.

A Week on the Concord and Merrimack Rivers, ed. Carl F. Hovde et al., Princeton: Princeton University Press, 1980.

Faith in a Seed: The Dispersion of Seeds and Other Late Natural History Writings, ed. Bradley P. Dean, Washington, D.C.: Island Press, 1993.

Todorov, Tzvetan, *The Conquest of America: The Question of the Other*, trans. Richard Howard, New York: Harper and Row, 1984.

Turner, Frederick Jackson, "The Significance of the Frontier in American History," in *The Frontier in American History*, New York: Henry Holt and Company, 1920, pp. 1–38.

Turner, Orasmus, *Pioneer History of the Holland Purchase of Western New York*, Buffalo: Jetwett, Thomas and Company and George H. Derby and Company, 1850.

Vizenor, Gerald, "Socioacupuncture: Mythic Reversals and the Striptease in Four Scenes," in *The American Indian and the Problem of History*, ed. Calvin Martin, Oxford: Oxford University Press, 1987, pp. 180–91.

Wadlington, Warwick, *The Confidence Game in American Literature*, Princeton: Princeton University Press, 1975.

Wald, Priscilla, *Constituting Americans: Cultural Anxiety and Narrative Form*, Durham, NC: Duke University Press, 1995.

Walker, Peter F., *Moral Choices: Memory, Desire, and Imagination in Nineteenth-Century American Abolition*, Baton Rouge: Louisiana State University Press, 1978.

Wallach, Alan, "Making a Picture of the View from Mount Holyoke," in *American Iconology: New Approaches to Nineteenth-Century Art and Literature*, ed. David C. Miller, New Haven: Yale University Press, 1993, pp. 80–91.

Walls, Laura Dassow, *Seeing New Worlds: Henry David Thoreau and Nineteenth-Century Natural Science*, Madison: University of Wisconsin Press, 1995.

Weinstein, Arnold, *Nobody's Home: Speech, Self And Place In American Fiction From Hawthorne To Delillo*, Oxford: Oxford University Press, 1993.

Weiskel, Thomas, *The Romantic Sublime: Studies in the Structure and Psychology of Transcendence*, Baltimore: Johns Hopkins University Press, 1976.

West, Michael, *Transcendental Wordplay: America's Romantic Punsters and the Search for the Language of Nature*, Athens: Ohio University Press, 2000.

White, Richard, "Discovering Nature in North America," *The Journal of American History* 79 (1992), 874–91.

Whitman, Walt, "Song of the Open Road" in *Complete Poetry and Selected Prose*, ed. James E. Miller, Jr., Cambridge, MA: Riverside, 1959, pp. 113 and 455–501.

"William Louis Sonntag," *Cosmopolitan Art Journal* 3 (1858), 27.

Williams, Raymond, *Marxism and Literature*, Oxford: Oxford University Press, 1977.

Willis, N. P., *American Scenery; or, Land, Lake and River Illustrations of Transatlantic Nature*, 2 vols., London: George Virtue, 1840.

Wolf, Bryan Jay, *Romantic Re-Vision: Culture and Consciousness in Nineteenth-Century American Painting and Literature*, Chicago: University of Chicago Press, 1982.

Wroth, Lawrence C., *The Voyages of Giovanni da Verrazzano, 1524–1528*, New Haven: Yale University Press, 1970.

Zafar, Rafia, "Franklinian Douglass: The Afro-American as Representative Man," in *Frederick Douglass: New Literary and Historical Essays*, ed. Eric J. Sundquist, Cambridge: Cambridge University Press, 1990, pp. 99–117.

Zwarg, Christina, *Feminist Conversations: Fuller, Emerson, and the Play of Reading*, Ithaca: Cornell University Press, 1995.

Index